The Best
Little Magazine
Fiction, 1970

The Best
Little Magazine
Fiction,
1970

Edited by Curt Johnson

New York: New York University Press
1970

Acknowledgments

"Archie and the Dry Ninth Hole" reprinted by permission of Barding Dahl.
"The Wind Chandelier" reprinted by permission of Cynthia Buchanan from
Epoch, Winter 1968.
"The Conspiracy Against Mr. Mann" reprinted with permission from *The
Fair.*
"Sixty Acres" reprinted by permission of Raymond Carver. Copyright ©
1969, 1970 by Raymond Carver.
"Tenderloin" reprinted by permission of *Colorado State Review.*
"Spending the Day," by J. M. Ferguson, Jr., 1969, reprinted by permission
of *Descant.*
"The Whereabouts of Mr. Haber," which first appeared in *Transatlantic
Review,* is reprinted by permission of Fred Gardner c/o International Famous
Agency, Inc. Copyright © 1968 by Fred Gardner.
"Shake the Dew" reprinted by permission of Gary Gildner.
"The Other Kingdom" reprinted from the *Carleton Miscellany.* Copyrighted
by Carleton College.
"Voice of the Town" first published in *TriQuarterly* 16 © 1969, North-
western University Press.
"Lykaon" reprinted with permission from *Epoch.*
"F." reprinted with permission by *Northwest Review.*
"The Monopoly Story" reprinted by permission of *TransPacific.*
"Friday Night at the Project and Tenuous Relationships Reaching to Long
Island," reprinted by permission of *Duel,* Sir George Williams University,
Montreal, Canada.
"The Anniversary" reprinted by permission from *The Colorado Quarterly*
(Summer, 1968). Copyright, 1968, by the University of Colorado, Boulder,
Colorado.
"Kick" reprinted from *Shenandoah*: The Washington and Lee University
Review with permission of the Editor.
"Voyeur" reprinted from *The Literary Review* (Autumn, 1968, Volume 12,
Number 1), published by Fairleigh Dickinson University, Rutherford, New
Jersey.
"Unmailed, Unwritten Letters" reprinted by permission from *The Hudson
Review,* Vol. XXII, no. 1 (Spring, 1969). Copyright © 1969 by The Hudson
Review, Inc.
"The Naked Man" reprinted by permission of *Minnesota Review* and Bill
Rodriguez.
"From Image to Expression" reprinted by permission of *Minnesota Review*
and Henry H. Roth.
"The Rhyme of Lancelot" reprinted from *South Dakota Review.*
"Down in the Eighth" reprinted by permission of *Colorado State Review.*
"Smitty's Haven" reprinted from *The Western Humanities Review,* Volume
XXIII, Number 3, Summer, 1969, with permission.

Foreword

This is the first annual collection of the best fiction from little magazines. (The editor's definition of what constitutes a "little" magazine must be deduced from the list at the back of this volume, "Magazines Consulted.") The reason for publishing this collection is to find as many readers as possible for stories originally published in noncommercial, small-circulation magazines.

The editor considered calling this book *The Best of the Best,* the first superlative referring to the stories themselves, the second to the type of magazine in which they first appeared. As witness, on the second, the words of Martha Foley, who each year edits *The Best American Short Stories,* the fine annual collection of stories selected from both commercial and noncommercial magazines; Miss Foley, interviewing herself in the Foreword to her 1968 volume, responds to the question "Which magazines published the best stories this year?" with this comment:

The small circulation magazines, called "little" because of that limited circulation. They are not little in quality. Many, many readers would enjoy them if they only had access to them. But they do not have the money to finance the lavish promotion campaigns of the mass circulation magazines primarily interested in money and not in literature.

The year before Miss Foley's statement, the editor of *Prize Stories: The O. Henry Awards,* said this about little magazines in the Introduction to his collection:

As homes go, the "little magazines" have a good deal to offer. Suppose, then, that they did not exist? Suppose that in one year they were all together to cease publication, having run afoul of creditors, having lost the good will of a foundation or a patron or a board of regents, or for whatever reason—the effect upon the American short story would be immediate and lamentable.

(Amen, of course, and we urge you, then, to support your local little.)

The stories in this volume were mostly printed in 1969, some in 1968. Next year's collection and those after will include only stories printed the previous year. In selecting the stories, the editor has tried to offset his known prejudices of taste by informally seeking the opinions of others whose judgments he respects, notably this year those of Bob Wilson and Carole Spearin McCauley. Next year this may be done on a more formal basis, perhaps by asking half a dozen little magazine editors from all parts of the country to recommend stories that have especially impressed them in their own or in other littles. Volunteers will be welcomed.

It is customary in a Foreword to a volume such as this to remark upon a detected trend. Here is a trend we detected: More and more and more—in both little *and* commercial magazines—short-story writers are writing about writers and writing, or writing and teaching, or writing and the teaching of writing. (This is done in both bad stories and good. For example, in last year's *O. Henry* collection, the two characters of the first-prize story are writers; in the second-prize story, two of the three characters are writers; and in the third-prize story, the tale is told by a writer about a boy who is going to become a writer, with tips on how to write tossed into the telling.)

This is an unfortunate trend. It is unfortunate because the stories are often boring, and they are so because the subject does not have enough to do with the *many* varieties of experience we live and know. True, most American writers must earn their livings by teaching English and/or creative writing; but if barbers, bricklayers, and neurosurgeons can find a great many things interesting in life outside their crafts, can't we reasonably expect writers to do the same?

There were other trends—the most alarming being the widespread feeling among the young that fiction has had it. This feeling apparently arises syllogistically: Words have been used to mislead; stories are made from words; therefore, ... It is to be hoped that this trend, together with the conditions that created it, will soon be reversed.

We now quote in full an editorial by Barding Dahl that appeared in Vol. 5, No. 4 (1963) of the little magazine *Coastlines*. We do this not only because the editorial is a lively short story, but also to introduce little magazines and their writers and editors to those unacquainted with them. Here, then, is Barding Dahl's editorial, "Archie and the Ninth Dry Hole":

No rain this season. Farmers shaking their heads. Who asked them to be farmers. Little mag editor. Nobody asked him either.

Going around trying to get book stores to carry you. Contempt lying like limpid pools in their flaccid eyes in their gelid stores. The impossible has happened: somebody beneath them. Convicted of microscopism, you stammer your confession. Unworthy to be in the same rack with *Fun in the Sun*. Might as well accept it, grin fungously, phosphorously. Lie down dismally in the path of Juggernaut Mediocre.

Coming home you feel for warmth, a sign, small flags announcing though in last place you are *somewhere* in the flotilla. A number of ominous brown envelopes. A weight on the rainless day. Scraping at you with their SHOULD YOU FIND THE ENCLOSED STORY UNACCEPTABLE YOU WILL FIND A RETURN ENVELOPE. Your contributors, let's wipe a tear. *They're* rooting for you, *they* know what it's like, getting out a dinky mag. NORTH AMERICAN SERIAL RIGHTS ONLY! Our scheme for a big killing with the South American rights gone smash.

Cold coffee. Radioactive cream. Krushchev says when all's said and done it's a mighty fine wall. Fingering the brown envelopes. Idle notions helping you stall. A marker in the sky, way out there, the break-even point, reach and reach. Then you could have a secretary, at least part-time. Students glad to get a dollar an hour to break into the publishing game. Wig them with a dollar and a quarter.

YOUR SNIDE COMMENTS ON MY STORY WERE MOST UNWELCOME, WHY CAN'T YOU JUST SEND THEM BACK. Looking out your window, millions are looking out of windows. You are different, you are a little mag editor. They'd never know it to look at you, but that's the beauty of it, incognito. No sign on the door, no diplomas. Self-made, you're there because they can shake the tree all they want to and you're still there. They are not there. They are sniggering at stale jokes at stale cocktail parties. You are in the vanguard, a regular spearhead. YOUR REASONS FOR REJECTING MY STORY ARE TRIVIAL TO SAY THE LEAST. I HAVE GOTTEN HANDWRITTEN REJECTIONS FROM THE BEST OF THEM. WHO ARE YOU TO—

Crops drying out. Brown envelopes drying out. Private visions worthless unless made public, enacted in the formal laws of excitement. Like canned movies on dusty shelves, inferior to the bored shufflings of clerks. In impotent need of a projector, and when it comes you are already too old.

Only a little mag editor, and you mapped empires. The burden of tolerant smiles from friends who have already made their deal. Are you really crazed? Are you really the Castro of the magazine world, hunting for Henry Luce in the canyons of Manhattan? Does he really demand your privates on a platter for his paycheck? IT IS NOW SIX WEEKS SINCE I SENT YOU MY STORY, ENTITLED, "A SURPRISE FOR ARCHIE." I REALIZE A *BIG MAGAZINE* LIKE YOU MUST BE *SWAMPED* WITH SCRIPTS, BUT I WOULD APPRECIATE—

Trapped with Archie by the vast cunning of authors into dancing out the last full measure, the author knowing in his heart he is counting on our polite surprise. Archie and we *are* too polite to dissent, for in the little mag world we are all alright, politically. That is to say, we sit down though gingerly next to coloreds. We throw away our votes on Democratic candidates on pretext of not throwing them away on an honest man. Archie knows his business. Properly surprised. Heads for his niche.

And the Archie's of MGM, and Doubleday, and M.C.A., differing in nimbleness and salary, join hands with their counterparts in the little mag world. Art is only makebelieve. Transport within reason. Protest within reason. Love within reason. In youth we take pride in private lunacy, dismayed later by the shock that everyone else seems to be playing the same game. There is an appalling, one may say an absolute, lack of personnel in the chart room.

I THINK YOU ARE FOOLISH NOT TO PAY YOUR CON-TRIBUTORS. IT WOULD AMOUNT TO (I'M SURE), A VERY SMALL PART OF YOUR PUBLISHING BUDGET, AND IT WOULD MAKE SUCH A DIFFERENCE TO THE WRIT-ERS. IF YOU WANT PROFESSIONAL WORK YOU SHOULD BE PREPARED TO PAY FOR IT. But we may say, must in all honesty say, the little mag world seethes with hate. It is not over-stating the case to say that passions run deep among our people. If our enemies (who are everywhere), do not cease their machina-tions against us, we will issue the ultimate ultimatum. We will go so far as to blast them with an even more scathing, damning, pulverizing editorial.

Sadists are attracted to the jailing profession. What may we say (then) of the little mag editor, taking his ease in an arbor of net-tles. Small wonder his laugh rings hollow, his handshake slips. Nervous coughs for creditors, unbelieved excuses to contributors, spreading measly shreds of hope before anthologists and writers' conferences, abjectly arranging his cravat before the concordat of fat cats.

For if you are not with us, you are certainly against us. *With* us in our greased careen to blank acceptance and waffle-iron faces, *against* us in our (important) plan of surprising Archie, whom everyone else was so sure could never be surprised again.

For, like maids, butlers, and all categories of men Fridays, hav-ing not and wishing much, we keen with appetite. Preening our worn livery, we wait in the wings for an unscheduled cue. Sched-uled, perhaps, to pass all our days in those wings. Darkness, dust, an easy prey for maudlin tears.

But on the few boards that are given us, the words come trip-ping, measuring, cutting the cloth that covers our ideas. But *our* cloth, *our* ideas, nothing made to order, never two of a kind. In-dignance laid aside, we accept our humble station. For though a butler may be a tiger in dreams and on his night off, he is never far from the trappings of his trade.

We grumble, and sweep the way-station for future greats, learn to feign gratitude, like granny mouthing thank-you's for a remem-brance card. Playing our small trumps in the game of picking front-runners, those giants forever straining after huge explosions of the blood, even on their knees still sifting to isolate the unique virus of their name.

We envy, for a butler is after all a butler, and we are surprised. By smaller things than surprise Archie—no miraculous encounters, no violent slaughters that sum up so beautifully, no changes of heart that smack of magic. We deal in the small coin of reportage, recounting voyages of the heart with faithful exactness. Thus it was, or really seemed to be, and no one may alter the stacking of the bones. PLEASE RETURN MY MANUSCRIPT ENTITLED A SURPRISE FOR ARCHIE I SENT IT TO THIS OTHER MAGAZINE AND THEY KEPT IT SO LONG I THOUGHT THEY HAD LOST IT AND SO I SENT IT TO YOU AND NOW THEY WANT TO USE IT YOU WILL UNDERSTAND I'M SURE AS IT IS ONE OF THE BIGGER PUBLICATIONS.

Mr. Dahl wrote a happy ending for Archie's author, but was unable to do as much for his own magazine; death, as it must to all littles, came to *Coastlines* with its next issue.

First thanks, respect, and our admiration go to the writers whose stories are included in this book; next thanks go to the magazine editors who first published them. May you all prosper.

C. L. J.

To DR. MARVIN SUKOV, who has done much for many years in many ways for many little magazines.

Contents

Contents

The Best
Little Magazine
Fiction, 1970

The Wind Chandelier

Cynthia Buchanan

from *Epoch*

The day of her birthday, the old woman reached up slowly and felt of her hair. The unmarried daughter Lillian kept it clean and cut as short as a paper boy's.

Lillian had washed the old woman's hair today. When she sat her mother down in the living room afterwards, she said, "And you *stay* that way, hear?"

"Sister," the old woman said, "when I was fourteen, my hair was heavy, and it traveled clean down to my waist. Sid . . . he was near twicet my age then . . . Sid, he never let me cut it. So, by God, I wore it in coils . . . top of my head, you know. Oh, every oncet in a while, I let it go wild about my waist until it came caught against them splintered posts. Or in Sid's hands. 'I'm going to tie you up in them ribbons,' he would tell me, meaning my hair, don't you know. And he would smile."

"Yes, yes, yes, I know," Lillian said. "Lord, what time is it? I've got to call Maxine!" She bounded into the kitchen, and the old woman listened to her dialing the telephone.

Where was that remote punch for the television? She looked around for the small hand device with the buttons. She punched one of them, and the television tube whined forth an image.

3

"Mother!" Lillian yelled from the kitchen. "Mother, if you would kindly turn that down a minute I could hear what Maxine is saying. What, Max? What? Hold on a sec; Mother's got that TV going until I think my head is going to split in two. Hold on." She opened the swinging kitchen door.

"Mother! How do you suppose we can talk with that Queen for a Day show splitting my head in two? Now, you can just wait until I'm through on the phone in here." She retreated with the swing of the door. "All right, Maxine; go on."

"Whuh?" the old woman said. "Didn't know you was on the telephone." She punched the remote control, and the television picture melted into a distorted white dot. She stared at the electronic point on the tube and said, "Turn it off. Clean off, that's what we'll do." Resting her head on the back of the armchair, she stared into the living room of the tract house. She had it memorized down to the contents of the odds and ends drawer. A few *How-to* books on the shelves. Beige carpet with sworls. Scrabble game in the closet for certain of the company. Oleander bushes next to the front porch. Toaster had a crocheted cover. Flamingoes on the bathroom shower curtain. Sewing basket in the bedroom with Lillian's aprons-in-the-making stacked on top.

"She's got it fixed up nice for my birthday," the old woman said and looked into the dining room where the party preparations waited on the table. All the family would come today by four o'clock and have cake. Someone's Pekingese would have to be fussed over and put in the bathroom, so he wouldn't wet on the rug. Lillian had put a paper tablecloth on the table in the dining room, with paper "Happy Birthday" lettering taped on the mirror.

She heard Lillian say, "Mother's calling, Maxine. I'd better go see what it is now. Yes, bye. See you at four. Uh-huh. Yes, Hawaiian's fine. You can get it in those pint bottles. Mixes up enough to feed an army. Yes, uh-huh, okay then, four o'clock or a little tinsy bit before."

There were saucers of nuts and pretzels on the end tables at the couch, and all the magazines were straightened in their stacks. The napkins on the table cooperated in a symmetrical diamond design.

"I wonder what ever happened to Celia Franks," the old woman said to herself. "She married that boy. She should have gotten rid of those moles." She folded her hands in her lap. "But she got that boy. Moles or no, she got him. Her family was a shameful, thieving lot, but *she* turned out, moles and all. All right that Celia Franks."

Lillian came through the door. "Yes, Mother? What is it, Mother?"

"Nothing. I was just saying to myself you got the house fixed nice. I been taking notice of the things in the dining room and what all."

Lillian smoothed her hands on her apron.

"Yes, it does look rather festive, if I do say so myself. Now, are you ready for your bath? Go on in, and I'll be in in a minute. Pratt and all of them will be here early."

"He came yesterday."

"Well, yes, he came yesterday. Pratt can come visit his own mother without it being her birthday, can't he? He can come two days in a row, I should think. You don't mind seeing Pratt, your own flesh and blood, do you?"

The old woman tapped the end of her fingers absently on the arms of the chair and pursed her lips in and out.

Lillian rearranged the zinnias. "Well, you don't, do you?"

"No, miss, I don't mind seeing him two days in a row, and I don't see reason for you to talk to your mother so, either."

"Are you going to be peevish today? On your birthday? Come on. You better get your bath."

The mother had her bath and her Yardley talcum. Lillian put on a jersey dress and stood before the mirror, pulling her hair back at the temples with two combs. The old woman sat on the edge of the bed holding a satin brassiere in her hands.

Lillian saw the reflection in the mirror and turned abruptly. "Here, here, here! What are you doing, Mother?"

"Getting dressed, Lillian. For my party."

"I thought I put that silly thing away last Christmas. And now what do I find you doing?"

The old woman put the brassiere down in her lap. "You don't need to concern yourself with my things."

"Oh no, no, I don't need to concern myself with your things." Lillian sighed and pulled the venetian blinds open. "No, I, Lillian, have never had to concern myself with your things, Mother. Never in my life have I had to look after you . . . or care for you . . . or stay in this house and rot! Here, give me that brassiere."

"It's my birthday, and I'm going to wear it. Leave it be. Nancy's girl ordered that for me from Frederick's of Hollywood."

"Oh, yes. And if that doesn't take the cake!" She scratched around in a dresser drawer, laying amber colored jewelry out on the dresser top. "No, I never have to concern myself with you or with your belongings or your happiness. Never once in the past millennium have I ever given a thought to your happiness or comfort. I've lived entirely for myself. Yes, wear that silly bra from . . . Frederick's of Hollywood! What in the world Jennifer thought you would ever do with a . . . a . . . provocative . . . and expensive . . . French brassiere, I'll never know."

The old woman looked at the piece of lingerie. It was white . . . as white as seagulls . . . whiter than her wedding dress. "She knows I like pretty things. Nothing wrong with giving a person pretty things."

"Well, don't we all like pretty things, Mother. Every last one of us, I'm sure."

She answered that Yes we did, all of us, and her daughter said that that was no reason to waste good money on impractical items like French brassieres.

"It's almost . . ." Lillian smiled with one side of her mouth but did not quite laugh. "Oh, go ahead if you want to try and actually wear the thing. It's no business of mine. I only live here. I certainly wouldn't try to see any things of yours. I never have in my life, why should I start now?"

The old woman put on the brassiere. When she was buttoning up the little rhinestone buttons slowly at the front of her nylon dress, Lillian said, "Here, here, I'll do that. We don't have all the time in the world to be buttoning ourselves together when Pratt and all of them will be getting here just any time."

The old woman sat on the bed after Lillian went into the kitchen to see to the cake and paper cups. She rose and looked in the mirror at her cheeks and neck. They were criss-crossed with grooves; it looked as if the sewing machine had stitched the pattern of wrinkles. "Well, birthday, birthday, birthday," she said and sat on the bed again. She would like a little coffee-colored volume of poems for her birthday. She could read them just as well as the newspaper or the TV Guide or the Milk of Magnesia bottle. "What did they do with all those books any more? I used to have some pretty little poem books among them. One was E. A. Poe, and it had a pressed pansy on top of the poem about Helen. Sid or someone or I stuck that flower there. Little books with ribbons to mark your place if you wanted to stop reading and go some place for a while and then come back and read some more. Could keep your place." Maybe somebody today would give her some colored cotton balls in a round plastic box like Lillian had here the other day to give away as a bridge prize. They were pastel cotton balls, gentle and almost candy or magic, nestled one next to the other in that clear-plastic box. Pretty and delicate and pastel. "Or say, I know what I'd like to have." She smiled. "I'd like to have a hammer. Brand new with a new yellow wooden handle and a shiny, heavy head. Fresh from the hardware place. A hammer that could sit on the night table, or I could hold it in my hand when I wanted." With the head of it cool and firm in her hand, like a cool stone from the seashore. Oh, a hammer was a beautiful thing once you thought about it.

She plicked at the chenille on the white bedspread and wondered whatever did happen to that girl with the moles, that Celia Franks. She and Celia Franks used to hide oranges in the mesquite trees on their way to school and then find them on the way home. Sure, sure did, though, think this white brassiere

7

was pretty. Maybe Nancy's girl would come today, and maybe she would bring her a hammer or some pastel cotton balls. "Say, I wouldn't mind having any of those things."

"Mother!" Lillian called from the kitchen.

"Yay-oh?"

"Mother, come here a minute and tell me where you want this cake. In the middle of the table, like this, or do you want it more towards the living room for everybody to see?"

"What you want. It's the same whatever's best," she whispered.

"Mother? Mother! I *said* would you come here a second to tell me about this birthday cake. Where you want it put? Do you want it . . ." Lillian was nearly shouting; she turned as her mother entered the kitchen. "Oh! I didn't know you were here already. Why didn't you tell me you were standing there, so I wouldn't be yelling? Now, where do you want your cake?"

"Is Nancy's girl coming today?"

"What does that have to do with the price of eggs? I asked you where you wanted your cake." She opened and slammed the refrigerator door after taking out some Philadelphia creamed cheese. "I don't know if Jennifer's coming or not. I can't keep track of neighbors. I've got my hands full here as it is."

"I can hear you. You're shouting, sister." The old woman shuffled through the kitchen and looked at the arrayed table in the dining room, with the plastic ivy leaves hanging on one wall. "Yes, Pratt's said he's going to find out if that tomcat got run over or not."

"What?"

"Pratt. He's going to ask about that orange tomcat that was around here, if he got run over by a car out in the road or not. Haven't seen him for some while." She looked out the window at the two palm trees in the backyard. There was nothing in the yard but the two trees and a pink dust storm.

"Haven't seen him for a while? He was just over here yesterday, Mother! He came to show us the trophy he won bowling in the city semi-finals."

"Who?"

8

"Why, Pratt, Mother, *Pratt!* Why don't you listen? Now, do you or do you not want your cake on the dining room table, or do you want it closer so everybody can see it?"

Lillian put the cake in the middle of the table and began unceremoniously punching candles ("just . . . a . . . few . . . here . . . and . . . there!") into the white frosting. She told her mother that if she wasn't going to cooperate with her own birthday party, she'd do best to go sit in the living room and no, of course that cat had not been run over. "I, Lillian, gave it away to the paper boy. Why, we couldn't have any more cat hairs flying around here, coming in the door and into the kitchen where the food is kept, food that you eat."

The old woman sat in the living room and looked out the picture window to where a glass thing hung from the front porch. She sat and waited for her guests, liking that little glass thing more and more as the minutes passed. It was Japanese or Chinese, made of short striplets of glass that hung by threads and tinkled in the wind. Kind of like a wind chandelier, she thought. And those tiny brush strokes of the designs painted there by some Jap or some Chinaman. Just as little and delicate as you could want them. Nancy's girl had brought her the gift that swayed and played crystal notes in the breeze. Nancy's girl went to Chinatown in San Francisco, and when she came back, the two of them had had a fine time fixing the string and glass thing up on the porch.

A breeze now brushed across it, and the wind chandelier talked to itself in little crystal laughs. It talked to the old woman and made her think of oceans and seaside things and love and jade and then of Sid when he was a young strapping man.

"Nancy's girl brought this thing hanging out on the porch, didn't she?" she called into the kitchen. Come to think of it, Nancy's girl did bring that tender glass thing. Brought it some months back.

Where were those cigarettes? She looked over her shoulder at the kitchen door. She picked around in the pocket of her dress, her eyes still on the door. She then put a single crumpled cigarette on her knee and attempted to straighten it out and pinch some of the falling tobacco back into one end. She stood up slowly and lighted the cigarette with a book of matches whose cover asked her if she had psoriasis. She exhaled and closed her eyes, placing one hand lightly on top of the television set.

And to have some poems with a ribbon.

"Huh? What are you saying in there, Mother?" Lillian shouted over the grindings and flushings of the automatic dishwasher. The noises stopped abruptly, and the old woman stuffed the cigarette quickly in the vase of fresh zinnias, where it died in the water.

Lillian appeared, wiping her hands on a towel. "What is it? All the muttering. What do you want, Mother?"

When she found that again it was nothing and nothing, always nothing, she wondered if Pratt was or was not going to come early and said she would like to see the day *she* would try to wear a silly satin brassiere when her own daughter advised her against the silliness of it. "Say, wait a minute! Do I smell smoke?" She strode around the living room with her head cocked to one side and her nostrils flared and sniffing.

"Is that Nancy's girl coming for my birthday?"

Her daughter stopped and threw her hands out at her sides; they dropped with a slap to her thighs. "Oh, Lord. I ask you if I smell cigarette smoke, and you are still going on about Jennifer. That takes the cake." Deciding she did not smell anything, that her mind was playing tricks on her because of all this overwork in preparation for the party, Lillian went back into the kitchen.

At three-thirty, Pratt arrived with his hefty wife and their three bickering sons in YMCA T-shirts. After Pratt and his family, more and more family arrived, plopping in chairs and divans. The children turned the television on, ate the pretzels and socked each other. Nineteen family came. One grandchild brought blow-bubbles-through-a-plastic-ring and got whipped when the bubbles exploded on the newly polished coffee table and left little soapy rings on Lillian's clean furniture.

The offspring talked among themselves, jumping up from

their chairs from time to time to tell the guest of honor that she was looking younger every year.

Pratt kissed her gingerly, shying away from the smell of dentures and age. "Bet you're itching to get your hands on those birthday presents, eh, Motherkins?" He laughed and winked at her. "Hey, Maxine, hand me another cup of that Hawaiian, will you?" Then he piled her gifts in her lap. "Dig in, Mom!"

The old woman opened the packages and found three pairs of brown winter-warm stockings for her circulation, a round tin of stuffed dates, a bathmat with rubber suction cups to hold it to the tile of the bathroom ("Then nobody slips and gets hurt, right, Mother?"), and a framed family picture of Pratt and all of his. Then there was a shoehorn, a box of See's candy, which was passed around the room, an envelope with a subscription to *Senior Citizen!,* and a bottle of Pacquin's hand cream with the pricetag on it.

She opened each gift carefully, putting the ribbons in a pile and folding the wrapping paper to save it. She thanked for each item and thought, Nancy's girl should be here soon. She will come through all them and light upon my knee like a little moth, and I won't dare to move my hand so that her wings will be just so.

She said, "Pratt, what time is it, son?"

"Eight o'clock or a hair before."

"I'm thinking Nancy's girl ought to be popping in here any minute."

"Nancy whose girl?"

The front door opened suddenly, and the old woman leaned forward rigidly in her chair. That would be Nancy's girl from across the oceans and the wind chandeliers! It was one of the grandchildren who ran in after another one. She sat back slowly in the chair and folded her hands in her lap. It was very late. Only parts of the party were left around. She stared at her hands and tried to remember a poem about a hummingbird. Or a moth. Was it a moth? Nancy's girl was off flying around the light somewhere too far or too high and away. Oh and oh and oh.

Lillian moved around quickly wadding up wrapping paper.

"I know somebody who's had a pretty big day." She winked at the family and turned to her mother, "Come on, birthday girl."

"No, I think I'll wait a spell."

Lillian squeezed a ball of crumpled paper so tightly her knuckles turned white. "Mother . . . Nancy's girl is not . . . N . . . O . . . T . . . coming."

"I expect not, but I think I'll wait some anyway."

"I don't think you will, Mother."

"Says who?"

"We'll . . . we'll pretend that you didn't say that. Now, let's bundle ourselves off to bed, shall we? Say goodnight to Pratt and to . . ."

"I'm going to wait for my birthday to finish itself up. I'm going to stay up until midnight."

Lillian shot a look at the guests and said to her mother, "Now, you go on in the bedroom and go to sleep, and if you have to use the bathroom, call me or Pratt first, so that Chow-Chow doesn't get out and ruin the rug. I'll come in and help you get undressed in a minute."

"Lillian, lady, I'm telling you that I'm going to wait my birthday out."

Pratt grunted forward in his chair as he reached to snap on the television remote control. "Oh, now, Mother, let's not get testy on our birthday . . ."

In a high, tight voice, Lillian said, "Oh no, Pratt; that's all right, little brother, if she wants to be petulant . . . she can just be petulant until she rots." She opened the door to her mother's bedroom. "But she's not going to spoil our day with her little obsessions. If you, Mother, want to wait your birthday out, you can do so in here."

The old woman struggled to her feet and shuffled in to the bedroom. "I think I'll do that, lady." She sat down in a chair and stared through the venetian blinds.

"And thank you, Mother," Lillian said before shutting the door, "for being so very very appreciative of your birthday party that I was such a fool as to try and make nice for you!" With the light out, the room was filled with moonlight.

But through the closed door, the old woman could hear the wives and daughters scraping the party into the garbage disposal. The children would be going to sleep on the rug as the men watched the wrestling matches on the television.

She sat and sat and presently heard all the guests leaving and the refrigerator door opening and shutting. Lillian would be taking her carton of yogurt to bed with her.

Lillian opened the bedroom door and stood holding the yogurt and a spoon. "Oh, my my, you're still up, are you? I see. Well, wait on until dawn, if you like. Your birthday should surely be over by then." She slammed the door shut, and the old woman continued to sit in the chair.

She fell asleep there but awakened sometime before she heard the clock in the hall chime midnight. She stared at the white tufts of chenille on the moonlit bedspread and blinked, thinking of someone's hair falling down her back like long long wild ribbons.

The Conspiracy Against Mister Mann

Jerry Bumpus

from *The Fair*

Mr. Mann supposed it was a literary cocktail party, for everyone was talking about poetry. There were a number of men who looked like poets, there were men who appeared to be professors, there was a great abundance of young people who were no doubt students, and a great many women were on hand who were between the ages of thirty and fifty. These women, Mr. Mann guessed, were literary camp followers. They were the wives, mothers, aunties, and sweethearts of the poets. The ladies were haggard and as a whole had harassed, badgered expressions. All of them wore, as if it were the uniform of the cause to which they were devoted, baggy knit dresses.

The party host was a young bearded poet whose father did well on the North Side as a lay analyst. Elma had told Mr. Mann that the young poet hadn't yet received the recognition he deserved as a poet. Mr. Mann knew nothing about the host or poetry, and presumed Elma did; Mr. Mann usually believed whatever he was told. Thanks to his father, the young neglected poet lived well. His apartment wasn't luxurious, but it was enormous. Nearly two hundred people were in the main room of the apartment, and there were more people in the other rooms.

The host was short, had gentle eyes behind the thick glass of his spectacles, and he frequently tugged a sprig of kinky hair out from his face and let it recoil back into his thick black beard. In fact he was doing this as he stood talking to Elma across the room from where Mr. Mann sat in a corner drinking rum.

A famous American poet stood in the middle of the room surrounded by people. He was chatting with students and smiling politely as the young people competed with one another in a contest to prove how much each knew about the famous poet's personal life. The students' expressions were a mixture of blank entreatment—as if some of them were sure the poet was a god—and crafty-eyed incredulity—as if these particular young people were convinced the poet was a colossal liar.

Mr. Mann didn't know the name of the famous American poet; he knew only one person in the room—Elma. He knew he was in Chicago, near the University, but he didn't know how long he had been in this city, and he had no idea why he was where he was. For about thirty minutes he had been trying to think of a way of getting out of here. Neither he nor Elma had an automobile. He would have called a taxicab, but there wasn't a telephone in the apartment: a young woman Mr. Mann had asked about the phone had demurely told him the host was opposed to machines. There was the alternative of leaving the party and setting off on foot. But that was out of the question. Not long ago—was it several weeks or several months ago or even longer?—Mr. Mann had wandered around Istanbul for days and days. He shuddered at the thought of being again lost on foot in a strange city. His only hope was in Elma's finding someone at the party who had an automobile.

Blankly gazing off into space, Mr. Mann became aware that a tall woman across the room was staring at him. Then she winced as though she had been jabbed with a pin, and she started cutting through the crowd toward him.

He watched her coming. He finished his drink and started to get up from his chair and escape her if he could, but it was too late.

She had long black hair and her face was violent. She wore a great deal of make-up and her lips were coated not with lipstick but with thick red paste, perhaps medicine. Her large mouth dominated her face: it was a large thing of anger, vindication and, no doubt, triumph. Her nose was large and in any other face, on any other person, the nose would have been remarkable, but on her it was barely noticeable. Her old knit dress fit tightly and displayed her matronly breasts, amazon thighs, and broad hips.

When she was closer, Mr. Mann was fascinated by the red, wild glare in her eyes. The thought occurred to him that possibly in her youth, when she was innocent and still vulnerable to the whims and ways of humanity, she had been beaten at regular intervals.

Mr. Mann felt he had met the woman somewhere before and he tried to remember what he owed her.

"What're *you* doing here?" she said. She jerked her head from side to side to see if anyone noticed that they were talking.

Mr. Mann smiled dubiously.

Her eyes narrowed. "Did Peter bring you?"

"I . . . don't know Peter," he said, "do I?"

"Yes. But I like Richard Wilbur's poetry *so* much more," she said loudly, smiling fiendishly at Mr. Mann. A mumbling, gray-haired poet passed nearby, giving them a close scrutiny.

"Yes. His poems are very good," Mr. Mann said loudly.

She glanced over her shoulder at the poet's back and said low, "God damn him."

Mr. Mann looked at the man again and it struck him that the mumbling poet looked vaguely familiar. Had he met him at another party?

The woman was again glowering at Mr. Mann. As he looked up at her from his chair she seemed tremendously tall. He smiled. "You shouldn't've come here," she said, her large lips moving slowly, her enunciation perfect and full of rage. Then she leaned forward and whispered into his face, "If Howard gets done at the auction in time he's coming here."

"The auction?"

16

She straightened up, glanced around her, then looked back to him.

He blinked his eyes and said, "Whom are you talking about?"

"Don't play *games,*" she hissed. He supposed it was frustration, hate, ennui, perhaps menopause madness that made her this way. "He knows everything about us," she said. "Peter showed him some of those nasty photographs he took of us."

Mr. Mann blinked. "He did?"

"You *let* him, didn't you? Peter wouldn't have thought of doing that on his own. You put him up to it. *I know you,* you sly old fart."

"You do?" Now he was very interested. He tried to remember a detail of her body, any detail. She stood frowning and waiting for him to say something. He gazed at her big breasts and tried to remember what they looked like bare and sagging down. He knew, but he couldn't remember actually having seen them.

"Well?" she said.

He thought of apologizing. But that would incriminate him; it would be admitting everything. But apology was his natural inclination. It was the saint and the fool in him. So he said, "I'm terribly sorry, but you see I am a stranger in Chicago, if indeed that is where we still are; and I have no memory at all of your friend Peter or your own self or the nasty photographs or . . . anything, for that matter. I am very sorry."

Her expression changed as she listened: the fury eased and was replaced by a smile of amused cynicism.

He could tell that it was this fey helplessness in him that made her love him. She shook her head and said, "Roscoe, you old fart, you're one in a million."

She turned and made for the kitchen where the booze was.

Mr. Mann's brow hunched into three deep cracks and his eyes slowly faded out of focus. *Roscoe.*

He sat with his face sagging and his eyes closed. Maybe Elma knew the woman. He would ask Elma to have a calm, sensible talk with her.

Then he thought of Howard. Mr. Mann knew he wasn't physically a match for Howard if it came to settling things that

17

way, and eventually it always came to that. It was the only way. He reached behind his chair and got the rum bottle and poured some into his glass. The ice had melted away over an hour ago. He sighed and sipped the rum.

There was the wire-thin chance that when Howard came from the auction he would like Mr. Mann at first glance. It was not totally impossible that they were a veritable Damon and Pythias combination that had been kept apart by bad luck. Just like that—Mr. Mann tried to snap his fingers—they would be fast friends and go off, arm in arm, laughing and leaving behind the big woman with red eyes.

But there was no hope of Howard's liking him. For no doubt the woman had convinced him that Mr. Mann did horrible things to her that Howard couldn't come close to. And of course there were the photographs. Mr. Mann wished he could see them. He imagined grotesque, pathetic scenes in which his flaccid, scarred body was the star performer.

Mr. Mann felt the familiar constriction in his throat, the reaction he felt each time he was accused. The tightness, he believed, was what he would feel if he were drowning, a death he particularly feared.

At the thought of death the word *Conspiracy* entered Mr. Mann's mind. He opened his eyes a crack and viewed the complex conspiracy around him. Everyone in the room was involved in it. The conspiracy wasn't directed at him alone, Mr. Mann consoled himself. His paranoia, he sadly knew, wasn't a psychic debility to which he could abandon himself and, by indulging, survive. The real sorrow was in that he felt he wasn't paranoid. That indeed all these strangers were conspirators.

Howard, or for that matter anyone in this room, could walk over to Mr. Mann and pull a Luger from a scabbard inside his jacket and blast Mr. Mann's head with a nine-millimeter bullet. Or Howard, or anyone, could crawl along the baseboard of the wall to the side of Mr. Mann, get behind his chair, like Satan behind a rock, and at the most opportune moment draw the pink line of surprise across Mr. Mann's throat with a dagger. With Conspiracy everything was possible. Mr. Mann's business partner was killed by a conspiracy just before the invasion of France. Otto Krum had eaten a salmon that wasn't just tainted, but sodden with arsenic. And Otto Krum had been a gourmet. For him to have fallen victim to ersatz lox meant all things were violable; the universe was disintegrating from its lock of small, meaningful gravities; the Master Juggler of the universe, the clown-suited master of spheres, had got drunk on rum with Mr. Mann and was now prey to whim and idiocy. The gravity of the balls he was still somehow managing to keep spinning suddenly became their own masters and their weird and deranged course through time pulled the Master Juggler himself, and Mr. Mann with him, and everyone else as well with them, and the whole bag of cats went yowling through space.

Mr. Mann's mind spun in the sickening vortex, and as he closed his eyes he saw again his old friend, Otto Krum, his big nose almost touching the cold, blunt nose of the poisonous salmon, the man and the fish staring aghast at each other throughout eternity.

He must have dozed for a few minutes. When he opened his eyes he could still feel the presence of dread about him—it was as if dread even had an odor, the severe, sharp smell of raw meat. He knew dread had fended him away from sleep and he tried to recall what it was.

Perhaps it had been the beginning of the recurrent dream Mr. Mann had about the Swiss lad. It happened in Madrid just after the war. The Swiss youth had been standing ahead of Mr. Mann in line in a butcher shop and he had commented on the unexplained disappearance of The Leader at the most crucial stage of fighting in Berlin. The butcher held the rest of the people at bay with the cleaver while with his other hand he snagged the young Swiss with a meat hook, hung him screaming on the wall, his feet just short of the floor, and hacked him to pieces. Of course the butcher was insane, the police told Mr. Mann and the other witnesses after the butcher had been quietly led away and while the Swiss youth's remains were being gathered up and wrapped not in the butcher's heavy waxed paper but in newspapers. Later Mr. Mann learned that the butcher had committed a similar crime in Dusseldorf before the war. In his dream, Mr. Mann saw first the dripping cleaver, then the Swiss boy's bare white chest. Always in his dream Mr. Mann picked up the cleaver.

Mr. Mann sighed heavily and gazed about him, his eyes burning. He had absolutely no idea where in the world he was.

He watched the crowd of people and saw two young poets standing behind a very beautiful young girl. She stood with her back to them, admiring a picture on the wall. Her hair was lovely, soft and blond. Her skin was light and had the smooth texture of youth and health. "Beauty is . . ." Mr. Mann muttered.

He watched her; then he said quietly, "My eyes have given me madness. My eyes are to blame." Still the young woman stood there, a lovely intimation of a white kingdom beyond death.

As he watched her he realized the two young men behind her were snickering. They moved slowly closer to her.

Then the party's host stepped in front of Mr. Mann and from behind his beard and thick glasses he said, "I'm Jeffery Traum. How do you do? You are Hermann Mann, aren't you? The famous German literary critic?"

Mr. Mann remembered he was in Chicago.

"I am Hermann Mann, yes. But I am sure I am not the one . . ."

But, as happened so often, Mr. Mann wasn't allowed to further explain who he was. Jeffery Traum was already saying, "I read *Existence and Truth* in translation. I believe it is the best analysis of the human condition I have ever read."

Mr. Mann sighed, considered, and then finally said, "Thank you very much, Mr. Traum."

Mr. Traum nodded his head once, and, as he reached into his beard, pinched a wisp of hair to give it the stretch treatment, he asked Mr. Mann how his translation of Henry James into German was progressing. Mr. Mann pondered the question, wondering how the translation *should* be progressing, and was answering in more hesitant English than was actually necessary for him, when again the large woman with the violent face came through the crowd toward him. She announced hysterically, "I talked to him on the phone. He's on his way over here."

She and Mr. Traum stared at Mr. Mann. He looked down into the tiny sea of rum in his glass.

"He'll kill you," the woman sighed.

Still there was no reply from Mr. Mann. The woman turned and headed back for the kitchen.

"She must have gone out the kitchen window and climbed up the fire escape and used Goring's phone upstairs," Mr. Traum said. "Goring has the only phone in the building."

"Could you perhaps tell me who that woman is?" Mr. Mann asked him.

"I've never seen her before in my life. Don't you know her?"

"No."

"Really?"

"Absolutely not."

"God damn it," Mr. Traum said slowly. "You come to this country to get away from the Nazis, you're an honored person, and what happens? Crazy goddamn women sic their crazy goddamn husbands on you. That's no way to treat a great person like you, an important, good person who has done so much. My God, I can't imagine what in the hell is happening." Mr. Traum's eyes bugged behind his glasses.

"I am surprised that you, a poet, and a very good poet," Mr. Mann said, smiling benignly, "should be so concerned over such a trifling and, I might add, drunken matter as this."

Mr. Traum brightened for a moment at these kind words from the famous critic. But his despair was deepening, Mr. Mann could tell. The young poet's eyes squinted and he was suffering behind his spectacles and behind his beard. Mr. Mann was impressed by American youth. It seemed their constant companion was a tragic depression. Was this nervous despair the result of their fear of the next war?

"I've been thinking," Mr. Traum said slowly, heavily, the expression of the idea causing him pain, his face scowling, "I've been thinking of a poem about the assassination."

A shrill scream silenced the room and froze the two men in the word.

It was Mr. Mann, naturally, old man, old tortured fart who had too often alone survived to tell the tale, who moved first. His hand jerked and his empty glass flew into the air in a smooth, beautiful arc. Its slow flight attracted the attention of many people in the room and they looked up at the glass, their mouths open, their eyes large with awe.

Mr. Mann gripped the arms of his chair and waited just one moment before closing his eyes and holding his breath—for years ago he had decided that it would be best to wait with his eyes closed for the nine-millimeter bullet that would reduce him to oblivion.

But the moments passed and he opened his eyes and saw across the room the beautiful blond young girl who had been admiring the picture on the wall. The two young poets now stood one on each side of her, and though their faces were young, they were deeply creased with intense expressions, their lips drawn back, their teeth gleaming. One of them held the girl's arm and the other was leaning against her as if he were whispering something in her ear. The girl's face was strained, not pretty, as she tried to remain dignified.

"What is happening over there?" Mr. Mann asked.

Mr. Traum shrugged his shoulders. "There are strange things," he said.

"Yes, but . . ."

And in the few seconds it took for this to be said, while Mr. Mann glanced at Mr. Traum, there was another high, terrible scream from the girl, and when Mr. Mann looked at them again the girl was kneeling on the floor and the two poets were stepping back from her, their mouths snarled with toothy, hideous grins.

"What has happened?" Mr. Mann said out loud, unaware of the total silence in the room until he heard his own words like clear echoes from a great distance, and people turned and looked at him, waiting for him to answer the question.

There was a restless scuffling in the room and suddenly five young men dressed identically in gray suits and immaculately white shirts burst from the crowd. Mr. Mann was sure they were young businessmen, but they had the faces of beasts. They glared a moment at the two poets and then they charged them at a dead run.

"Don't fight!" Mr. Traum yelled as they crashed into the poets.

The leers on the poets' faces were stunned into vacant expressions as the two of them were slugged over the head by blackjacks three of the young businessmen pulled from straps on their belts. "My God!" Mr. Traum yelled.

One of the fallen poets lay on his back a moment, staring up at the man who struck him. Then his entire body quivered and he flopped over onto his belly, his legs and arms flying.

Other fights broke out and soon all over the room women were screaming, men were cursing and shouting, people were heaving to and fro as they were shoved and beaten. The pandemonium was so great it was as if a thousand hogs were being butchered in the room. Bottles and glasses and some furniture were hurled through the air. Everyone who was physically able was fighting, and those who weren't able to fight were either yelling, clutching to someone, or being victimized by the others.

Through the gray-brown blur of writhing people Mr. Mann saw a young girl with a child-like face, and her eyes were big and gleeful, her nose crinkled like a snarling puppy's: "The joint's up for grabs!" she screamed at Mr. Mann.

He nodded and replied, "It certainly is," as he watched her go dashing by, carried under the thick arm of a giant.

The floor of the apartment shook ominously and Mr. Mann crawled over the back of his chair to hug the wall in case the floor fell through. The rum bottle was handy, so he took a quick drink.

When he lowered the bottle he saw a huge Negro he hadn't noticed earlier at the party. The Negro picked up a man by the ankles and after spinning him around a few times, sailed him over people's heads into a far corner of the room where the man crashed face first into the wall above a crumpled professor who had, Mr. Mann guessed, made the same trip just a little earlier.

The Negro pounced on new victims. He adeptly upended a short, fat man who was trying to fight him off, a broken bottle in each hand, but the Negro sent him against the same wall.

After the fat man, he threw two more people and then stopped to catch his breath. When he stopped he was attacked by the five young businessmen. The three with blackjacks were slugging away at him, swinging very slightly short, Mr. Mann realized—not going for bone, but tearing at the flesh. As Mr. Mann watched, the scene slowed and he saw with perfect clarity one of the young men draw his arm back straight from his shoulder and he saw the man's wrist flick and the blackjack snap erect for an instant as the forward swing began, and then the young man hunched down slightly as he swung forward and the blackjack went taut and sleek through the air and Mr. Mann heard the splat as it smacked into the Negro's mouth.

One of the young men suddenly bent double, his face blank, gagging, his tongue thick between his lips. The others didn't stop and now the Negro was giving ground, his face torn, large chunks gouged out of his face, blood and flesh spurting as the blackjacks snipped the air around his head, and now as each blow landed there was a wet sucking sound.

Still behind the chair, Mr. Mann took off his jacket and began carefully wrapping it around his left arm, gripping the collar in his hand and tucking in the end of the coat when the arm was covered up to his elbow.

He continued watching what they were doing to the Negro and just before the man collapsed, Mr. Mann hunkered as far as he could behind the chair and closed his eyes and held his breath.

Concentrating to achieve a deep well of blackness within himself, he forced out the shouts and screams and other sounds of crashing turmoil, and for just one moment there was a soft apparition: his wife's lovely face, so many million miles away in Berlin, years ago, a precise world of crystal and beautiful children, music in the warm mornings, tea in silver cups upon a table, nearby a frog pond with marvelous bright goldfish, the beauty of childhood, his wife's voice the sound of love. . . .

"Come on."

He rose, his eyes closed, not lifting his coat-padded arm to defend himself. He turned toward his death.

But the touch at his elbow was light and when he calmly opened his red and burning eyes he saw his gentle host, Jeffery Traum, and he walked straight and calm behind the young man who was dodging and ducking as they crossed the room, stepping over people, and once Traum let go Mr. Mann's arm and fought a bloody, drunken woman who attacked him with an icepick.

They made it to the kitchen. They climbed out the window and up into the black night.

Mr. Mann looked down between his feet as he climbed the steel ladder of the fire escape and below him there was perfect blackness.

Then they went into the kitchen of another apartment.

He was surprised. Sitting around a kitchen table were a dozen or more people. The famous American poet was there and his chin had been cut. Most of the people in the kitchen were middle-aged women in knit dresses, and everyone was very nervous and worried about what was happening down below. Up here the noise from Traum's apartment was muffled, but now and then a shout or a scream carried out into the night and occasionally the walls shook violently.

Mr. Mann stood staring at them and then it occurred to him that he should unwrap his jacket from his arm and put it on.

While he was doing this, one of the middle-aged women said to him, "Elma's sleeping in the back bedroom."

Mr. Mann blinked his eyes. Then he remembered that there was a person called Elma, and he smiled at the people and said, "Thank you."

The famous American poet hiccupped harshly and said, "Mr. Traum, I must say your party was completely lousy from the point of view of dignity and peace, but I *will* say this shows that poets are human."

Mr. Traum sat down at the kitchen table while Mr. Mann

backed up and leaned against the sink and everyone listened closely as the great poet told a tale about his experiences in Japan when he was a Guggenheim Fellow. Mr. Mann listened as closely as he could, but something seemed left out of the poet's story.

Tranquility is found in a state of silence and immobility, the poet explained. He described a scene for them. He spent a great deal of time trying to create in their minds a picture of one thousand Japanese virgins on the beach sitting cross-legged in the Lotus position. They were contemplating. All around these thousand virgins the world was exploding and erupting. The poet said that all around the virgins the world was molten and bubbling. But the virgins were cool to it all.

"Perhaps they were cool to it all because they were virgins," Mr. Mann mumbled.

"What was that crack?" the poet said, his eyes narrowing as he turned his head slowly and stared at Mr. Mann.

"Has anyone called the police?" someone said as a man in the apartment below began yelling. The screaming voice choked and there were hoarse coughs; then apparently the man was attacked again for his voice rose even higher than before in a terrible cry of agony.

Jeffery Traum asked the famous American poet, "Did you actually see these virgins sitting on the beach?"

"I don't want to be around when the Man makes the scene," a broad-shouldered henna-haired lady said.

Mr. Mann recognized the light in the eye of the famous poet as he stared at him. The poet's nostrils flared and quivered slightly. His mouth tightened. Mr. Mann wished he hadn't unwrapped his jacket from his arm. "I feel ill," Mr. Mann stammered.

"Give him a drink," a woman said. "When they get that look it means they need a drink."

"Yes," Mr. Mann agreed, smiling exaggeratedly. The poet had put both hands on the edge of the table and he was now leaning forward to get up.

Someone handed Mr. Mann a tall water glass full of a yellow

liquid. He sniffed it—it had the quality—and he downed it. Everyone in the room was watching closely.

"What was it?" someone asked.

"Paregoric," another person answered.

They watched Mr. Mann avidly. "Ah," he sighed, his eyes watering, the room spinning around a few times.

"How did this rotten old junkie get up here?" the famous American poet roared.

Most of them shrugged their shoulders. "He's the critic, Hermann Mann," Jeffery Traum said.

Mr. Mann smiled.

"Like hell he is," the famous American poet said, "and I should know. I happen to be one of Mr. Mann's most intimate friends and I can tell you straight that this old hopster isn't Hermann Mann."

"Who gives a rat's ass *who* he is?" Mr. Traum said. He tugged a hair out from his beard and twanged it with the fingernail of the little finger of the same hand. "He's a decent person. One of the most decent persons I've ever met. So what the hell?"

Nodding judiciously, Mr. Mann began edging down the sink toward the door that led to the front of the apartment. He smiled wanly at the famous American poet, who was still staring at him in a deadly way as he listened to more of Traum's praise of Mr. Mann.

Then he turned away from the sink and stepped out of the kitchen.

The next room of the apartment was black and Mr. Mann hadn't gone three steps before his foot touched a piece of furniture. He stopped and waited for his eyes to adjust to the darkness. If the American poet came after him he would, Mr. Mann hoped, have trouble finding him. He stood waiting, weaving in the darkness, his hands out before him, and then he heard voices in the distance, from the other end of the room. It seemed to be an unusually long room. He waited longer, but the room seemed to grow even blacker. Mr. Mann began shuffling forward, moving his hands up and down slowly before him. He was, he reminded himself, looking for Elma. Or was he escaping from the American poet? He paused and listened to see if he could hear the poet coming after him. Again he heard the voices from the other end of the room.

Mr. Mann went on into the darkness, and though he was dragging his feet, it was as if he were plunging headlong through time.

He stood back from the door of the small room where the two men sat talking. He was sure they couldn't see him even if they hadn't been arguing so intently.

He inched closer, careful not to bump into anything. He stopped. Still he wasn't close enough to hear them distinctly, though now he could see them fairly well in the dimly lighted room. They sat facing each other on small stools, their knees almost touching. One of them was a small young man wearing a white shirt with the collar open at the throat and no jacket. He spoke very excitedly and as he did his voice rose high and his eyes bulged, his lips twisting and contracting as he shouted.

The other man was large, heavy, and balding—in his late forties. Perhaps they were father and son; they resembled each other a good deal. When the older man spoke, his words were snapped. He gestured quickly, his large hands quick and dangerous, and he leaned forward on his stool. As he spoke, suddenly shouting louder than the young man, he flung his arms and shook his hands in the young man's face, his fingers crooked like the talons of a great bird.

But the young man didn't flinch or even blink his eyes as the hands flew near his face. His expression changed as the other man shouted at him. His eyes squinted hard and his mouth pursed in an expression that was smug and childish.

Mr. Mann was sure the two men would soon be fighting, but he was drawn still closer.

He moved to the side, out of the weak light coming from the room, and approached silently. Now he could hear what they were saying. He was so close he was afraid to look into the room, afraid they would see him. But, very gradually, in the middle of a long harangue in which both of the men were shouting wildly, he peered in the doorway. He was so close he could have touched their shoulders.

Now the room seemed full of light, as if floodlights were shining into the room. The men were sweating under the bright, glaring light, their faces glistening like the pale faces of wax figures. Their eyes were large and intense, unblinking.

"No, no, no," the big man bellowed, the veins standing out in his thick neck. "They can't wait there in the boat for us 'cause somebody see the boat, get the cops." Then his voice dropped suddenly; his tone became cajoling. "It's 'cause you're stupid." As he went on he was no longer shouting, but he spoke in a reasonable, calm manner and only slightly did his words take the choked quaver appropriate to the pained, desperate expression on his face. "You're a stupid fink hate everything they give me you."

The young man's sneer was complacent. He licked his round, full lips and said, "See, we get down there, the boat's setting . . ." He blinked his eyes a few times as he talked, and as if there were a meaning beneath his words which only he understood; his eyes and mouth assumed an appalled expression and his voice rose. His mouth again became vicious and he was shouting, "We take off for Mexico. We get a *plane* there. They have a plane *waiting*. For us. A jet. A Boeing Seven-o-seven jet. We get on it, see; then *nothing* can get us, nothing."

"Hold it," the big man shouted, the words exploding, and he held up both arms against the world's movement.

For an instant they were silent, panting and staring at each other, and they resembled each other more and more, their profiles frozen in the white glare, face to face, their noses nearly touching, a frozen tableau of the soul's sudden self-confrontation.

The older man opened his mouth to speak and hesitated one moment, his tongue between his teeth, his face tightening into a terrible scowl. Then he spoke, "*Where* we get the jet? Tell. Tell me that."

"It's there. Look, Man. Trust me. You got to trust me." The young man put his hand on the big man's knee.

"You think somethin' like this just . . ." and again, uncontrollably, he jerked both arms up against the sky, "Wham! Outa nowhere just up and happen. You are a *punk. Punk.* So you do it. Okay. That is okay *fine!*" he screamed. "But you are a . . . *stupid.*" His voice dropped and he repeated, his voice quite level, "You are a stupid."

"You want me to be like that?" he was answered by the young man in a tone just as gentle as his had been when he finished speaking. But then the voice became more firm as the young man said, "But I am *not* stupid. I done a lot of stuff, I tell you." His head rolled back and he gazed up at the black ceiling beyond the glaring white path of light shining on them, and as he stared away, his eyes became glazed, and from the shadows, from the secrecy of the ceiling, he developed the new dark rhapsody of his mood. His voice peaked to a wail, lost and profound in its loneliness. "We get a boat and we get in the boat, we go out into the Gulf of Mexico at night. We take lights because it's black and dark out there, the water black, everywhere." His eyes were closed. The big man, listening closely, also closed his eyes. Then he opened them after a moment, wanting to say something, wanting to interrupt the young man, but he couldn't interrupt him, even when he tried, for he was entranced.

"The water splashing up against the side of the boat . . . ," he lifted his hand and waved it slowly from side to side and the big man nodded his head. "We'll have stuff to eat, so don't worry. We'll have stuff and we won't get seasick because the Gulf of Mexico isn't like that." He licked his lips. "The dark stars everywhere in the sky, the sky dark like sleeping." He smiled, his eyes closed. "Like bein' daid, Man."

The big man licked his lips and moved a little closer to the young man, putting one knee between the young man's knees. "Out there in the Gulf of Mexico we'll have a captain on the boat and he'll have all the stuff we need. He'll take care of everything. Huh?"

"Yeah," the big man grunted.

"Then in the morning we'll be there and they'll have everybody out standing around to see us. Yeah. We'll come up on deck the submarine and they'll start greeting us. They'll hail us." His voice rose as he said, "I been there. I know it. I seen it happen, Man. It's . . . my God, *every*body out there."

Then again they were shouting furiously at each other, their eyes open, tense, straining toward each other like wild dogs, the big man screaming like a woman now, his voice from another world, "Submarine. Submarine Man nobody no no no. Goddamn submarine to me. No Man. No submarine me."

The young man stopped yelling and listened to the last part of what he said. The smug, coy smile came onto his lips, for even with his eyes open he could see all of them standing and waving flags and screaming and hailing, everything for him; and then he said to the big man, "Okay. So they send something else. Not a submarine. Just a regular boat that goes on the top. It don't matter."

"They send a de-stroyer."

"Okay. Yeah. A de-stroyer. So like I say, they're all cheering us, we come up on the deck, and there's everybody you ever knowed. They've come down there to see you and shake your hand. Jesus Christ. Beautiful girls everywhere and those big black guys . . ."

Then the big man was shouting, "Doan gimme *that* jazz, Man," his hand on the young man's knee, and, as if on signal, they moved their stools an inch closer together.

"All the sky beautiful like no clouds or anything and all of 'em got out their flags, big trucks, and they got, even they got *army* tanks, Man, and they got our picture on it, you and me, see, Man . . ."

"Baby . . ."

"Yeah. All over the world, everything, all the sky and I beat it all over and we get there all the candy blood shoot rifle clear in the blue sky like he was a big long bird flying his arms wings fly falling. . . . He is falling, not looking at me, no, Man. He will never know I done it don't know it is I it is I it is I it is I . . ."

"Baby . . ."

"You son of a bitch," the young man screamed, his eyes now closed, his face savage. He lunged forward for the big man's throat and the big man caught him, his eyes also closed, his lips moving as he repeated the word over and over, and they fell down, the young man on top the big man, and they were grunting and whining and struggling on the floor when Mr. Mann staggered back from the doorway into the darkness behind him and he hung his head to disgorge all the sour bile of alcohol and life, and as he stared down he saw, cast perfectly white in the immense black bubble of the soul of the universe, what at first he thought was another person's face; but then he realized the face he saw reflected from the night was his own face, splattered with blood, smiling back at him, his own face, the face of the young assassin.

"Poor Mr. Mann. He has had a bad time." A woman's voice. Speaking German.

"A man his age should take into consideration." Another woman's voice, in English.

Slowly he opened his eyes, admitting bit by bit the light and pain.

"Elma is waiting to see you," one of the two squarefaced, blank-eyed nuns said to him.

"Elma?"

"Elma is your wife," the one said in German.

"My wife," he said dully.

They waited a moment, alternately smiling sympathetically and frowning solidly. He stared at them for a while and then heard a man cough nearby and turned his head and looked around him. He was in a large ward of beds and there were over one hundred men here. He recalled having earlier looked around this same hospital ward. Or had it been a hospital years ago? The walls were yellow, the ceiling high, with barred windows high on the walls.

He slowly sat up in the bed and looked down at his body and found no harm done. Gently, with the tips of his fingers he touched his head and face. There were no bandages, no tender lumps, no clumps of stitches. He lay back and now that he was completely awake he realized his mind was clear, extraordinarily clear, too clear. Every color, sound, every scent of the stringent atmosphere of the ward bore into him.

Mr. Mann felt the beginning of a long monologue inside his mind, the blatting lecture that, once begun, he knew, would continue its blaring enumeration of all the meaningful facts that all together conspired toward his destruction. To think at this stage, was to relive a lifetime, as though the switch had been thrown on a machine that, once started, continued its operation, infernally, to the conclusion.

He heard the voice, the shrill, inexhaustible voice shouting. It was still in the deep distance of the past in his memory, but it was started: it was the prologue to the end of the world. All youth was standing in the stadium cheering and waving the red flag with its bent, angered cross. The sky was limitless. His eyes burned across the distance, the steel of his face severing all doubt. Mr. Mann's soul was stunned to silence by the angelic strength of his voice, by his furious wisdom. All manifestations of his power and dreadful beauty commanded God and the universe to listen to him.

"Our Motherland lies pillaged under the black hands of enemies. Our Motherland weeps—but we are silent. Our Motherland weeps—but we stand weak and unmoving. Our Motherland *lives*," the word like lightning in the mind. "Our Motherland is calling to us and now we answer. We answer."

A roar rising in the stadium, a million voices lifted in deep passion: "We answer."

Mr. Mann got up from the hospital bed. On the foot of the bed was a faded blue robe and pinned to it was a pink card with the word "Pass" on it. He put on the robe and clutched the pass in his hand. He glanced up. Men were watching him from their beds. The pulsating roar of the voices in the stadium flooded the long hospital ward: *We answer. We answer.*

He went to the door and through the small window in it he

saw a large woman with hideous long black hair and a violent, grimacing face. She was showing some photographs to the old policeman who sat guarding the door of the ward.

Mr. Mann turned around. At the far end was another door and he hurried down toward it. Not looking at the dead men in the beds, for he knew they lay with their right arms lifted, frozen in the salute of death, he held his eyes on the door and still the world echoed with the shouting in the stadium and *He* was smiling at all of them and they knew He would say more and they loved him.

He held up the pink pass to the window and a policeman nodded, got up, and unlocked the door. Mr. Mann nodded and hurried by him down the hall, one hand holding the faded blue robe together in front, his other arm swinging briskly at his side and clutching the pink pass.

Sixty Acres

Raymond Carver

from *Discourse*

The call came an hour ago, when they were eating. Two guys were shooting on Lee Waite's part of the Toppenish Creek, down below the bridge on the Cowiche Road. Joseph Eagle had sounded upset. It was the third or fourth time this winter somebody had been in there, he reminded. Joseph Eagle was an old Indian who couldn't get around and who lived on his government allotment in a little place off the Cowiche Road, with a radio he listened to day and night and a telephone in case he got sick. Lee Waite wished he'd let him be about that land, though, do something else about it, if he wanted, besides call.

Out on the porch, Lee Waite leaned on one leg and picked at a string of meat in between his teeth. He was a small thin man with a thin face and long black hair. If it hadn't been for the phone call, he would have slept a while this afternoon. He frowned, and took his time pulling into his coat; they'd probably be gone anyway when he got there. That was usually the way. The hunters from Toppenish or Yakima could drive the reservation roads like anyone else, they just weren't allowed to hunt. But they'd cruise by that untenanted and irresistible sixty acres of his, two, maybe three times, then, if

35

they were feeling reckless, park down off the road in the trees and hurry through the knee-deep barley and wild-oats, down to the creek—maybe getting some ducks, maybe not, but always doing a lot of shooting in the little time before they cleared out. Joseph Eagle sat crippled in his house and watched them plenty of times. Or so he told Lee Waite.

He cleaned his teeth with his tongue and squinted in the late afternoon winter half-light. He wasn't afraid; it wasn't that, he told himself; he just didn't want any trouble.

The porch, small and built on just before the war, was almost dark. The one window-glass had been knocked out years before, and Lee had nailed a beetsack over the opening. It hung there behind the cabinet, matted-thick and frozen, moving slightly as the cold air from outside came in around the edges. The walls were crowded with old yokes and harnesses, and up on one side, above the window, was a row of rusted handtools. He made a last sweep with his tongue, tightened the lightbulb into the overhead socket, and opened the cabinet. He took out the old double-barrel from in back and reached up into the box on the top shelf for a handful of shells. The brass ends of the shells felt cold, and he rolled them in his hand before dropping them into a pocket of the old coat he was wearing.

"Aren't you going to load it, papa?" the boy Benny asked from behind.

Lee turned, saw Benny and little Jack standing in the kitchen doorway. Ever since the call they'd been after him—had wanted to know if this time he was going to shoot somebody. It bothered him, kids talking like that, like they'd enjoy it, and now they stood at the door, letting all the cold air in the house and looking at the large gun up under his arm.

"Get back in that house where the hell you belong," he flared.

They left the door open and ran back in where his mother and Nina were, and on through to the bedroom. He could see Nina at the table trying to coax bites of squash into the baby, who was pulling back and shaking her head. Nina looked up, tried to smile.

He stepped into the kitchen and shut the door, leaned back against it. She was plenty tired, he could tell. A beaded line of moisture glistened over her lip and, as he watched, she stopped to move the hair away from her forehead. She looked up at him again, then back at the baby. It'd never bothered her like this before when she was carrying. The other times she could hardly sit still and used to jump up and walk around, even if there wasn't much to do except cook a meal, or sew. He fingered the loose skin around his neck and glanced covertly at his mother, dozing since the meal in a chair by the stove. She squinted her eyes at him and nodded. She was seventy years old and shrivelled, but her hair was still crow-black and hung down in front over her shoulders in two long, tight braids. He was sure she had something wrong with her because sometimes she went two days without saying anything, just sitting in the other room by the window and staring off up the valley. It made him shiver when she did that, and he didn't know any more what her little signs and signals, her silences, were supposed to mean.

"Why don't you say something?" he asked, shaking his head. "How do I know what you mean, mama, if you don't say?" He looked at her for a minute and watched her tug at the ends of her braids, waited for her to say something. Then he grunted and crossed by in front of her, took his hat off a nail and went out.

It was cold. An inch or two of grainy snow from three days past covered everything, made the ground lumpy, and gave a cold, desolate look to the stripped rows of beanpoles in front of the house. The dog came scrabbling out from under the house when it heard the door, started off for the truck without looking back. "Come back here!" Lee called sharply, his voice looping and bouncing in the thin air.

Leaning over, he took the dog's cold, dry muzzle in his hand. "You better stay here this time. Yes, yes." He flapped the dog's ear back and forth and looked around. He couldn't see the Satus Hills across the valley because of the heavy overcast, just the wavy flatness of sugarbeet fields—white, except for black places here and there where the snow hadn't gotten. One place in sight—Charley Treadwell's, a long way off—but no lights on that he could tell. Not a sound anyplace, just the low ceiling of heavy clouds pressing down on everything. He'd thought there was a wind, but it was still. "Stay here now. You hear?"

Lee started off for the truck, wishing again he didn't have to go. He'd dreamed last night too—about what he couldn't remember—but he'd had an uneasy feeling ever since he woke up this morning.

He drove in low gear down to the gate, got out and unhooked it, drove past, got out again and hooked it. He didn't keep horses any more but it was a habit he'd gotten into, keeping it shut. Down the road, the grader was scraping toward him, the blade clanging sharply every time the metal hit the frozen gravel. He was in no hurry, and he waited the five or ten minutes it took to come up. One of the men in the cab leaned out with a cigarette in his hand and waved as they went by, but Lee looked off. He pulled out onto the road after they passed. He looked over at Charley's when he went by, but there were still no lights, and the car was gone. He remembered what Charley had told him a few days ago; about a fight he'd had last Sunday with some kid who came over his fence in the afternoon and shot into a pond of ducks, right down by the barn. The ducks came in there every afternoon, Charley said. They *trusted* him, he'd said, as if that was what really mattered. He'd run down from the barn where he was milking, waving his arms and hollering, and the kid had pointed the gun at him. If he could've just got that gun away from him! Charley said, staring hard at Lee with his one good eye and nodding slowly. As it was, he didn't stand a chance; couldn't even get the license number of the kid's car. Lee hitched a little in the seat. He didn't want any trouble like that. He hoped whoever it was would be gone when he got there, like the other times.

Out to the left he passed Ft. Simcoe, the white painted tops of the old buildings standing behind the reconstructed palisade. The gates of the fort were open, and he could see cars parked around inside and a few people in coats, walking. He'd never bothered to stop. Once his history teacher in high school had brought all the kids in his class out here—a field trip, she called it—but he'd stayed home that day. He rolled down the window and cleared his throat, hawked it at the bridge abutment over a drain.

Another five minutes and he turned onto Lateral B, and then came to Joseph Eagle's place; all the lights on, even the porch-light. He drove past, down to where the Cowiche Road came in, and got out of the truck and listened. He began to think they might be gone then, and he could turn around and go on back, when he heard the group of dull, far-off shots coming across the fields. He waited another minute, then took a rag and went around the truck and tried to wipe off some of the snow and ice in the window edges. He kicked the snow off his shoes before getting in, drove a little farther until he could see the bridge, then looked for the tracks that turned off into the trees, where he knew he'd find their car. He pulled in behind the gray sedan and switched off the key.

Lee sat in the truck and waited, squeaking his foot back and forth on the brake and hearing them shoot every now and then. After a few minutes, he couldn't sit still any longer and got out, walked slowly around to the front. He hadn't been down here to do anything in—four or five years. Leaning against the fender and looking out over the land, he couldn't understand where all the time had gone. He remembered when he was little, wanting to grow up. He used to come down here often then and trap this part of the creek for muskrat and set night-lines for German brown. He looked around, moved his feet inside his shoes. All that was a long time ago. Growing up, he heard his father say he intended this land for the three boys, but both his brothers had been killed, and Lee was the one it came down to, all of it.

He remembered: deaths. Jimmy first. (He woke to the terrific pounding on the door; dark, the smell of woodpitch from the stove, a car outside with the lights on and the motor running, and a crackling voice coming from a speaker inside the car. His father throws open the door, and the enormous figure of a man in a cowboy hat and wearing a gun—the deputy sheriff—fills the doorway. *Waites? Your son Jimmy has been killed at a dance in Wapato.* Everyone had gone away in the truck and Lee was left by himself. He'd crouched petrified and alone the rest of the night in front of the wood stove, watching the flickering shadows dance on the wall and hearing in his mind the dry, whooping sounds of his father. Later, when Lee was twelve or thirteen, Jack was in a car wreck on Highway 97 and killed instantly, but when the sheriff came, a different one, he only said there'd been an accident, that they'd better come along. He remembered Jack better. They'd shared the same room, and in the mornings he used to watch him in front of the mirror, smoothing back with his palms his black, shiny hair. Sometimes, after chores, late in the long summer evenings, they used to play catch with a hardball Jack had. The nighthawks would be out, wheeling and darting silently overhead after insects; Mt. Hood, where spirits once lived, towering up at the end of the valley, with orange and purple-colored clouds pulled in around its top. At the funeral, though, he wouldn't have known it was Jack; his hair was combed in a different way, and his head seemed larger.)

He pushed off from the truck and walked the few feet over to the edge of the field. Things were different now, that's all there was to it. He was thirty-two years old, and Benny and little Jack were growing up. And there was the baby. He shook his head. Time, what was time? A bird flying up the valley against the wind until it disappeared. He closed his hand around one of the tall stalks of milkweed that swayed and rustled in the slight breeze that had come up. He snapped its neck, felt the sticky sap ooze into his palm. He looked up when he heard the soft chuckling of ducks over his head; their wings made a rapid, whistling sound as they cut the air. He wiped his hand on his pants and followed them for a moment, watched them set their wings at the same instant and circle once over the creek. Then they flared. He saw three ducks fall before he heard the shots. He turned abruptly and started back for the truck.

He took out his gun, careful not to slam the door, and moved out into the trees. It was almost dark. He coughed once, and then stood with his lips pressed together and his body rigid, surrounded by the trees and staring impassively down the creek.

They came thrashing through the brush, two of them. Then, jiggling and squeaking the fence, they climbed over into the field and crunched through the snow. They were breathing hard by the time they got up close to the car.

"My God, there's a truck there!" one of them said, and let go with a thud the ducks he was carrying.

It was a boy's voice. He had on a heavy hunting coat, and in the game pockets Lee could dimly make out the enormous padding of ducks all around his body.

"Take it easy, will you!" The other stood craning his head around, trying to see. "Hurry up! There's nobody inside. Get the hell in the car!"

Without moving and trying to keep his voice steady, Lee said, "Stand there. Put your guns right there on the ground." He edged out of the trees and faced them, raised and lowered his gun barrels. "Take off them coats now, and empty em out."

"O God! *God* almighty!" one of them began.

The other didn't say anything but took off his coat and began pulling out the ducks, still looking around.

"Jesus, my father has a weak heart, sir. God! For Godsake, this'll tear him up. It really will. He thinks, thinks the sun rises and sets just on me." His voice was wavering. He waited a moment and then took off his coat.

Lee opened their car door, fumbled an arm around inside until he pulled on the headlights. They put a hand up to shield their eyes, then turned their backs to the light. He wasn't sure what he was going to do with them, but he felt better now that they were unarmed.

"Whose land d'you think this is?" he said. Then: "What d'you mean, shooting ducks on my land? Huh?"

One boy turned around cautiously, keeping his hands up before his eyes. "What're you going to do?"

"What d'you think I'm going to do?" Lee said. His voice sounded strange to him; light and insubstantial, like he was talking into a wind. He could hear ducks settling on the creek, chattering and quacking to other ducks still in the air. "What d'you think I should do with you?" he asked. "What would you do if you caught somebody trespassing on your land?"

"If they said they was sorry and it was the first time, I'd let them go," the boy answered.

"I would too, sir, if they said they was sorry," the other boy added.

"You would? You really think that's what you'd do?" He stalled for time. He didn't know what else to say and, try as he might, he couldn't really summon up anger against them.

They didn't answer. They were still in the glare of the headlights, and they'd turned their backs again.

"How do I know you wasn't here before," he went on. "The other times I had to come down here."

"Word of honor, sir, we never been here before. We just drove by, decided to stop. That's all. For Godsake," he faltered, "we're sorry we stopped."

"That's the whole truth," the other put in. "Anybody can make a mistake once in his life."

It was dark, and a thin drizzle was coming down in front of the lights. Lee turned up his collar and stared at them. From down on the creek the strident quacking of a mallard drake carried up to him. He glanced around at the dark shapes of the trees, then back at the boys again.

"Maybe so." He moved his feet. He'd let them go in a minute. There wasn't much else he could do unless he took them into town, and he didn't want to get involved in anything. Besides, he was putting them off the land; that was all that mattered. "What's your names, anyway? What's yours? You. Is this here your car, or not? What's your name?"

"Bob Roberts," the one boy answered quickly, and looked sideways at the other.

"Williams, sir," the boy said after a moment. "Uh, Bill Williams."

They tried to look up into the glare, then again turned away.

Lee knew they were lying. He couldn't understand it, why it bothered him so. They were just kids, punks, and they were lying to him because they were scared. The two boys stood with their backs to him, facing across the fields toward Toppenish, ten or twelve miles away, and Lee stood looking after them.

"You're lying!" he said suddenly. "Why you lying to me? You come onto my land and shoot my ducks and then you lie like hell to me." He laid the gun over the car door to steady the barrels and pointed them off toward the trees. He could hear the branches rubbing in the treetops. For an instant, he thought of Joseph Eagle sitting up there in his lighted house, with his feet on a box, listening to the radio.

"All right. All right," he said. "Liars. Just stand there a minute." He walked stiffly around to his truck and got out an old beetsack, shook it open, had them put all the ducks in that. When he stood still, waiting, his knees unaccountably began to shake.

"Go ahead and go. Go on!"

He stepped back as they came up to the car. "I'll back up to the road, you back up along with me."

"Yeah, yeah," the one boy said as he slid in behind the steering wheel. "But what if I can't get this thing started now? The battery might be dead, you know. It wasn't very strong to begin with."

"I don't know," Lee said uneasily. He looked around. "I guess I'd have to push you out then."

The lights went out, the boy stamped on the accelerator pedal a few times and hit the starter. It turned over slowly, but it caught, and he held his foot down on the pedal and raced the engine before turning on the lights again. Lee looked at their pale, cold faces staring out at him from inside the car, waiting for him to move.

He slung the bag of ducks into his truck and laid the double-barrel, still loaded, across the seat. He got in and backed out carefully onto the road. He waited until they were out, then followed them down to Lateral B and stopped with his motor running a few minutes, watched their taillights disappear toward Toppenish. He'd put them off the land. That was all that mattered, wasn't it? Yet he couldn't understand why he felt the way he did, that something crucial had happened that night which he could not find words to describe. But nothing, nothing had happened, that was just it. He thought for a while. One thing, he had not *been himself,* that was partly what bothered him now. He couldn't explain it, but somehow he had not been himself. He felt that very strongly. He had been like a play-actor standing there in the snow, making sounds, raising his arms. But if he was somebody else, if he wasn't Lee Waite, then who was he, what was he?

It was cold and patches of fog had blown in from down the valley. He couldn't see much over toward Charley's when he stopped to open the gate, only a faint light burning out on the porch that he didn't remember seeing that afternoon. The dog waited on its belly by the barn, jumped up and began snuffling the ducks as Lee swung them over his shoulder and started up to the house.

He stopped on the porch long enough to put the gun away. The ducks he left on the floor beside the cabinet. He'd clean them tomorrow, or the next day.

"Lee?" Nina called.

He took off his hat, loosened the lightbulb, and before opening the door, waited a moment in the quiet dark.

Nina was at the kitchen table. The little box with her sewing things was beside her on another chair, and she held a piece of denim in her hand. Two or three of his shirts were on the table, along with a pair of scissors. He went through to the kitchen without saying anything, pumped a cup of water, and picked up from a shelf over the sink some of the colored rocks the kids were always bringing home. There was a dry pine cone, too, and a few big papery maple leaves from summer that had been left in a little jar. He glanced in the pantry, but he wasn't hungry, and then he walked over to the doorway and leaned against the jamb.

It was a small house and there was no place to go. In the back, in one room, all of the children slept, and in the room off from this, he and Nina and his mother slept, though sometimes, in the summer, Nina and he slept outside. His mother was still sitting beside the stove, only now she had a blanket over her legs and her tiny eyes were open, watching him.

"The boys wanted to stay up until you came back," Nina said, "but I told them you said they had to go to bed."

"Yes, that's right," he said without thinking. "They had to go to bed, all right."

"I was afraid," she said.

"Afraid?" He tried to make it sound like he was joking her. "Were you afraid too, mama?"

The old woman didn't answer, but her fingers fiddled around the sides of the blanket, tucking and pulling as if there were a draft.

"How d'you feel, Nina? Feel any better tonight?" He pulled out a chair and sat down by the table.

She nodded. When he didn't say anything else, only looked down and began scoring his thumbnail into the table, she asked "Did you catch who it was?"

"It was two kids," he said. "I let them go." He got up and walked over to the other side of the stove, spat into the wood box and stood there with his fingers hooked into his back pockets. Behind the stove the wood was black and peeling and overhead he could see, sticking out of a shelf, the brown mesh of a gillnet wrapped around the prongs of a salmon spear. He squinted at it, and then said again "I let them go. Maybe I was too easy on em."

"You did what was right," Nina said.

He glanced over the stove at his mother, but there was no sign from her, only the black raisin-like eyes still staring at him.

"I don't know about that," he said uncertainly. He tried to

think about it, but it already seemed like it'd happened long ago. "I should've given em more of a scare, I guess." He looked over at Nina. "My land," he added vaguely. "I could've killed em, I guess, easy as not, if they'd started anything."

"Kill who?" his mother said.

"Them kids down on the Cowiche Road land. What Joseph Eagle called about." She didn't answer. From where he stood he could see her fingers working in her lap, tracing delicately over the raised design in the blanket. He leaned over the stove, wanting to say something else, but the rising upsurge of heat made him draw back.

He wandered over to the table and sat down again. He still had on his coat, though, and he got up, took a while unfastening it, and then laid it on the table. He pulled up the chair close to her knees, crossed his arms limply and took his shirtsleeves in between his fingers. "I was thinking, Nina, maybe I will lease out that land down there to the hunting clubs. No good to us down there like that. Is it? Our house was down there, or it was our land right out here in front, would be something different."

In the silence he could hear only the wood snapping in the stove. He laid his hands flat out on the table and could feel the pulse jumping in his arms. "I can lease it to one of the duck clubs from Toppenish. Or Yakima! Any of them would be glad to get hold of land like that, right on the flyway. That's some of the best hunting land in the valley. . . . If I could put it to some *use* someway, Nina! Would be different then." His voice trailed off, and he looked at her.

She moved in the chair and said, after a moment "If you think we should do it. I don't know. It's whatever you think. I don't know."

"I don't know either, Nina. I think so. I can't see," he said, "what they could hurt down there." His eyes crossed the floor, raised past his mother without looking and again came to rest on the spear.

He got up, shaking his head. As he walked over, the old woman crooked her head and laid her cheek on the chairback, eyes narrowed and following him dully. He reached up, worked the spear and the mass of netting off the splintery shelf, and turned around behind her chair. He looked? at the tiny dark head, at the brown woolen shawl covering the hunched shoulders. He turned the spear in his hands and began to carefully unwrap the netting.

"How much would you get?" Nina asked.

He didn't know. It even confused him a little, and he waited before answering. He plucked absently at the netting once or twice, then laid the spear back on the shelf. Outside, a branch scraped faintly against the house.

"Lee?"

He still wasn't sure. He'd have to ask around. Mike Chuck had leased out twenty or thirty acres last fall for five hundred dollars. Jerome Shinpa leased some of his land every year, but Lee had never asked how much he got.

"Maybe a thousand dollars," he guessed.

"A thousand dollars?" she repeated.

He nodded, felt relief at her amazement. "Maybe so. Maybe even more. I will have to see. I will have to ask somebody how much. I guess we could use a thousand dollars right now, huh?"

It was a lot of money, all right. He tried to think about having a thousand dollars for several fields he didn't use any more. He closed his eyes and tried to bring the land into mind, saw vaguely a few scattered fields with clumps of trees at the edges, a slow side-stream that came in from someplace and which beavers had dammed. Then, for some reason, he thought of Day's cows wandering slowly across his fields, going slowly into one field and then another, snapping off the barley and tall grass, chewing it and working it in their cuds a long time before swallowing. He held it all for a moment, and then it began to fade—the land, trees, even the beavers he imagined living someplace on the side-stream, until there was nothing left, only a herd of cows he'd seen once, airily suspended in his mind.

"Now that wouldn't be selling it, would it?" Nina asked. "If you lease it to them, that means it's still your land, isn't it?"

"Yes, yes it's still my land!" He came over and leaned across the table. "Don't you know the difference, Nina? They can't *buy* land on the reservation. Don't you know that? I will lease it to them, for them to use."

"I see," she said. She looked down and picked at the sleeve of one of his shirts. "They will have to give it back then, won't they? It will still belong to you."

"Don't you understand?" he said. He gripped the table edge. "It is a lease! A lease, that's all."

"What will mama say?" Nina asked. "Will it be all right?"

"Mama!" he said.

They both looked over at the old woman, but her eyes were closed and she seemed to be sleeping, her cheek still against the chair.

"What is it, Nina? Don't you want a thousand dollars?"

"A thousand dollars," she repeated, and shook her head.

A thousand dollars. Maybe more. He didn't know. But even a thousand dollars! Still, he wondered how he would go about it, letting people know he had land to lease. It was too late now, for this year, but he could start asking around in the spring. He crossed his arms and tried to think. Suddenly it seemed so entangled, there were so many things moving inside him in such different directions, that his legs began to tremble slightly, and he leaned back against the wall. He rested there for a moment, and then he let his weight slide gently down the wall until he was squatting over the board floor, arms across his thighs.

"It is just a lease," he said. "I will just be leasing it to them. It is still my land. You can understand that. It is still my land." He stared at the floor. It seemed to slant in his direction and as he watched, he had the feeling that it was moving. He shut his eyes again and brought his hands up over his ears to steady himself. There was no sound at first, and then he heard a muffled roaring in his ears that was like listening to the wind howling inside a seashell.

Tenderloin

Rick DeMarinis

from *Colorado State Review*

"Is it well done, is it cooked enough for you?" She looked over her shoulder at Bill who was seated at the table, chewing slowly, pausing every five or six chews to deliberate. Evelyn looked over her shoulder again. "Is it well done, is it cooked enough for you?" Her five cats were moving between her legs, coaxing her. She tested the large beet to see if it was done. Her legs were aching again. Bill fished in his mouth, pulled out a torn piece of tendon. He wiped his fingers on his pants. He took another beer from the six-pack at his feet, removed the cap, drank deeply. Earlier he had said, "You are not my mother. You are not anyone's mother," and had regretted saying it. Evelyn drank too much, and in the bar where Bill had said it, she began to cry. She had put her face into Bill's shoulder and moaned over and over, louder each time. She was nearing seventy and her heart was weak. Wine seemed to make her strong. She was proud of her strong handshake and she shook the hands of working men up and down the bar. She had good hands and liked to display their strength. The flesh was falling in her face and she was well known as a character. She had never married. For many years she had lived alone in a little house by the railroad bridge on the edge of Cutter Creek. The creek is full and green and explosive against big rocks in the spring, but by late summer it is nothing more than a trickle, ugly with rusted cans. Evelyn looked over her shoulder and watched Bill chewing slowly, reflectively. He was squinting with the care of deliberation. The large veins in the backs of her knees were beginning to ache. She tested the large beet to see if it was done. A log train carrying great pines made the small house move to its own slow rhythm. "Is it cooked enough for you?" Bill searched the crevices of his teeth with his tongue, drank deeply from the tall brown bottle. He had regretted saying it, but the regret was dim in his mind now. He chewed the next piece of meat slowly and with careful deliberation. He had said it again in the cab on the way home, "Evelyn, you are not my mother," but this time it was not meant to hurt. He said it with tenderness this time, her head against his shoulder, her hand tightening on his. In the bar her crying had been unconsolable, it grew until there was the sound of death in it, a mortal wailing. In the cab she whimpered demurely and with great femininity. She had dabbed her puffed eyes on a small silk hanky painted with violets. She was much older than Bill, who was only forty-three. They had been friends for ten years, and had seen happier days together before Evelyn's health had deteriorated. Bill knew she would not live much longer, her heart would often leave her legs and fingers numb and cramped with pain. It was on these occasions that she would coax Bill to rub her feet and then her hands and arms. And Bill would agree, usually after explaining that he had some errands to run first, some important things to do. Bill had retired from logging. A tie chain on a lumber truck had snapped, breaking three vertebrae high in his back. The rolling rhythm of the log train sent a memory of pain radiating from the healing vertebrae. He knew he had had to say it again in the cab, and said it deliberately, firmly. Tenderly, yet with masculine dignity. The cab driver had turned his head but not completely, then glanced in the rear-view mirror. Bill knew this would happen but said it again, anyway. "Evelyn, you are no one's mother." Evelyn turned from the stove, her eyes swallowed by their surrounding flesh, her flesh sweating through its rosy make-up. "Is it well done, is it cooked enough?" Bill's mouth was full. He swished the remaining beer until it was milky in the bottom of the brown bottle. He glanced up at Evelyn, raised his eyebrows as if to speak, but said nothing. He drank the remaining beer, giving moisture to the heavy mass of meat and bread that filled his mouth. Evelyn's five cats rubbed against her thick legs, some rising slightly, their mouths begging. She tested the large beet to see if it was done. Bill fished in his mouth, pulled out a torn piece of tendon. In the cab she had said her legs were gone. The cab driver looked back, impatient to end the afternoon shift. Bill had watched her knuckles turn white against the small hanky painted with violets. Bill said aloud, "Ten years ago I was thirty-three." The cab driver and Evelyn looked at Bill together, then separately away. The driver and Bill helped Evelyn into the small house. She was heavy with age and they entered sideways, the driver, Evelyn, then Bill. They eased her to the couch and she sank into its faded tapestry, sighing deeply, then coughing. Bill paid the driver and the man left, letting the screen door slam. There had been an alarming moment for Bill when Evelyn seemed lifeless, staring dimly, a thin rasping deep in her breast. Bill remembered the rasp of chain saws deep in the trees. Evelyn pushed her fork into the large beet. She looked over her shoulder at Bill. Her cats rubbed against her legs. Bill looked up, squinting carefully, swishing the remaining beer until it was like milk in the bottom of the brown bottle. He had regretted saying it. He had never said it before. And when Evelyn had asked him to do her legs, her feet, her hands and arms, he had said yes he would and that he had nothing important to do just then. She looked up at him, the thin rasping in her breast gone, her pale eyes small and liquid. The stinging haze of distant chip burners was in the room. He knelt and removed her shoes. Her feet were splotched and swollen. The toes yellowing. Evelyn leaned back into the stuffed cushions and closed her eyes. It was the end of summer and the small house was filled with the heat of day. The thin ribbon of water that was Cutter Creek made delicate music against the large stones that lined its bed. The air was perfectly still. "Is it well done, is it cooked enough for you?" Bill searched the crevices of his teeth with his tongue, and squinted with the care of deliberation. He drank the whitened beer slowly. He had regretted saying it. He had never said it before. And when Evelyn asked him to do her legs, her feet, her hands and arms, he said yes. His hands were hard with years of logging and he worked her veined calves with great gentleness. Evelyn leaned back into the stuffed cushions and closed her eyes. She reached out and touched his head and her fingers went into his hair. She was proud of the strength in her hand and she brought his face down, slowly, into her lap. Evelyn looked over at Bill then tested the large beet to see if it was done. Her five cats moved between her legs, coaxing her. Earlier he had said, "You are not my mother, you are not anyone's mother," and had regretted saying it. Evelyn brought his face slowly down to her lap. Bill's hands gripped the backs of her knees, working the hard knots of veins, his face buried in the steamy darkness of her lap. Evelyn looked over her shoulder at Bill who was seated at the table. Her legs were aching again. Bill fished in his mouth, pulled out a piece of tendon. Her hand was strong on the back of his head and her fingers moved willfully in his hair. He had never said it before. It's all right, you didn't mean nothing by it. She looked over her shoulder at Bill. Bill glanced up as if to speak. He swished his beer until it was milky in the bottom of the brown bottle. "Is it well done, is it cooked enough for you?"

Spending the Day

J. M. Ferguson, Jr.

from *Descant*

Harry wasn't really Harry and his wife Ida wasn't really Ida. These were just names that came to Harry one fall day while they were driving along in the Sierras in their little blue Chevy with their blue-eyed daughter. Blue was Harry's favorite color. His own blue eyes, however, were often bloodshot now. He claimed they were a symptom of his anxiety, a condition that had plagued him strangely since the war. Ida told him he was a hypochondriac.

"Who would you rather be," he blurted as they climbed through Tioga Pass into Yosemite, "Edna or Ida Mae?"

"For Christ's sake, Merton," Ida scowled. "Do you have to start that stuff?"

Harry had an irrepressible way of coming up with questions that annoyed Ida.

"Which?" he insisted.

"Ida, I guess."

"Just call me Harry," Harry said. "I've always wanted to be Harry."

"Christ, Merton. You and Harry Truman."

When Harry had first come courting before the war and

ventured his admiration for F. D. R., Ida's father had turned red around the neck and ordered him out of the house. Naming their daughter had caused a family crisis. Harry had wanted to name her Eleanor after Eleanor Roosevelt. "A great lady," he explained. But Ida had once known an Eleanor whom she detested, and besides her father had voted Republican for forty years. So they had named the baby Elaine, which Harry suggested as a compromise. It seemed to Harry that his life was composed of compromises with Ida.

"Harry and Ida," Harry murmured without satisfaction, his finger in his nose.

It was late September, and at that altitude the leaves on the aspen were already turning. The car had begun to descend into Yosemite Valley, and they had dropped into a rolling mist that was infiltrating the great pines. Harry really didn't know why he said such absurd things. He was a poet by nature and next to being Harry he would have preferred to be called Homer. A hawk was circling above them, and Harry could see that Ida was watching it, her face pressed sullenly against the car window.

"Harry and Ida," he said again, flatly. And the names stuck.

When Harry and Ida were married the war was already on in Europe. They lived in a small walkup apartment near the university where Harry was finishing his graduate work. They were poor and Ida was not used to it. She made the first months of their marriage miserable with her complaining and went home in the third month.

Harry decided to be grateful for the experience of cohabiting with a woman. It gave him a new perspective on things and made his poetry seem like the purest dribble. He decided to call it growth on his part. He watched the moon drop down his window and walked to his classes under the bare winter trees and thought he could always be happy in his celibacy. But then one night he had a dream about a girl he thought he had forgotten. Tall and blonde, she was his kind of girl. Harry had dated her briefly in his undergraduate days, and he had fancied he was in love, but then one night she had turned suddenly cold to him. Harry never knew why.

Ida was back after a week. Her father had turned red around the neck and told her to lie in the bed she had made.

Harry received her gracefully.

"Who would you rather be," he asked quietly, "Ralph Waldo Emerson or Henry David Thoreau?"

Ida looked at him queerly.

"Why?" she asked.

"I dunno," Harry said. "Thoreau never married."

"Henry David Thoreau, then," Ida said.

Harry nodded silently.

As it turned out they both got their wish. Harry's graduate career was broken off before he could finish his dissertation on Henry David Thoreau. It was the year of Pearl Harbor and Harry was drafted by mid-term.

Ida cried when she saw him off on the troop train for his induction. Harry was touched. She went home to her parents to wait it out. Harry didn't see her again for five years.

Harry came home from the war looking tired and, of course, older. He had been unfaithful to Ida during his last years overseas. He had picked up a girl in the Soho district of London on the day Roosevelt died, but he did not tell Ida. His eyes were bloodshot, and Ida remarked on his disgusting new habit of picking his nose. Harry explained it all as a symptom of his anxiety.

Ida seemed to bear some grudge against him for being gone so long. He sometimes had the uneasy feeling, looking into her steel gray eyes, that she was uncanny. She seemed to have divined his infidelity, and Harry knew he would never atone for it.

Harry couldn't face any more graduate school. His father had died during the war and he felt obliged to help his mother. Ida was jealous of Harry's mother and got herself pregnant in order to claim more of Harry's attention. So Harry took a job in a teachers' college out West. He spent his small savings on a used Studebaker. It broke down before they got there, and Harry had to buy the blue Chevy with money borrowed from the college credit union. Later he had to borrow more when the baby was born.

Ida found her first year at the teachers' college not much different from waiting for Harry in the war. There was never enough money, and when Harry was home he sat over a stack of papers to be graded, rolling his eyes distractedly and fingering his nose. Sometimes she wished she were dead, and she started to drink. She smoked a lot too, and when Harry came home he found loaded ash trays scattered all over the house. He couldn't get the smell out of his head at night and he slept fitfully. Sometimes in bed he had the feeling that Ida was glaring at him when he was half asleep on his pillow. They often quarreled before they could get out of bed in the morning.

"I'll be damned if I'm gonna sit around this house doing nothing all my life," Ida would say. "Why the hell do I need a college education? I wish I was *dead*."

Harry sometimes caught himself thinking it was too bad she wasn't, and too bad they let women go to college, except for the ones in his classes—Ida was suspicious of him on that count. Sometimes he would try to explain to her about education.

"That's not the point of education," he would begin. For a while he thought he would write a long philosophical paper on education, but he wore himself out thinking about it, and he was discouraged whenever he thought of all the people who were already writing about education. So finally Harry quit trying to explain.

They were both restless, and almost as soon as the baby was old enough they took to driving in the mountains on the weekends. But Ida didn't like Montana. She complained that it was too cold and that there wasn't any blue grass.

"Blue grass your ass," Harry retorted one morning before they had gotten out of bed. He rather liked Montana.

In the end, however, they went back East for Harry to work on his doctorate. Harry contended that he would never need it at the teachers' college, but Ida couldn't stand it any longer. It was one of Harry's compromises.

"Which would you rather be," Harry asked on the way back, "a two-thousand pound Montana grizzly or a Kentucky thoroughbred eating blue grass?"

"For Christ's sake, Merton," Ida scowled.

Harry had his finger in his nose and his eyes were bloodshot.

Harry began to allude to his new "split personality" as he worked on his doctorate. He tried to explain that he didn't want to be a scholar but a poet, but no one seemed interested. Ida wasn't any happier in Kentucky, and although she complained herself she got tired of listening to Harry gripe.

"Go ahead and quit then," she would say. "I don't give a damn what you do if you'll get out and get some money."

"Get out and get me some money," Harry mocked. "It's the same here as Montana and it would be the same anywhere."

"Go on back if you want," Ida taunted. "But you can damn well count me out."

Harry would have gone, too, but it broke his heart to think of parting from Elaine. She had Ida's dark hair but Harry's blue and sensitive eyes, and Harry couldn't bear to desert her. He felt sorry for her, knowing that his frequent quarrels with Ida struck wonder and confusion in her face. She seemed to be a nervous child and Harry feared she was developing asthma. Ida said he was imagining, but Harry felt guilty about it.

Harry noticed that his handwriting had begun to change. Sometimes, for example, he would print his s's, which he had never done before. But only sometimes, and without rhyme or reason, as far as he could see. Then he noticed that the same schizophrenia afflicted his capital D's and I's. Ida bought a paperback book on handwriting at the supermarket, but her only verdict was that Harry's r's indicated he was conceited.

It wasn't the handwriting itself, however, that disturbed Harry. He began to attribute his confusion to some frightening indecision and purposelessness in his character. The more he studied at the university the more often he found his meagre collection of convictions untenable, and Harry felt that he needed some convictions to sustain his identity. After all, he thought, wasn't it asinine to be confident about how to make one's s's when one did not know why he was bothering to make them at all? Distraction upon distraction seemed to prevent him from discovering the real answers. He felt that he was a man torn in two, but he didn't mention his handwriting to Ida again.

What he said instead was "I'm a man torn in two," and he read a passage from a book to her: " 'Let us spend one day as deliberately as Nature, and not be thrown off the track by every nutshell and mosquito's wing that falls on the rails.' You know who that is?"

"Who?" Ida challenged.

"That's Henry David Thoreau," Harry beamed.

"Christ, Merton," Ida scowled. "You and Henry David Thoreau. I'm sick of that bastard." Harry had been quoting Thoreau to her while he was writing his dissertation on him.

"You really want to be Henry David Thoreau?" Ida taunted. "Then go be Henry David. I don't give a damn. You can get yourself a little shack and sit and roll your eyes and pick your nose and write poetry for all I care."

Ida was always saying something like that, but Harry knew some of it was true. He had read somewhere that his habit of fingering his nose was a symptom of his need for identity, and that there were certain sexual implications connected with it which disturbed him. Harry didn't tell Ida but he had taken to girlwatching on the campus. He didn't know what Ida meant about rolling his eyes, though.

"Well," he said, "I don't know what you mean about rolling my eyes, but I'm sure as hell not writing any poetry. I never get a minute to write what I want, and all you do is gripe."

Ida was about to offer a rejoinder, but before she could Harry began to beat on his head with his fists in utter exasperation. Ida was concerned then and said she was sorry about always wishing she were dead—she didn't really mean it—and that everything would be better when he could finish up the degree.

"Yeah," Harry grunted. But in his heart of hearts, he didn't believe everything would be better at all. Sometimes, sitting up alone at night, he was torn between working on his degree and writing a poem he had been nursing along in his head. He could do nothing but finger his nose. It was at such a moment one night that he caught himself rolling his eyes.

Harry never did finish his doctorate, and things didn't get better. He took a job in one of the California junior colleges he had heard about. He told Ida he could finish his dissertation "in absentia," which was a lie, and that they could move to a university somewhere when he finished it.

The pay was better than it had been at the teachers' college, and Ida was able to resign herself to her new situation except on Friday nights. She continued to smoke heavily, and Harry had to keep a bottle of bourbon in the house for her. It got to where Harry could count on coming home to a drunken wife on Friday nights, the nights Harry liked to relax after a hard week of teaching. One such night Ida didn't get supper on the table until nine o'clock, and when she did she got mad at Harry and turned the table over on him. She called Harry a son of a bitch and staggered off to her room and locked the door. Harry spent the night at his office, but he was finding it increasingly difficult to coax the poetry out of his soul. He didn't have much heart for his teaching, either, and he found himself watching the girls on campus more than ever. He was afraid it was becoming an obsession.

The life he was leading seemed intolerable. He toyed with the idea of becoming some kind of salesman so he could spend most of his time away from home. He thought of divorce again, but he still couldn't bear to abandon his daughter. She was then nearly four years old, and definitely asthmatic, Harry thought.

Harry tried to pacify Ida whenever he could on the weekends by driving her to scenic points around California in their little blue Chevy, and it was during one of the first of these trips, to Yosemite, that Harry thought of the names, Harry and Ida. Harry recognized that these outings were an escapist impulse, the same habit that they had fallen into in Montana. On one trip, in an out of the way green valley between some mountains, a man working with a hoe near the road raised his dusty face as they drove by and showed them a healthy animal smile. Harry couldn't get the man out of his mind. He made him think of some of D. H. Lawrence's characters. He knew their little excursions were only temporary stays—from what, he was not sure—and he was usually anxious about a stack of themes left behind that had to be graded. He felt his life slipping through his fingers while he drugged his spirit with the beautiful scenery.

"Who would you rather be," Harry blurted one Sunday afternoon while the sun was going down, "Henry David Thoreau or Lady Chatterley's lover?"

"Jesus, Harry," Ida snapped, "watch the road."

Harry quit his job abruptly in the middle of his second year at the junior college. He never offered any explanations. He came home one afternoon mumbling something incoherent in a hollow sounding voice and flopped into a chair with his finger up his nose. Ida questioned him, but Harry only said "I have nothing to teach." That was all she could get out of him.

Ida wrote to her mother that she suspected Harry was having an affair. They had been to a party not long before he quit his job and Ida had seen him slap a willowy blonde on the buttocks. Harry drank himself into oblivion on gimlets and went around telling everyone he was throwing his hat into the ring for the presidency. He cited some Chief Justice that Ida had never heard of as a distant cousin. It was election year and Harry Truman had announced his plans to retire.

Harry found employment as a technical writer for a corporation in Sacramento that was doing secret defense work for the government. He had to pass a security clearance to get the job. He found the work boring and the routine tedious, but he was beyond caring and he never complained. Ida thought it was the best job he had ever had: it paid the most money. Harry realized there were easier ways to make money than teaching or writing poetry. He began to work overtime on Saturdays.

But again Harry's job ended suddenly. He was working overtime one Saturday when his supervisor caught him fornicating in a broom closet with one of the secretaries. Ida heard about it from the supervisor's wife. Harry made feeble allusions to his anxiety, but he didn't try to deny it. Both Harry and the secretary were dismissed, of course, as poor security risks.

Ida took Elaine and spent her six weeks in Reno, and then they were back to the blue grass country to live with her parents. Harry found himself alone, divorced, and saddled with a judgment for alimony and child support. He was still carrying the debts he had incurred at the teachers' college, transferring them from one credit union to another as he moved about.

It seemed to Harry that the world was being run by Republicans, who had won the November election. And he felt guilty about Elaine.

Harry did his best to pull himself together. He had long nourished a secret desire to be single again, but time was suddenly heavy in his heart. He didn't feel young again, as he had imagined he somehow would. He was just thirty-four, and he knew that he was not too old for a new beginning, in spite of five years wasted in the war. Yet he felt his back against the wall, and his anxiety was unalleviated. He had more time for his poetry, but he couldn't find a poetic phrase in his head. He began to send out some of his old poems to editors, feeling that it was time he tried to publish something, but they came back one by one, rejected. He finished off Ida's cigarettes and the bottle of bourbon she had left—he had had to ship a whole crate of her things to her. When these were gone Harry bought another carton, and another bottle.

He needed, he knew, a good job in order to meet his

obligations and maintain himself. He wanted to be able to send a check to his mother once in a while, but he had little hope of helping her. He knew he was all washed up as far as security clearances went, and his only other thought was for the business world. Harry didn't relish the idea, but there wasn't any line of work that really appealed to him. He wrote to as many college textbook publishers as he could think of, and he finally landed a job with a big company as their Midwest representative. It didn't pay as much as he had hoped, but he thought he would manage if he stayed in the second-best hotels and saved some of his expense money. He rented a small furnished room for himself in Kansas City, the site of his company's regional office. It was an old building inhabited by elderly people, but he didn't mind because the rates were cheap.

Harry had one more brief affair and a chance for a second on his new job. He was in line by himself in a Kansas City cafeteria when he heard someone behind him calling his name. It was one of his former students from Montana. They had lunch together, and she explained that she was working as a beautician—she had never finished at the teachers' college. Harry remembered that he had never been able to picture her as a teacher, and he also remembered that she had sat in the first row of his class with her skirt pulled casually above her knees. She had nice thighs, he remembered, and she was not unattractive in a rather plain and insensitive way. Harry thought that for the relationship he had in mind it was fortunate that she was not especially sensitive. When he told her he was divorced she volunteered her phone number.

The first time he called her they spent the night in Harry's room—she had two girl friends sharing her apartment—and the following day Harry was served an eviction notice by his landlord. Harry changed his mind about old people for neighbors, and he began to wonder whether he had some kind of proclivity for making his lovemaking public. He took another place nearby, but in the end it turned out to be more than he could afford, and he had to move again. He missed the peace and quiet of his first room, and only then did he realize how well the place for old folks had suited him.

Harry never saw his former student again. He had to travel shortly after their first date, but he called her again one winter night after he had been to a cheap theatre that showed burlesque films. One of her roommates told him that she had married. Harry was a little stunned. He wished that Ida would marry too, and take the burden of alimony off his back, but then Harry couldn't recommend her to anyone.

Harry had a chance for a second affair with a young woman who was an instructor at the university in Columbia, Missouri. It was early March on a Friday afternoon, Harry's favorite time of the week, and he was in her office trying to interest her in a textbook. He looked up and noticed that she seemed more interested in him. She had taken off her glasses and was smiling at him. Harry was suddenly aware that she was an attractive woman, but she looked sensitive and intelligent and maybe a little too slender for him. He decided she was not his kind not at the moment, anyway.

"Well," Harry said, "I have to make St. Louis tonight. I thank you for your time."

It was a lie, of course, and she put on her glasses and quit smiling.

Later, walking up the Strollway and looking in the shop windows on his way back to his hotel, Harry wished that he had at least asked her to dinner. On the second floor of his hotel he could see men and women embracing behind drawn shades. It looked for a moment like a Roman orgy, but then everyone suddenly changed partners and he remembered the dance studio which operated there at odd hours. Starlings were clustered on the building ledges, making a tremendous racket as the sun went down. The still luminous sky southwest of the earth silhouetted black branches of elms that loomed on the horizon of the city like a network of roots by which the planet clung to the universe.

Then it was dark and Harry felt lonely.

Spending the Day

The following September Harry was forced to go to a finance company to meet his obligations to Ida. He tried to adjust to hotel rooms that were worse than second-rate, but he found them too depressing. In one, a St. Louis hotel where an exposed light bulb hung down from the ceiling on a cord, he smelled flesh in the bathroom. Later, taking a bath, he discovered on the edge of the tub several large callouses that someone must have pared from his feet.

He was passing through Columbia on a Friday night, and on Saturday morning he strolled about the campus, hoping faintly to see again the woman who had smiled at him. The campus was quiet, and as he walked Harry felt an emotion he couldn't name. Turning a corner, he thought the woman who came into view on the walk ahead of him might be her.

He presumed she was on her way home, but before she left the campus she entered a building that looked only recently completed. Harry followed cautiously, with curiosity and long- ing, thinking he ought to be framing an alibi in case he should come suddenly upon her, yet unable to do so. Within the building there was the smell of fresh paint and plaster, but no living being, as far as he could determine. Then he heard a noise echoing from a far stairwell. Pursuing it, he looked with surprise down the winding metal stairs which must have descended several stories below the ground. He hesitated before plunging into what his imagination kept suggesting was some secret tunnel he had discovered to the bowels of the earth. For an instant, Harry was struck by the incongruity, the implausi- bility of his situation, as if at that moment he were removed from and observing himself. He felt unalterably alone then, his longing overcoming his uneasiness, and he descended the stairs in search of the noise he had heard, of which some person, he reasoned, must surely have been the source.

At first he saw no one. The stairway ran into a closed door, and, opening it, Harry thought he had reached a cul de sac. He stood before a dimly lighted room of metallic shadows that he recognized as boiler room equipment, and he was about to retrace his steps when he heard the noise again. Something moved in the dim room and emerged between amorphous pieces of dark machinery. He was confronted by a white-haired, trembling figure: a wrinkled, molelike old man in gray janitorial attire, leaning on a mop. Harry felt the squinting eyes fasten upon him inquisitively.

Back in his hotel room, alone with his bourbon, Harry wondered what the woman at the university had seen in him in the first place. He had noticed that his hair had begun to thin. His eyes were bloodshot, and he thought his nostrils seemed slightly enlarged from his nervous habit of picking them.

"I could never afford to marry her," he said aloud to himself in a voice that was strangely hoarse. He hated himself for having preferred the beautician, his former student, to this young woman.

He dreamed that night again of the blonde of his college days whom he had loved. She was as tall as Harry. They met at a party, in a room full of people, and later, leaving together, she pressed close to Harry and told him she had never been able to forget him.

Harry awoke unnerved by the fact that she should occur in his dreams again. Remembering how abruptly his romance with her had ended, he thought now that he could understand why.

"Can it be," he asked himself, "that she knew me better than I knew myself?"

Later that fall things went from bad to worse for Harry. He didn't keep to his traveling schedule for his company. He went anxiously to his burlesque films and he spent long hours in newsstands looking at girlie magazines. And he bought more bourbon.

He was staying in a motel in Joplin when he came down with the flu—he hadn't been taking care of himself. For two days he just lay in bed with his bottle and a fever. He got back to his office three days behind schedule and found himself dismissed. His supervisor told him the company wasn't satisfied with him anyway.

It occurred to Harry that all he had in the world were his clothes and his books. With a kind of perverse and defiant logic he gave all his clothes, except an old army trenchcoat and the ones he was wearing to the Salvation Army. He donated all his books, except Henry David Thoreau's *Walden,* to the nearest library. He notified his landlord that he would be out the following day. Then he went to the burlesque theatre and saw a marvelous big stripper whose flaming red hair hung down to the small of her back.

"You marvelous big thing," Harry sighed to himself after he had begun to drink in his room. His mind wallowed freely in his lust, and he was tormented by a desire to relieve himself. He tried to think of something else he wanted to do.

Harry started to read Henry David Thoreau's *Walden.* He read the last chapter first, and he lingered on the part where Thoreau described the butterfly coming out of the farmer's applewood table, like some kind of resurrection. Harry wondered whether Henry David Thoreau meant to imply a resurrection, and whether he could be resurrected, himself. He didn't believe in immortality. He surmised that Thoreau must have been talking about a man's potential in this life, and thinking about his own life, Harry saw how he had succumbed to shameful sensuality. It was no good, he knew, blaming it all on his anxiety. He decided then upon a pilgrimage. He would hitchhike to Walden Pond and spend the rest of the winter there, where Thoreau had lived a century before.

But then Harry read the introduction to *Walden* by a scholar in his own century, and when he finished he was sorry he had read it. The scholar explained that Thoreau's pond had been made into a public beach and that authorities had found that the pond ranked high in urine content among the waters of the greater Boston area. Moreover, he advanced the Freudian theory that Thoreau's practice of immersing himself in Walden Pond was a manifestation of his suppressed sensuality.

Harry decided not to go to Walden Pond after all. He

remembered how blue the water had looked when he had last passed by the Lake of the Ozarks, and he decided to go there instead. Blue was Harry's favorite color.

Ida told the investigator that she didn't know whether Harry could swim or not. She had never seen him try, but she thought that he probably could and that he was just pulling a fast one. The investigator explained that a copy of *Walden* with Harry's name in it had been found in the boat drifting near the middle of the lake. It was a big lake and they might never find the body, he said. It had happened before.

Ida's alimony stopped coming and there was nothing she could do about it. Harry's body was never found in the lake, but it couldn't be located anywhere else either. She felt a little uncomfortable about Harry and about the drifting boat. She decided she would forgive him for deserting her. Besides, her father had died and she had inherited all she needed for herself and Elaine.

Ida taught Elaine that her father had been a disgusting creature and that she should never, never trust any man. Harry had often feared she would teach her something like that.

The Whereabouts of Mr. Haber[*]

Fred Gardner

from *Transatlantic Review*

The man in the doorway waved me into his dark apartment and said, "Two years ago I had my picture in every magazine you mentioned."

To make me comfortable he motioned to the edge of a big brass double bed that took up half the area of the room. There was no kitchen, no bathroom, only a sink in one corner. On the far edge of the bed sat his wife, knitting. She was the thinnest person I had ever seen. Her hands resembled the vu-thru illustration of *human hand* in my high school biology text book.

"It's some coincidence," he was going on, "the only other person to visit all this time was also in the magazine business. *Newsweek* magazine. He wanted to interview us for the 'Where are they now?' column."

I must have looked blank because he explained, "You know, like whatever happened to Tony Zale?"

I nodded.

"He was like yourself, a young man from college. Comes to

* This tale won first prize in the *My Toughest Sale* story contest. I have now changed the title.

the door asking if I am Haber of the 4-A quads. Yes, I says, I'm the father. He asks me a few questions, then he wants to leave. Can you imagine? Said there was no point getting the story because he knew they wouldn't print it."

"Why not?"

"Well," he began, glancing at his wife, "I'll tell it to you in case you ever get to the writing end of your . . . profession." His wife gave him a mild you-talk-too-much look, then continued knitting.

"Up until May 7, 1962, I was a conductor on the West Side IRT. My service was served, my hair had stopped thinning, I was kind of happy. My wife got pregnant: fine. I did what I was supposed to, got her everything she wanted, made sure she followed doctor's orders. I even went along to an educational film about how a baby is born (the key to it all is these tubes, I forget the name. It's like everything else. I forget it now but I understood it then).

"The big night comes. There I am waiting at the hospital. Scared? A little, sure. Then the nurse comes in and says 'your wife just gave birth to something very interesting.'

"Interesting? Once I read in the papers how this 16-year old gave birth to puppies. What can be so interesting?"

" 'Guess.' she says.

" 'It's a little boy.'

" 'Nooo.'

" 'It's a little girl.'

" 'Warmer . . .'

"What did she want me to say, 'a little fairy?' I may not be so well educated but I'm not dumb. I know it's the environment causes . . .

"Anyway I see these newspapermen start stomping through the waiting room, right through the door where my wife probably is. Then guys with cameras, tv cameras. The nurse starts fixing up her hair. "Your wife gave birth to four charming little girls.'

"I fell down. I fell down like I was Floyd Patterson. I wanted to get up on my feet but I couldn't. Finally a newspaperman lifted me up. I remember he was shouting. 'Hey here's the father, look how little he is!'

"To this day I resent that. At the time the quads were born I stood a good 5′ 5″, and considered myself very average."

I began to doubt his truthfulness, for he could not have been taller than 5 feet that evening.

"Before she became pregnant my wife weighed, I think, 88 pounds. That gave them what they call an angle. We were small. *Time* magazine, to give a for instance, ran our picture with a thing that said: 'From their small packages, good things.' Did you know a lot of people wrote in that I should be man of the year? But they gave it to the Police Commissioner.

"Not too much comes back about that night. Before I was allowed to see my wife this representative of the 4-A had made the deal with her about naming them all with A's. I was smashed from all that State of Ohio champagne I endorsed; and blind from the lights and flash bulbs. There was a fight between the people covering it for CBS and the others from NBC. I got caught in the middle.

"Next morning I couldn't get out because the front door was blocked by cartons of milk. We lived in a nice little apartment in Washington Heights then. I called a neighbour who cleared a path to the door. It seems that Borden's had donated a year's supply of milk, but like you might guess, it didn't keep more than a week. Oh we had diapers and cribs and bayonets and carriages, all free. I had to be there all morning to sign the endorsements. I phoned in that I couldn't come to work. In the afternoon I went to the hospital to visit my wife and Alice, Alexandra, Alma and Andrea, whose names had already become household words. The 4-A quads. You know what the 4-A gave us for using those names? This bed, this golden bed, our prized possession."

Only then did I notice the gleaming eagle at its head, holding in its claws a ribbon that said "The American Association for the Addition of Americans." Not brass after all: gold.

"How healthy they looked that morning, their eyes closed to this world, screaming, spitting, peeing, crying. . . . The reporters asked if I felt proud. 'Real proud,' I said, and kissed my wife. Then they made her kiss me while I kissed the babies' heads (a nurse kind of held them together in a bunch so's I could kiss them all at once). Wet, phew. Then they wedged all the babies around my wife's face so it would look like they were kissing her while she winked at me. Hot with all those cameras. Finally I was allowed to leave.

"Mr. Fendel was waiting there when I came home and he told me he was my business manager. Also there was a telegram from a Mr. Heym, a landlord. He offered us a 5-room apartment free for a year. In Queens, nice.

"I don't know how Mr. Fisher became my writer but I think it was arranged by *Life* magazine. *Life,* like you yourself just said a minute ago, is a family magazine, very worthwhile. They wanted a story from me about the night the girls were, you know, conceived. That's the family angle, see? I learned a lot about how magazines operate. Anyway I wasn't too sure what night that exactly was and they said not to worry. They sent along Mr. Fisher and he worked it out so's we had gone to a movie at Loew's and then took this romantic walk to a certain place on Riverside Drive where you can see the Spry sign. We used to go there when we first met. I enjoyed the story, to tell you the truth.

"Personally, I want to make one thing clear. I was permitted very little contact, actually no contact, with the quads. Mr. Fendel said I'd drop one or smother it in a diaper, so he hired some nurses and after that I wasn't really entitled to touch them. I went to see them in the movie, Delivery Ward Hootenanny; they were *featured.* But this did not fulfill my natural affection of a father, a father's affection.

"As you might imagine, a lot of money was coming into our hands in those days, but a lot was going out, too. Taxes. And the nurses and advisers. Also I wasn't working because they thought I'd cause jams and riots what with people trying to get a glimpse of me. Things would have worked out all right— I mean I made mistakes, like I endorsed this Barbie family planning kit which made 4-A so mad they cancelled my contract as something or other—but things would have been all right if Alice hadn't passed away God forbid. She was the skinniest of the quads. ABC had the best coverage at the funeral but CBS was waiting there when we home. I'm not sure who had the best, finally. At the time I was getting a lot of criticism for not crying enough. I want to take this opportunity to repeat that I am not an unfeeling person. But before Alice died, I'm not sure I'd ever actually been alone with her. Or any of them. The staff was so large, so possessive in those days.

"The endorsements came few and far between after that because, as Mr. Fendel said, we had broken the set. One thing, though. Placid Valley provided a grave which had compartments for all the girls, God forbid.

"Another thing. This Mr. Michael Boccacino from Roslyndale, Long Island, wrote an article claiming to be the father of the quads. My wife had never seen him before in her life and so we sued (even though Mr. Fendel said we shouldn't). What happened? Mr. Boccacino sued back, a maternity suit against my wife. We had to go through many hung juries and a great deal of grief and anguish. Public grief. The story of Boccacino's about the night the quads were conceived was a lot more convincing, between you and me, than the one Mr. Fisher wrote.

"Finally we agreed to settle if Mr. Boccacino would grant my wife custody of the girls. This he did, and that night we celebrated with the last of the State of Ohio champagne, and ate the last of the turkey in the freezer. Then we sold the freezer because we had to pay the rent to Mr. Heym, $290 a week for five rooms, you believe it? We began looking elsewhere but landlords are not anxious to have you with three squealing babies. The other tenants complain. Anyway we couldn't find a place and just kept selling our appliances to pay the rent. Naturally we dismissed the staff, what was left of it, and I started looking for work.

"That's funny, huh? Did you ever try finding a job after you couldn't hold one with the city? Impossible. After a while I told them I was willing to work for less than the machine. They let me answer the phone at the Cinema Avant and say 'This is a recording. The air-conditioned Cinema Avant is currently showing . . .'"

He cracked his knuckles.

"Tell you the truth I was not at this point a very stable person. My wife was down to 79 pounds, two of the girls were sick and I was beginning to lose faith. One evening somebody called and I picked up the phone and said 'This is a recording. I was once a human. Now am a machine. Once human. Now machine . . .'

"I was sent away to rest at an institution. The rest did me a whole lot of good and I think you'll agree that even though the road has had its ups and downs, the person standing about 2 feet in front of you right now is a rational person."

I agreed, of course, remembering rule number one about the customer.

"During my absence, unfortunately, Alexandra succumbed. Her death was covered only by NBC. A coup for them, I read in the papers. My wife, for the first time in her life and against all her instincts, filed for welfare. But we were ineligible because of our previous year's income. The welfare people suggested that we write the New York *Times*.

"When I got out of the funny farm—see how I can joke about it now?—the doctor said relax. I said I'm unemployed. He said you can't work, you're sick. I said I'm sick of being out of work. My wife had been dispossessed while I was gone and she found this little place. Andrea had passed away God forbid— I had not been allowed to get that news where I was—and my wife was forced to sell Alma, our one remaining quad. My wife, who is a moral and honest woman, had certain misgivings about saying Alma was in perfect condition when she had, for a long time, been running a fever. But you also have to figure she was worth something extra as a collector's item. So she got a decent price and we were able to pay the month's rent and security for this place. It's not bad, is it, the place?"

I shook my head, no, it's a lovely place.

"We got it through the New York *Times* classifieds. At least we got something through the New York *Times*."

He was going ha ha. I asked, "Had you also applied for a job through the *Times*?"

He kept going ha ha and opened an Ohio champagne carton that seemed to serve as a file-box. Soon he pulled out a letter which he handed me to read:

Dear Mrs. Haber,

We regret to inform you that your application to become one of New York's hundred neediest cases has been rejected. If it is any consolation, you finished 114th in the contest, and we certainly think your chances of qualifying next year are excellent.

In case you choose to re-apply, let us provide some advice. "Neediest" applications should make specific reference to

(a) alcoholism, many children

(b) war disability, few children

(c) educational needs, one child

so that the Catholic, Protestant and Jewish charities who generously sponsor our project can specify to whom their donations will go.

Merry Christmas,

THE NEW YORK TIMES.

In the silence granted while I read the letter, I took the initiative. "Well," I said, "if you don't care to receive any of these magazines at the *present* time . . ."

"No, no," he interrupted, "the point is I'm receiving four copies of every magazine on your list. And will till the day I die."

"Perhaps," I suggested, "you would like to divert some of these to your friends and relatives in the form of gift subscriptions. The transfer charge is *virtually* nothing."

He agreed that this would be a good idea and I left him with the appropriate forms.

Shake the Dew

Gary Gildner

from *December*

Freddy Hill used to say, "Shake the dew!" Or if he was surprised, "Well, shake the dew off my goddam lily!" Can I use that? Freddy knocked up his girlfriend, married her, and when I last saw him he was a fireman on the railroad; he said he took his 22 rifle along on night runs and shot at things moving in the weeds. He is not important.

Who is? Is the mysterious Linda Maxwell? Who sends me letters and (surely) dreams about me? There's a pleasant thought. Linda Maxwell is important and I think a little chubby (otherwise she would show herself, no?).

She comes to all the readings, and then writes me letters about them, about how I look. "Lanky . . . angular." I think she's built like Thomas Wolfe's Aline Bernstein—round face, soft, a good cook. I'll have a ham on Polish rye. Any cold beer? (The truth is, I'm built like an arrow.)

"At thirty-one," she writes, "I pride myself at being able to control my thoughts."

Why?

And why tell me she's thirty-one?

Because she's more like forty?

Linda Maxwell who says I am lanky, are you chubby, forty and in full control?

If she's fat she's out of the question. There are limits.

Don't worry, I have her return address.

Here's something. Today I saw the painter Karl Mattern, and his wife Mary. They knew Bodenheim in Chicago.

Promise yourself you will not be too subtle, baby. Think of B. Franklin, think of H. D. Thoreau, think of R. G. Dunn, Uli Beigel and Richard Purina.

A detailed plan is in the works.

Why?

Jessica stopped in to see me today. She hoped she didn't upset me with the bad news. "It isn't all that terrible," she said. "I have at least a fifty-fifty chance."

One of my girls, an alleged vegetarian, wants to write a novel about a beautiful mute named Amy who falls in love with a gas station attendant named Ned. But Amy's parents think he's up to something sneaky. I said to her, "They should wail for joy that he's willing to take damaged merchandise off their hands." That sure stumped her, and putting her thoughts between her tits, she returned to the sorority house, an imaginary toad in virgin's clothes. (If I had any guts I would have fingered her on the spot.)

Vegetarians fart a lot.

OK, I checked out Linda's address. Nice shady little street. A blue star in the window. You know what that means: little kids in trouble can run up and get protection. She has kids of her own maybe? I'd say four—three of which have different fathers. The first kid, however, was a miracle, a gift from God. No, its father was a mailman—part-time—Christmas help.

Casanova once laid a nun who kept saying, *"Fiat voluntas tua."* I'll use that someday—but how?

A little note on pink paper: "I have decided that your poetry is best described as 'consummated rape'—an old familiar behavior of mine." Under her signature (looks mannish) a postscript: "Saw you in the book store today—pretty green shirt. Who was the girl?"

None of your goddam business!

Someday when you least expect it, ask yourself, "What do I really know about Wordsworth?"

I'd like to know what fatty means by "consummated rape" for Christ's good sake. I'd also like to know if Jessica's going to make it. October's a lousy month.

My virginal vegetarian returns to say that Ned is really the only son of a fabulously rich Michigan auto maker. I said, "Do you *believe* that, Cissy?" "Oh God," she said, "we have to believe in *some* things, don't we?" She was serious, dead. I wanted to lick her eyes.

I'm thinking today of my aunt Sophie Skolnik, who raised three sons. Two became priests, and the third, poor Andrew, married (in Aunt Sophie's words) "a piece of ass." She offered this opinion at least twice in my presence. Once was at Thanksgiving-time. There is a marvelous story here but no one would believe it, including Cissy A. Smith, from St. Louis, Missouri.

The city came out today, declared the big elm in my back yard dead, and painted a red X on it. The piece of paper I was handed said I had a month to remove it. I ripped the paper into Cissybite sizes and flushed them down the toilet.

I have decided that on Monday next I will knock on Linda Maxwell's front door. After dark, when all the kids are tucked in.

Shelly was a vegetarian.
The American Tree Co. wants $300 to chop down my tree; that does not include the stump.
Hump the stump!

Jessica in tears. Word got to the Dean of Women about her private treatments, and the Dean thought she ought to withdraw from school—"in all fairness to the other girls."

Told Cissy I'd see her, but first she had to take off her shoes so I could smell her toes. She wanted to know if that was relevant. When I said it was, she collected her thoughts. Then: "You make me feel funny inside." Then: "I have to go now."

Freddy Hill, Linda Maxwell, Uli Beigel, Shelly, Cissy Smith, poor Andrew, Amy & Ned . . .

Got up early to play tennis but couldn't find my good white socks. When the phone rang (my partner) I ignored it.

Jessica went home to Illinois. I gave her my copy of *The Bourgeois Poet*.

Through a small window in the door I could see a sofa, a coffee table, and on the table a half-full bottle of Dr. Pepper. I knocked. In my pocket were copies of my poems—gifts (which later I would offer to sign). I leaned against the house. It's brick. A car went by slowly and the driver looked at me. I'm thirty years old, holder of B.A. and M.A. degrees—who in the hell are you! I knocked again, lightly. I neglected to shave—to scratch her a little. An interior door slammed. Feet on the floor.

"Miss Maxwell?"

"Consummated rape," says Linda, "means pretty much what it says."

She's not fat or chubby, not thirty-one or forty. Average weight, twenty, a drop-out from Wells, married. No kids of any kind.

"Why the blue star?"

"It was here when we moved in."

How we got from the hornet in the kitchen, to rum on the rocks, to her bed is important. I killed the hornet, on the fifth or sixth swipe, with a flyswatter. We had been talking about her husband's attempted suicide. Pills (that's ugly) and a bottle of milk for chaser, so he wouldn't vomit. She said, "Stop calling me Miss Maxwell," and that's when I saw the hornet. In the process of killing it, I knocked down a plaster pear hanging on the wall; it broke into several pieces. I didn't finish my rum, nor she hers. We did, however, sip at the bottle of Dr. Pepper after our tussle in the sheets. She hadn't been to bed with a man, she said, for two weeks. Apparently this had something to do with George's suicide try. She was very lovely, especially her smell. I bit her on the ass once or twice and she liked it. George would be confined at least a month, if not longer.

The Other Kingdom

James B. Hall

from *Carleton Miscellany*

I did not at once gain their confidence.

Now, however, I live in a house beside marshlands that stretch rustling towards the shut-down Potash Works, and all night I listen very intently but hear only the jet aircraft in the overcast, burning towards the runways. Beneath these sills I know storm sewers converge, then lead offshore to the first shelf of the sea. Not there, but by parallel to your own city lies their Other Kingdom.

Twice I talked calmly with your government (city) officials—told everything. Twice behind my back they winked slyly and said, Is that so? Whereupon I moved secretly to this house. But isn't it now only a matter of time?

Obsession is no issue. What began in innocence became disinterested study; from understanding came the final intimacy of full knowledge—as they had planned from the beginning. (Fully explained, below.)

Even as a boy my instincts were normal (in all respects). That spring an Ohio thunderstorm had just passed across the town. At noon by the pond's edge, between a railroad siding and the maze of cattle pens, my terrier foraged the cattail stalks. Suddenly, overhead, the sky was a split-open bale of sunshine, and my airgun barrel became a straight tube of purple light. Beneath the great steel tick-tick of noon, I saw a round, grey stone twitch—then run. As though a woman's stocking of nylon floated up the post, and then trotted in full view across the top board of the cattle pen, shining, outstretched against the clouds and the red water tank beyond, I saw it.

My terrier rose upward from the gravel, seemed for a full minute to remain suspended in mid-air until he struck flat against the cattle pens yelping. The dog fell back. But the rat (*Rattus Norvegicus*) was gone.

Hatred was what I felt. From that moment until I was eighteen and moved to your city, I killed them. I harried them from Kennet's barn; by cage-trap and immersion in water, alone, I cleansed the Slaughter House. Where their incisors chewed the upholstery of cars in wrecking yards, or where they ran on beams across the grain elevators, I pursued them. Or so The Old allowed me to believe, at the time.

All *highly approved.* (Note: very central to character.)

In the home, highly approved by my grandmother, for I lived with her after my father was killed in the woods. In the schools, highly approved by all teachers who knew from my oral reports and my display boards about the row-upon-row of tails, labeled and dated very nicely. Likewise, from my early paper in Social Living, "The Rodent: Familiar Haunts." I still retain my government pamphlets: "Breeding for Profits"; "The Threat of"; "Safe and Sane Poisons"; "Controls: Warehouse and Dock." (See tin-lined boxes, East basement wall.)

From the first my unique "interest" was noted. The first little story appeared in our high school news. Staring back at me from an inside page, I saw a young boy: ears perhaps overly large, the two nippy black eyes close together, the nose and chin coming to a distinct, intelligent point, and my smile—so engaging then—highlighted by my two large upper front teeth (not overly large). Boyish, outgoing. I was the very picture—of myself.

And who could have known my apprentice years were also

their Phase I? After all, had they not already engaged my interest?

Then one day with my government pamphlets and anatomical drawings packed neatly in suitcases, I came to your city. Slender of hand, clever at traps, mother not heard from since they found my father dead in the woods, I first saw the buildings of your city. There I heard what I knew was the *real* world humming in the washed-white dawn of youth. Alone I came there not to seek my fortune, but to pursue disinterested knowledge for its own sake.

Those first weeks perhaps you saw me walking the streets, looking intently at bouquets of flowers behind plate-glass windows. Later I rented clean airy rooms not far from a midtown university. Because I was a specialist, they hired me; daily I walked between cages wearing my white smock. There I witnessed experiments in psychobiology concerning drugs and memory. But at night, in my rooms, I studied much alone.

After heavy rains I heard water running in the storm sewers beneath my bed. Then, late one night, past Christmas, I discovered—and then articulated—the first sullen phonemes of their language. By way of sounds uttered in my own throat began the bridge, the long way to knowledge, the way into their Other Kingdom.

In personal habits I remained chaste (in all respects).

II

No matter. After hours, in my rooms, I had trained twelve *Rattus Albans* to trip the latch of their cage at sunrise and to pull the cord on my Venetian blinds. I can now believe this activity, done in unison, served as an ur-language: their movements in concert was something like music and was therefore understood by The Old without transliteration. (Complete explanation below.)

Therefore imagine my joy when I heard the first voice: that voice was intelligence, oh sought-for communication:

-Beet—Veat?

Their first envoy, at noon, was in the center of my study, in a diagonal ray of sunlight. She sat on haunches, light fawn in color, her exceptionally broad, wide-eyed face looking upward into my face.

Unquestionably, I say "she" because of the feminine timbre of the voice. As beside the cattle pens, in the burst of sunshine, I sat transfixed. Then discipline took over.

"Meat-meat?" I said in a high-pitched tone. I was on my knees, but not too close.

From my kitchen I brought back two squares of roast beef.

-*Beet—Veat!* she said, and in two trips returned the squares of beef to the refrigerator. I heard the refrigerator door swing open—and then smartly close. At once I knew: here was a higher order of kinetic capability.

Precisely then, I understood: their Other Kingdom is a version of our own, and therefore is roughly parallel in both patterns of conduct *and* in language. Therefore their "v" is our sound "kn."

"Knife? Knife?"

-*Kneef—Kneef!*

I handed over my small pearl-handled pocket knife, the one I had carried since boyhood. I held the knife, unopened, in the sunlight. I placed it gently in her overly long, highly articulate "fingers."

Without haste, but with great excitement, the most wonderful one I had ever seen turned, and still upright, vanished as though by liquifaction into the shadow of my bedroom closet.

Date: 26 February.

At sunrise the next day the twelve I had trained with such great labor ran in unison across my bed and very mechanically closed the blinds. For the first time I saw those twelve were of a lower order, perhaps genetically inadequate. By noon I had destroyed them. With their destruction I had left behind an epoch. I had stepped from an encircling woods into the first meadow of their Other Kingdom.

-*Ieets—Ieets?*

Two more of the fawn-colored order—save one shade darker

—came back at noon. Upright they stood, in the sunshine of winter. In unison their voices spoke. Their articulate "hands" were outstretched in supplication.

At once I understood their their new request.

"Steel, steel?" and I gave them two old razor blades from my bathroom cabinet. My usual scientific detachment, as when I walked between cages wearing a white smock, suddenly gave way to mere speculation. Passionately, I wanted them to converse. Could they really operate simple machines? (See below, "At the Forge.")

Yet how unaware I was about the larger issue of their plan. Even then I could actually believe they needed only metal with a cutting edge: *Ieets,* or *Fnor.* (See, "Their Metallurgy: Contamination, Toleration, and Release." Journal #6.)

III

Notes: all their data is held in "files"; this information is passed on by rote. Each individual memorizer (Slave, Class 5) is the equivalent of one manila file folder; each memory-group aligns tribally (i.e., by the subject matter they remember). To eliminate a body of knowledge, The Old denies those files (individuals) food. The Old, however, are also "files" of past *Ianimret* decisions; they, therefore, combine both jurisprudence and causistry. (See my tin-lined boxes, clothes closet.)

[Noted ascendencies: much like our own organized crime syndicates, each "state" of their Other Kingdom has traditional boundaries. Their government (equivalent to our exploitation) is dictated by The Old. Their supreme *Ianimret* (our Senate) convenes in their Capitol. Politically Fascist, all edicts are enforced by the *Sub-Ianimret* warrens, as follows: Public Works (i.e., our destruction); Welfare (our Prisons Bureau); *Iaerec* (Foods); Health (our hatcheries, pig farms, and other breeding establishments). Planned feeding aligned with forced breeding fills all worker requisitions. Their State itself is conceived by them as an *Iaerec-Inc* food-getter) system. Our central concern is "salvation"; their obsession is to obtain total food-world.]

Query: being authoritarian, does this account for the total absence in their language of our signals for "thank you"?

Those things I did not at all comprehend until I followed down into the storm sewers beneath my bed. Gradually, those sewers became illuminous because of phosphorent algaes. Suddenly the passageway became incredibly small. Only by kicking and squirming did I pass into a larger room, and then, by tunnels, into the chambers of The Old.

In the presence of The Old, in a halting version of their speech, I made a formal statement. I declared Good Will. I announced a good new Era of Communication. I declared—symbolically—an end to all prejudice between their domain and our world.

In unison I heard The Old reply, using my exact intonation, my precise words. Significantly, however, they repeated the last phrase: they declared an end to all prejudice—and all causes thereof.

That we could both understand this problem—and could agree—seemed to give my life a new meaning.

The three members of The Old were exceedingly broad-faced, intelligent. I had a dual impression: their polish was that of successful executives, the world over; secondly, there seemed to be an illuminosity about their presence which I felt very strongly. There were no other preliminaries.

-*Loitamrofni, Loitamrofni!* In tone their shouted order was absolutely military.

In the mouth of a nearby tunnel a "file" appeared. Before entering our conference chamber the "file" hesitated. Being administratively trained, he awaited further orders.

An *Araug* (guard) snatched the informant and threw him with great force at the base of their three-sided desk.

Still dazed, the "file" very mechanically began to speak.

Behind the desk, on their scoop-like chairs where they half reclined, The Old attentively watched the expression on my face.

I heard a shrill outflow of names, places, dates. This file concerned a project of long standing, and of great importance to

The Old. What I heard was a thousand details of my own life: from the cattle pens, to the first words we exchanged: *kneef-kneef*. It was their version of my life, seen from "below." Having repeated the contents of its mind, the "file" turned his back on the three-sided desk.

Possibly a signal was given. More probably custom prevailed. But the information having been conveyed, the individual (a fawn-colored male) was struck down from behind with a truncheon.

The Old were already standing. Without another sign they led me through an exceedingly dry tunnel, downwards, towards the flames.

From a balcony, I looked out across a low, vaulted industrial room. The flames burned in a row of separate forges. As their smithies worked metal, the sparks flew upward towards my eyes.

Beside the sixth forge we stopped. A thousand small sticks seemed to snap, but this noise was their hammers of stone tap-tapping in the wind-sound of their bellows. Above each forge, running in harnessed teams of six inside a wheel, the largest ones I had ever seen made the bellows pulley spin.

The forge-worker ritualistically exposed his neck to The Old. When they did not strike him with a truncheon, the smith returned to his work.

Overhead the team running furiously inside the bellows wheel made the flames turn a fragment of blue steel to white heat.

-Your old razor blade, Sir.

Beside the forge, a cage door opened. A half-grown male came out. Its head was placed in a wedge of stone, and the forge-master's assistants twisted the head in such a manner that: 1) the body was immobilized; 2) the white incisors were exposed to the smith's hammer of stone.

I witnessed twelve attempts. First the smith clipped off an "ingot" of razor-blade steel. He held this metal first to his own nostrils. In panic he threw certain ingots at once into a pile of scrap. If he were satisfied *with the odor*, the smith then placed the white-hot steel on the worker's exposed teeth. If the subject screamed, he was struck with an iron bar, and the body thrown with great force into a chute which led to the feeder pens below. If the specimen's body could accept the metal (i.e., if there were no visible spasm) then the smith reheated the tempered steel.

Cleverly, the smith fashioned two cusps of steel. These caps were shaped to a cutting edge, then shrunk on the end of the exposed teeth. Thus shod, the blue razor-steel shining, the specimen was released. Joyfully he trotted past the other forges, splintering any pieces of wood in his way.

"Only one," The Old who was this day's spokesman said. "Only one worker's tooth in eighty can accept metal. This is our national tragedy."

And so it was: their bodies tolerated or rejected metals in direct proportion to individual intelligence. Being of a higher order, the smith first tried the hot metal on himself; only then did he give each worker a crude "Metal-Tolerance" test. Only much later I understood why The Old wanted their second envoy to take a razor blade from my own hand. Nevertheless, I asked the obvious question, but The Old stared at me in disbelief.

"Force? We should use force?" The Old finally replied. "You suggest we forcefully cap *all* Class Five and Six and also our Out-Runners . . . ah . . ."

He explained that when force was used the worker first attacked the forge masters, and then used the steel-cutter teeth for the destruction of Self.

"Ahhh, but *if* we could!" and they threw back their heads and laughed and laughed. When they did a little dance step before the hot mouth of the forge I saw their own back teeth were capped with tips of gold.

"Then, Sir, would it matter if there were tanks of steel around the vegetable oils? or even dikes that keep back the sea?"

Because I wanted to help them, I suggested caps of non-ferrous materials, perhaps diamond dust. Diamonds might be obtained at night from certain store windows . . .

Scornfully, The Old looked at me—savage that I was. The spokesman put it clearly:

"The wealth of nations is food-supply, *Iaerec-Vlppus*. This supply is in direct proportion to capability in steel. High-grade, tempered *Ieets,* Sir . . ."

Suddenly he paced back and forth along the row of forges. The teams running inside the wheels overhead stopped, and he shouted at me:

"No more so than *you,* are we to be forever the have-nots, the citizens of the sixth class, denied the efficiency, the total food-getter capability of *every other race.* Our struggle is Just. Our dedication shall prevail! We shall overcome the national tragedy of *our own blood,* our unjust inability to accept, yes, to accept genetically what is there—" He pointed to the world above the ceiling of that room—"up *there* for our foragers, for the packing away by the ton, yes, and also it lies as ore on the very surface of the earth itself. Oh, give us *Ieets, Ieets!*"

The forge masters and the assistants raised their clenched fists. They also pointed upward towards their poured-concrete ceiling. The applause re-echoed and their voices began to chant:

-Steel-for-all; All-for-Steel. (*Ieets pof Ill; Ill pof Ieets!*)

Such was one side of their national character.

Later I viewed their extraordinary Maze Hall where the young—up from the farrowing pens—were directed to the specific warrens of the social structure. As we walked, everywhere, continuously, I heard feet running on stone, and pelts rubbing, rubbing through passageways; everywhere, continuously, I heard the dark thud of truncheons on flesh, for in that place neither hope nor prejudice obtain. In their tunnels a fetid bran-smell hung like blue smoke even in their incubator stalls where crowns of females lay, their tails knotted, giving birth until they, themselves, were thrown down into the feeder bins, to be consumed by their own litters. We came then to the private chambers of The Old.

Daintily, The Old ate with their hands. To observe custom, I did the same. Our bran was warm, and tasted something like the fetid smell of the blue air.

"Therefore," I finally asked, for they answered all questions very candidly, "was my father's death in the woods entirely accidental?"

"Not accidental. Our interest, however, was in his almost precise resemblance to us, The Old."

Intently, they looked into my face.

True, my father's shoulders had sloped forward when he walked, and his small black eyes were close to a nose which was really overly long. Clearly, The Old had once believed my father's mere physical resemblance was enough.

"But not slain by us," The Old said. "Your mother ran away in a black automobile with the man who shot your father. That 'accident' was during squirrel season. His death naturally ended our interest—in his case."

"So you turned to me?" and everything that had ever happened in my life seemed to fall into place.

"But communication," said The Old, "is not . . ."

"Enough?"

"Precisely," and as we got up again The Old threw their wooden bowls with great force at the *Araugs*.

As we walked up ramps towards the light, The Old answered a final question concerning the tolerance of metal. Their Slave Classes are neither intelligent enough to select useful metals, nor are they genetically adequate to mouth-contacts with cutting or tempered steels. Therefore all metals must be *Aerutaned* (neutralized); this process is apparently an enzyme-triggered syndrome, systemic in nature. My pocket knife and razor blades explains all of this by example: as I affectionately trained the twelve *Rattus Albans* to pull my blind cord at a given signal, I also neutralized, in part, all objects of tempered steel within the radius of my bodily odors. That neutralization, however, was only mechanical in nature. Hence, communication—as they said—was not enough, was not totally efficient.

We stopped beside a heart-shaped door.

To my surprise, The Old handed me an all-white truncheon —probably a femur bone. The truncheon fit solidly into my hand.

When they stood aside, I entered the room alone.

The Other Kingdom

This room was a bower, the walls of grey velvet, the floor ankle-deep in the skins from small, white animals. The dais was covered with pillows, and I sat there for a long time, overwhelmed by the perfume of the moment.

An *Araug* appeared through a curtain of beads. After a ritualistic pause, another entered.

I felt a terrible excitement. She was tall, the face broad, the single white polished ornament—a tooth with a large polished cap of steel—fixed as a spot of light, a miniature crown, in the center of her head.

At first she seemed to be no fixed color for she was of light, changing as she moved: first fawn, then doe-brown, and then in shadows the color of wet pearls.

Having curtseyed, she then reclined on the dais. With pillows everywhere around her body, she looked up at me, eyes luminous and blue against the piled-high white skins of animals.

Desire, was what I felt. I, who was chaste (in all respects).

Ritualistically, the *Araug* kneeled before me—neck exposed.

My truncheon of bone seemed to rise by itself. With primitive force, I struck. Being now depraved by that act, I rolled the guard's body into the outside corridor. I did this in order to be here. Alone. Now.

For the second time I looked down into that face. The small skins of animals around the thighs quivered. The warm tip of the nose delicately touched the place where my shirt opened and exposed my own flesh.

And then she was mine (in all respects).

Afterwards, when as in a dream I saw the cereal factories of the world and the ground beneath skyscrapers give way beneath their tooth-armed assault, only then did I see the consequence of my act. What new tolerators of all metals might now be unleashed to bring the odor of bran and the dark thud of truncheons on flesh to all your cities? By my act I was now both their liberator and the new Adam of some dark teeming race.

Therefore, *only to save others,* I caressed that illuminous face with one hand. With my other hand I found the all-white truncheon.

James B. Hall

I hesitated. Then in a moment of revelation in those eyes, I saw not only the calculation of all governments, but also a genuine loathing—a loathing of me.

I struck again, and yet again, outraging her flesh with my truncheon of bone.

Once back in the chambers of The Old, I feigned raptures. I also ordered that the bower be not disturbed for sixteen hours —to insure gestation.

In feigned anger—and for revenge—I called for the "file" of their knowledge about the slayer of my father, so long ago inside a smoky woods.

Carefully, I listened. I heard repeated many of your own names. I slew my informant, and threw the body with great force into the corridor.

Greedily, I pretended to bargain with The Old for all diamonds in all the windows of all your jewelry stores—when Their Day came. With appropriate military dispatch, I accepted their offer of Liaison Chief for the world—when Their Day came.

Very clearly at that moment The Old foresaw the days of wrath to come when a new race of *Araugs* and every worker at the forge would come forth with steel-shod incisors glittering beneath the moon, come like water running upward from storm sewers, then go beneath street lights and along freeways until they overflowed the lawns of paid-for houses, their teeth making the shrubbery scream, splintering at last the sills of the world. The eyes of The Old glittered, and they cried out for joy.

At once I returned to my rooms near the University, carrying only the all-white truncheon.

Past midnight I fled (not on foot) past your city's edge and at last hid in this house beside a marsh that stretches rustling towards the shut-down Potash Works. But isn't it only a matter of time?

Until then, watch carefully for me in your city streets, especially at noon when I walk through crowds of Christmas shoppers, all prejudice forgotten—for the moment. At once you will recognize my overcoat of grey, the face which has two closely spaced eyes, the nose (admittedly a trifle too long) the shoulders sloping unnaturally forward as I go. It is the grey face which always floats past, the one almost too eager to smile, to speak, to tell everything: the face, in fact, of all your love.

Nor will you smile slyly and say, Is that so? when we pass beneath the tinsel and the decorations in the chime-noises of noon. You dare not smile for certain of your own faces each week tell me this: you also have known that Other Kingdom, and are haunted by a great longing to return. For in that place all men are born.

Voice of the Town

Curtis Harnack

from *TriQuarterly*

Theodore Rueff took on his life as if it held no mystery he couldn't solve. He tithed his income and served as elder in the Protestant church, sang the gaunt, sad hymns from his usual spot on the aisle in the fifth pew—even God seemed taken care of. But behind this amiable show of certitude we saw the loom ing figure of his youngest son, Danny, who by age fifteen was seven feet two inches tall.

As he began to sprout, Clara Rueff joshed with her friends about what a big boy she produced. They squinted behind their smiles and let her think what she wanted. Theodore was put to the trouble of buying special shoes and clothes in the city, but all he talked about was what a swell basketball player Danny would become. Years later Danny's surprising marriage to LaVonne seemed to fulfill his father's hopes of a normal life for his son—hopes which we of the town knew Danny could never possibly realize. All the time Danny and LaVonne lived and worked together. We saw their alliance with our own eyes but groped for an important truth lurking somewhere in their privacy. Who would tell of it? Theodore never cracked. He was Kaleburg's leading banker, keeper of the public confidence, and no one ever knew what torments of doubt or unease afflicted him. Finally he was to go to the grave clean and fast with a heart attack, before any audible whimpers could begin or any revelations. Because of men like Ted Rueff the general faith is held—or deeply doubted. One wonders why anybody likes to see himself in such a dubious role, and why we always expect someone to play it.

The Rueffs' was the third house in from the highway as you entered town, green clapboard with steeply pitched eaves and one hundred running feet of porch, all of it screened. There, on card-party evenings, Ted Rueff was the smiling host clearly visible through the windows to passersby in automobiles, as if he were on display. At the party everyone talked a great deal—but mostly about the tricks just taken and who should have trumped but hadn't. The four Rueff children, according to custom, were kept out of the way. But Danny the giant, dazzled by the company, would climb like Jack-and-the-beanstalk up into those rooms of people from the basement playroom. "What were you doing in the cellar, big fellow?" a guest might call. "Lifting the house?"

"Hey, how's the weather up there?" (This from one of Clara's twinkly friends.)

He never answered. Even his face was peculiarly unresponsive; his round jowls simply hung there like a peeled eggplant. "Danny, you get your sleep," Clara said, in her soft-sigh way. "Go on now—you're the youngest," an excuse she used to hide the fact that sometimes he got so tired he fell asleep standing up or sitting in a chair and had to be caught before he hit the floor and broke his flesh open. He couldn't bear the cold in winter like the others; he fainted from the heat if he went out in August without his blue baseball cap. Germs found a haven in his huge interior, and nothing could stop their proliferation—as if inside not all the caverns had yet been accounted for.

Clara was like the hen that sat on a duck egg along with her own and she refused to see a difference among her offspring. She was very bosomy, such an enormous pillow that it seemed ample not only for the Rueff family to cushion its fears upon but also for anyone who might need this reassurance. In winter she draped herself in a fox-collared coat, soft as a dog's shank. Her creamy pearls—a double strand, for years the only real pearls in town—stood for the things which were not of flesh, and she believed in them.

While he was young, Danny moved along from grade to grade, but at the start of high school the principal had a closed-door talk with Ted Rueff. Soon Danny showed up as clerk in his father's bank. "Hey there, big boy," customers called, "got your hands on the money yet?"

Cheerful as always and now even somewhat handsome in a blown-up way, he'd grin and wave his baseball-mitt hand. But he never said much. "He understands real good," said the teller. "He's taking it all in," said the cashier. "He'll be a banker yet," said Ted Rueff, thinking he was among friends, but it soon got around town.

Danny performed simple clerical errands such as going into the vault with a customer's safe-deposit key. He swept the floor and kept the cooler filled with water. Try as he might, he couldn't learn to work with figures. He found it hard to concentrate, sitting at a desk, his spine curved like a wishbone. Ted had new furniture built but Danny still couldn't remember the multiplication table. "What do they teach in that school!" Theodore shouted one day, and a farmer at the grilled window overheard and passed it along. "What do they *teach?* What do they *teach?*" was savored in taverns and stores all week. To think Ted Rueff hadn't been taught the difference between a soft-head and a normal person!

Danny was dismissed on orders from "someone higher up" and for a time not even the family seemed to pay much attention to him. The older boys were busy suiting-up for basketball after school; they dribbled down the glistening floor with the cocky good feeling of being loose in the joints. Girl friends tumbled to them quickly. They had no time to look after Danny, and even his sister ran out on the old tender responsibility. She became a cheerleader.

"Luckily, Danny's found something he likes to do," Clara

announced, smiling, imperturbable. "He just *loves* cars!" Although Danny couldn't pass the written driver's test, he knew how to operate them. He'd take the wheel whenever it was offered and barrel through the curves of the nearest winding road. Each hairpin turn and two-wheeled squealing corner seemed to thrill him into a skin-close consciousness otherwise unattainable. A couple of no-goods around town got a kick out of letting Danny loose on the highway. As he laughed aloud at the nearness of death, for a few vital seconds he did not feel buried alive in his body. The result was, however, he rolled a car over and was in the hospital half a year.

"He's not the same," Clara said, when Danny got out. "He's been affected," she told her card-playing cronies, shaking her head, and they let her talk. At last she'd been given a respectable excuse.

"He's got to learn a simple trade," said Ted, urging a farmer who was heavily in debt to the bank to take Danny on as a harvest worker. But it didn't work out. "The lummox," said the farmer, "he's always on the ground under the bundle-wagons, sucking on a lemonade jug."

In no time Danny was drifting around the pool halls again and one saw him drunk in the middle of the afternoon. Sometimes Theodore Rueff in his neatly pressed blue suit, gold-flecked tie, shiny shoes, and snap-brim hat walked right down the sidewalk past his sprawled, half-conscious son who was loafing on the bench in front of the family bank. They wouldn't look at each other or speak.

When the Korean war broke out, the two Rueff brothers, who were graduating from college, arrived home in their uniforms and made their last romantic impact upon the town: the one in Air Force blue with silver buttons, the other in ROTC Army officer's twill. One on each side of Clara, with Ted Rueff following behind, they walked down the church aisle under the eyes of God and the town. In the excitement they forgot to include Danny, who awoke from a late sleep to find the house empty, the church bells ringing for the world but not for him.

He wept, and he was still weeping when the Rueffs gaily tromped back into the house. "Danny—Danny! Don't be such a big baby!" called Clara, one arm still around Army, the other looped to Air Force.

"Hey there—" both brothers cried out and leaped to Danny's side to pick up the easy old romp of their childhood.

"Don't punch him," called Clara, "you know how easy he bruises."

"Leave me alone! Just leave me alone!" Face still shiny with tears, he loomed up and entered the stairwell, mounting the steps carefully to his room, a giant on business. The family was stunned, almost offended by the discovery that Danny felt he had a right to his own emotions—which might not be theirs. He would not come down to dinner, nor could he be persuaded to tag along as the Rueffs bade farewell to their patriotic sons, later that afternoon. "If they don't come back," Clara said finally, taking leave of him, the horn honking, "just *think* how bad you'll feel then!"

He looked at her angrily, stirring his huge limbs, and for the first time she felt afraid of him—and fled the house. She didn't tell her husband what had made Danny so furious, only that "he looked about to hit me!"

"If it gets any worse," said Army, "you know what you'll have to do."

"But we always said, your Dad and I" (Ted sitting right beside her in the back seat), "why have him put away when he's so harmless?"

"Some of the women in town are starting to worry," said Air Force, who'd spent most of his leave getting reacquainted with high school loves. Both boys had already confided to their father that Danny was actually no threat on that score, since he was impotent. They were certain of it. Some years back, in an attempt to explain sex to him, they'd sat on a pasture gate and watched a pony stud in action. Much to their surprise, Danny wasn't the least interested. Now the rumors of his threat to the local girls were just the dirty country gossip one might expect, given his outsize proportions in that department, too.

Everytime he was caught taking a leak there were guffaws and comments. But neither Rueff boy could bear to inform their father of the indecent nature of this talk—yet they felt some little warning should be voiced.

The following week Danny insisted he be allowed to enlist in the Navy. Theodore Rueff went through it all: helped Danny pack his bag, watched him bid farewell to his Mom, and drove him to the Navy recruiting office above the city Post Office. He and Danny walked up the steps as if they truly expected to get somewhere. "My son here wants—" Ted began, apologetically, while the Petty Chief on duty, red-faced from sea winds, widened his eyes, pushed back his chair. "My son—"

"I come to enlist in the Navy," said Danny, his deep half-muffled voice seeping out of the tower of himself. "I'm of age." A blush suffused his neck and lower cheeks, as if the blood of his life were coming forth, once he proclaimed himself a man.

The five-foot-three Petty Chief grinned and leaped to his feet. With a side wink to Rueff he reached up and thumped Danny on the back. "More fellas like you and we'd win this war in no time!"

"Where do I go?" Danny twirled his little satchel nervously, while Rueff blinked, looked embarrased, and turned to gaze out the window.

"Trouble is—you're so big you'd put the fleet to shame."

"I'm too big?"

"No, *they're* too small!" He marched Danny into the examination room, laughing to leeward all the way. It was a slack day, and the medical officer was waiting. "Look what I've brought you!"

They took great pains to describe the narrow, stacked seamen's bunks on a typical U.S. Navy vessel. They showed him skivvies and bell-bottoms so that he could see that none of them fit him. When the interview was over they shook hands with Danny, called him a fine American, urged him to stop in and see them whenever he liked.

"Well, son?" said Theodore. "Ready to go home now?"

Danny nodded agreeably but with a new independence. At last he'd gone beyond his father—and the family's network in Kaleburg. He'd been seriously discussing his life with representatives of the United States government. All the way home he couldn't keep the grin from his face.

Then, through a pool-hall friend, Danny got a job with a pinball machine company, Idle Hour Games. They helped him pass his driver's license exam and loaned him a car. His chief duty was to collect revenue from pinball machines and punchboards. Although illegal, most bars had several kinds of punchboards for the customers' amusement. You could buy a punch for a dime or a quarter, the whole card bringing the company ten times the cash value of the prize for the lucky-punch winner.

Danny took a room in a small hotel in the city, where he could receive messages that came while he was on the road. He collected coins from the pinball machines and learned to fix broken ones. Without his father close at his side, he managed to keep his accounts straight. After three months he was courier for half a dozen shady operations, including a numbers pool, ball-game pools, and a system whereby servicemen met girls. He was known and hailed as he made his rounds. Men would clap him on the shoulder and pump his soft hand, and Danny would bray with pleasure, showing his long-toothed horsey grin.

But suddenly Theodore Rueff received a call to bail Danny out of jail. He and the Idle Hour Games people had been arrested and charged with racketeering and procurement for the purposes of prostitution. An understanding judge commuted Danny's sentence, sending him home in the custody of his parents, who were henceforth to keep an eye on him.

"We've been all alone here, Danny," Clara whimpered. "This big house and all the children gone but you." However, she couldn't make him her baby any more. Before a week was out he fled. They didn't know where he'd gone and were afraid to ask the authorities to hunt him up, since surely then he'd have to be "put away." Both Rueffs became highly guarded on the subject; and while the addresses of the two boys in uniform and the girl in Los Angeles studying fashion were printed in the church bulletin, Danny was left out.

Soon everyone read of Danny's marriage—to LaVonne Zimmer—before a justice of peace in a town forty miles away, one of those many villages where Danny had become known as a traveling man. Clara said it was wonderful "to have somebody taking care of Danny." The Rueffs helped settle the newlyweds in a Kaleburg house available for twenty-five dollars a month, provided Danny and LaVonne would "look in" on the eighty-year-old lady who lived alone next door, their landlady. Wedding presents arrived, but Clara gave no tea to introduce her daughter-in-law and suggestions of a bridal shower were quashed for no reason, unless it was that Clara and Ted didn't want to pretend they expected grandchildren from this alliance.

The old rumors about Danny's sexual abnormality began to surface—*he* wasn't interested in girls, everybody knew. So, what was going on? LaVonne was tall and squarely built, as strong as Danny was weak. Her dark brown hair, the color of flaxseed, was done up in a coil over each ear and flat spit-curls just above her forehead were held in place by hairpins that seemed to staple her crown. She had deeply recessed, small blue eyes and run-together eyebrows. Her mouth was a neat, thin line, and except for her nose, which projected a modest distance, she seemed almost bereft of the usual features that distinguish one of us from another. Everyone thought she was up to no good and had probably married the village idiot in order to cash in eventually on the Rueff money. Clara made a point of telling her friends that LaVonne had nursed her father through a long illness, that she was a good, shy, devoted soul—hard to get to know, but in every way worthy of her son.

LaVonne didn't entertain in her home nor did she accept any of the invitations to join women's clubs. "He's being looked after," said Clara joyously, "that's what counts." The life of the elder Rueffs separated easily and decisively from that of their son and his wife. Soon nobody thought to remark that it was odd Danny and LaVonne were never seen in the big green house on Main Street. It was increasingly hard to remember he was a Rueff at all.

When the old drunk who ran the dray service got run over and killed by his own cart, Danny and LaVonne took over his business. They acquired a sorrel gelding used to plowing and corn-planting and shod him for service on town streets. La-Vonne showed the horse where to graze on the strips of pasture along the railroad embankment, and in the evenings he cleaned up the spilled oats and corn around the spouts of the Farmer's Elevator. The wagon was an ancient, heavy box on four thick wheels; panels slid into place making a rectangle four feet deep—or the wagon could be stripped down like a railroad flat-car. Originally there'd been a pair of horses for the outfit, but something had happened to one of them. Since the old man couldn't afford a new horse, he'd adjusted the rig; the load could be pulled from the whiffletrees, by a single brute in harness.

You may wonder what need there is for a dray service in a town as small as Kaleburg, since most citizens have cars and could make periodic trips to the dump with tin cans, glass, and junk that won't go into the back-yard compost pile. But some people hate to run the risk of having their tires cut by broken glass or nails. They detest the sight of rats among the refuse, should they go out there in daylight—or the bright little rat-headlights gleaming all over the place at night. They called Danny's Dray. Customers also phoned to have salvaged bricks hauled to the site of a foundation for a new house; or to carry lumber in a hurry, when the normal delivery couldn't be made. Even the stores employed Danny and LaVonne to transport heavy merchandise. The price for service wasn't high, and thanks to LaVonne the job was always done neatly and in good time, without much fuss.

In going about their business, Danny and LaVonne wore overalls and heavy work shoes, the leather so thick it didn't much matter what dropped on their toes. The only way to tell it was a man and woman on the cart, not two men, was that LaVonne wore a babushka, except in summer, when she was forced by the intense sun to wear a farmer's straw hat. Unlike junk carriers the world over, they never seemed interested in their burdens or considered their freight in any light except that it was something to be disposed of. No little trinket was ever filched and kept in secret at home. When something of possible value was included in the load, LaVonne would speak about it to the person employing her. "That hairbrush?" the woman might reply. "*Ach,* its bristles are mostly broken. No, it ain't good for nothing but curryin' your horsie." And then LaVonne would use it for that, as long as it lasted. She seemed to understand the dangers that might develop if she ever wised-up to the business she was in. She was, in short, incorruptible; but the town believed nothing of the sort. *They* thought she ignored salvageable items because she was waiting for the Rueff fortune itself, when the old folks died off.

Meanwhile, Danny's Dray made money, though they never seemed to spend any. Now and then they'd go to a movie, settle themselves in the front row where Danny had always sat, share a nickel bag of popcorn, and watch the cowboys galloping across the screen. They put a dime or two in the collection plate when they attended church, which was infrequently. They didn't drink liquor or even beer because LaVonne said (what everybody knew) it didn't agree with Danny. Their car was a beat-up 1939 Chevrolet. Every morning LaVonne was first at the bakery for day-old bread. She kept a sizable garden and canned all summer. She knew what farmers could be approached about picking the tart plums in a forgotten lane, to be made into preserves. The grocery supplies LaVonne bought were of the austere, pioneer sort: flour, sugar, salt. Even the meat was arranged for privately, during the country butchering time in February. The town speculated that perhaps Danny preferred the safety of his mattress or the sugar bowl for his hoard, rather than his father's bank.

Years later the true tale leaked out, in the surprising, appropriate way these revelations occur. In the prosecution of one of Danny's pinball-machine buddies, who'd been released after serving his term only to return to his rackets, the district attorney discovered that Danny Rueff had been paying hush-money sometimes amounting to two hundred a month. The convict had terrorized him into believing he could be re-arrested at any moment, and even LaVonne was convinced. Nowadays some blame Theodore and Clara for not inquiring into the reason why Danny's and LaVonne's back-breaking drudgery showed so little profit. But misery is often obscured because of the pride everyone takes in hard labor, the virtue it entails—the fact that "work never hurt anybody."

But it broke Danny—or rather the strain did. He was such a big, calm, plodding creature no one thought he might be a mass of anguish inside. One day he got into the Chevy and drove to the state insane asylum twenty-five miles away "to turn in." LaVonne was summoned for interview, and the authorities talked to Clara and Ted, each of them separately. Danny planned to remain safe inside the walls, LaVonne reported; "he's real happy there." She spoke without bitterness or even resignation. "Now I got to carry on with the Dray alone, I guess."

The town would have speculated at length about Danny's surprising action had not Clara succumbed to a stroke the same week. Her right side was paralyzed from top to bottom. She could only speak disjointedly with half a tongue, smile with half a mouth, and think with half a brain. It happened because of her grief over Danny's collapse—that's what people said. LaVonne immediately began to nurse her. In the morning she'd go over to the house on Main and fix Theodore's breakfast before he walked to the bank, then lift Clara from her bed, carry her to the bathroom, wash her and dress her and put her in the wheelchair. After a ramp was built over the front steps, Clara's trips in the mobile chair could be down the block or even to the stores, LaVonne always in attendance. The dray service dwindled, but she still maintained the business. She continued to live in the little house next to the very old lady (now in her nineties) and checked each morning to see if the woman was alive.

Clara was expected to regain use of her arm and leg; there

seemed to be improvement for several months. But Clara enjoyed being taken care of by LaVonne and wasn't much interested in using the doctor's spring-contraption to exercise her hand, biceps, and calf. She had no reason in particular to want to get up and walk again. "I've got it pretty easy, wheeling along," she'd say with a laugh, "I don't know's you folks have it so good." She would never be quite right in the head again, that was the trouble. There were no devices to fix that lesion. The doctor told Theodore that the end would most likely come suddenly, one of these years, with another series of strokes. Hard to tell just when.

During this time the three other Rueff children didn't come back. They had youngsters of their own, of course, which was fair excuse, but it seemed odd that in those four years none of them was able to make the trip home. Mostly it was thought the reason was guilt over Danny—and shame that he was where he was, when the Rueffs could certainly afford a private sanitarium. But who would start doing something? Theodore washed his hands of it—he had enough to think about with Clara; his face in profile was pewter gray and stern, the look of George Washington on twenty-five cent pieces. The letters between the Rueff children flew back and forth, from New York to California and Washington, guardedly speculating on what should be done about the home situation. But the last word was always, "Thank God for LaVonne!"

When Theodore died of a heart attack, all of them came back. What a strange procession they made: the children in their well-tailored dark clothes walking behind the coffin, along with dotty Clara, who was weeping, snuffling, and carrying-on aloud; and sober, lean-faced LaVonne, pushing the wheelchair down the church aisle, looking no more grim than usual—in fact, she was "just the same's ever!" She was about as tough as a mortal could be, in the best sense of the word, for no matter what was dished out, she took it without a whimper.

She was not entirely of iron, however. A few weeks after Theodore's burial, when she moved into the house on Main Street in order to be closer at hand in ministering to Clara, she put her horse in the barn out in back, which had been used as a garage. The city fathers said there was an ordinance against it. She received an official letter from the mayor, warning her that she'd be fined if she didn't remove the animal. But she *had* to have him close by, not in the shed giving onto a pasture (outside the city limits) where she'd formerly kept him. She was wildly attached to the beast who'd been her companion all these years. She wouldn't give in—no, she'd pay the fine.

But the penalty, it was explained, would be levied again next month and each succeeding month until she did something about complying with the city ordinance. Ladies who came to visit Clara got a full, emotional report from the invalid, slightly off-key, a peculiar wheezing screech, as if a half-melted phonograph record were being played on a faulty machine. "She got Theodore's pistol out—oh yes, she found that! And she cleaned it up real good, and dug up some bullets, too. Just you wait— anybody comes trying to move her horse—you'll see some shooting, you will. Our property, ain't it? They can't do this to us. And after all we've done for this town!"

That kind of talk, bruited about the village, was just the sort of thing the high school hoodlums liked to take up. They deviled LaVonne as she walked the streets or drove her dray cart in the alleys. They cackled and hooted and even threw firecrackers, daring her to shoot the pistol. She never gave them the satisfaction of paying any attention.

A special dispensation for the horse was finally granted "in respect to the memory of Theodore Rueff." Everybody knew LaVonne had won because of her strange, fierce love for that animal. In farm country you seldom hear of anyone getting affectionate over a cow or a pig or a workhorse because that sort of thing upsets the system. These beasts are in bondage to man; it's not the other way around. If only LaVonne had had the sense not to put that straw hat of Danny's on the creature, cutting out holes for his ears. If only the horse hadn't had such big blue eyes which did indeed resemble Danny's; if the animal had been given some name like Nick or Dobbin. But he had no name, and so the high school kids began calling him Danny.

Then you began to see other connections: the fact that he was a gelding; his lumbering gait and size; his sad, half-witted look. The effort LaVonne made protecting the horse got her into closer alliance, really a companionship. Cart, horse, and woman roamed the alleys even when there was nothing to be hauled, the cart empty.

Some village gossip must have written to the Rueff daughter in California, describing the situation and saying that Clara was being neglected because of LaVonne's infatuation with the horse. A practical nurse was suddenly engaged to come and live in the house. LaVonne was no longer to attend the invalid. The stranger, sent by a city agency, was a hearty, gray-haired, meat-and-potatoes sort. She was righteously indignant over the filthy condition of the house, which apparently hadn't been cleaned for a couple of years. Moths had infested the clothes, mice and rats had the run of the basement and attic, and even poor dear Clara Rueff herself was so dirty on the back of the neck that she had to be scrubbed hard with a rough washcloth and strong laundry soap. Purveyor of all this juicy news, the practical nurse was welcomed into every household on the block.

She told more than she should have. Or rather, she kept repeating everything Clara said, and these ravings were increasingly unreliable and not to be listened to. For one thing, apparently LaVonne had been in the habit of caressing the old woman in those regions where one would imagine only the young feel intense pleasure. Clara liked to be handled gently, dreamily, and for a good long time, until she went off to sleep. LaVonne, questioned about this by the practical nurse, who was shocked by such manipulations, was reported to have answered: "She'd smile and feel so good, I never had to give her no sleeping pills. That's more than *you've* done for her!"

The remark, coupled with Clara's own peculiar notion about LaVonne, began to spread. The nurse quoted Clara as having said: "LaVonne's got whiskers like a man. A girl ain't supposed to have a chin like that. No, I don't think she's a girl at all." Actually, LaVonne had always carefully shaved the stubble she'd been afflicted with, on her upper lip and chin. As these growths flourished in later years, she'd tried to cover them up with talcum powder. But one time Clara's hand had happened to reach out, in a moment that might have been ecstasy, in the evening when the light was dimming in the bedroom, and La-Vonne was soothing the old lady for the night. She touched LaVonne's face—her eyes widening—suddenly she thought she understood the mystery of this creature who'd come so accidentally into the Rueff household and now was such an indispensable part of it. "Always in overalls, she is. Works like a man. No wonder my poor Danny sent himself away!"

So when Clara died, and after the funeral and the dutiful visits from the far-off children, when the practical nurse lost her job and had to return to the city, in the settlement of the estate the clapboard house on Main went to LaVonne, plus a small income from farm property—largely because the Rueff children realized that she'd forever make those twice-a-month visits to the state hospital, keeping an eye on Danny. She lived alone and never went out in the streets or alleys with the cart any more. The horse was too old, and nobody phoned to have LaVonne do a job. They knew her circumstances had changed. By now LaVonne's hair was streaked with gray, and she wore it severely back in a bun and looked like some prairie sodhouse woman of the nineteenth century. You might guess that she'd be left alone to live out her years in peace, with whatever private hells she experienced, and wherever she found her heavens. But you don't know our town, if you think that.

The kids kept talking about the rumor that LaVonne was really a man dressed up in woman's clothing. One night in late spring a bunch of the graduating seniors, out drinking and celebrating, sneaked through the back yard and walked right into the Rueff kitchen—because nobody, not even widows and old maids, locks their doors. Maybe she knew why they'd come and what they meant to do to her. She did not shriek or run for the telephone. They tried to corner her in the front parlor, but she escaped up the stairs. Yelling like animals, they were hot after her. They thought she was merely fleeing—and she was in part —but she was also trying to remember where she'd last put

Theodore's Colt .45. Finally they pinned her down on a musty bed in a back room and ripped every shred of clothing from her body. She fought so wildly that the young athlete astride her got aroused—a local football hero I shan't name, for he later joined the Marines and died in Vietnam. With his teammates cooperating, as they used to do on the playing field, he made the full discovery of her womanhood, something no man had ever done before—not even her husband Danny. They saw the deep stain on the bedspread and knew her secret, a different one from what they'd come to find. She writhed free of their grasp in the moment her assailants saw the blood. The pistol lay on the washstand next to the only window with a clear view of the barn door. She grabbed the gun and, naked in the starlight, flung herself through the window, shattering the glass as she flew.

Aghast and suddenly sober, they raced downstairs, and out the front door, got into their cars and spurted away. They didn't even have the decency to go round back to see what might be done to help her. They just wanted to get away and not be caught. A neighbor heard the crash but couldn't figure out for a long time what had caused it. Then he saw the pale, nude figure on the lawn, slowly moving through the grass, long hair down her back. He'd have gone over at once if he hadn't also noticed that she was entirely naked, her breasts flat and loose. There seemed to be some dark stuff like paint here and there on her body. He figured that whatever she was up to, she wanted to do it alone. She squirmed across the long backyard lawn, hung awhile on the picket gate till she worked the latch open, then slumped down again to wiggle through the hollyhocks. It took nearly twenty minutes for her to get to the barn—the horse whinnying and trampling the earth as she came. She reached him at last and somehow managed to pull herself upright in the stall—so that she could explain to the horse and to herself what she was about to do—in a voice none of us ever heard give utterance to anything that mattered.

You can be sure she spoke. She got very close to his wall-eye, we know from the wound, and pulled the trigger. Then she shot herself, left hand clutching the mane, a fistfull of sorrel hair. Her head lay near his furry ear, as if she'd just stopped speaking. Those who came up after the pistol fired and saw the naked woman sprawled across the horse's body said, later, that Lady Godiva herself had not been more beautiful. Isn't it just like them to say something like that? Her leg had been broken, the doctor reported—*her* leg, not the horse's.

Lykaon

Robert Henson

from *Epoch*

One day Euneus king of Lemnos received an invitation to a royal wedding. The daughter of Menelaus king of Sparta was marrying Achilles' son. The father fancied having Lemnian wine for the guests, among whom would be a number of veterans of the War. Euneus would undoubtedly remember that he had supplied the troops (or at least the officers) with his famous wine. If it were still being made it would bring back many happy memories of those valiant times.

Euneus tugged his beard, gnawed his lower lip. Was he being asked to furnish such-and-such a number of jars free?—not to mention the cost of transportation? But if not, why was he being invited at all? He knew neither the bride nor the groom, and had met their fathers only in a business way. The message was exasperatingly neither personal invitation nor impersonal order for wine; it fell carefully between.

He suspected Menelaus of ambition. During the War he himself had maintained strict neutrality, provisioning both Greeks and Trojans with oxen, wine, cloth, medicinal mud. There had been some resentment of this among the Greeks—they felt that impartiality was especially unbecoming in a son of Jason. Ever since the fall of Troy rumors had floated over from the mainland that this or that Greek king was preparing to annex the island under the pretext that Euneus had aided the enemy during the War. So far nothing had come of such scares. Indeed, several of the more aggressive kings had themselves gone under—Agamemnon, for instance.

Still, Lemnos was in too favorable a position to be ignored forever, even by kings with no ready excuse. Euneus decided therefore that he had best cultivate Sparta's good graces. He wrote back begging to be allowed to offer the happy couple not one but three gifts. The wine, of course, the best vintage (Menelaus would remember how scrupulously the scribes had kept track of good years). A supply of medicinal mud (its proven uses had more than doubled since the War). And finally an evening's entertainment by Euneus' bard, who would sing a song in praise of Achilles. Euneus realized that Achillean bards were common as geese these days when the whole world united in idolizing the great man, but lest this third gift be valued too lightly, he begged Menelaus to know that this bard was extraordinary. He was none other than Lykaon, only surviving son of the royal family of Troy. He had been a servant in Euneus' court these nine years, had been taught the art of storytelling, and had proved very forward in it. Often and again he had brought audiences in Greece and Asia Minor to the edge of their chairs with the tale of his encounter with Achilles, whose heroism, of course, transcended partisanship and belonged to all men—

"Et cetera," said Helen, lifting a white arm to smooth her hair. She had recently stopped shaving under her arms—perhaps because the fashion for smooth armpits had at last come to Sparta. The glimpse of moist blonde ringlets gave Menelaus an agreeable little tingle. He believed now that he had never really liked it when she was statue-smooth.

He dismissed the scribe who had been reading Euneus' letter and growled, "What surprises me is that he hopes to put this hoax over on *us*."

"Why not on us?" Helen asked. Her "et cetera" had not

meant that she was skeptical, only bored with pompous phrases.

"He must know that we saw Lykaon slain by Achilles."

"I didn't. Did you?"

"Well, not personally, but there were half a dozen who did, who even heard the boy pleading for his life. Even without witnesses," he added, as if he had just thought of it it, *"you* would surely know."

She understood him too well to suspect a barb, and said placidly, "I wasn't exactly given free run of the palace. Toward the end I was never sure who had or hadn't returned from battle. Sometimes there'd be a perfect tempest of lamentation; then a couple of days later, the deceased would turn up safe and sound."

"I meant, love, that you would know Lykaon if you saw him now."

"Priam had so many sons," she said vaguely. When she was thinking hard her eyes had a way of changing color, shifting through a whole spectrum of melting blues, grays and lavenders. "Who was his mother? Not Hecuba. Did he have a brother named Polydorus? *His* mother, I'm almost sure, was Laothoë . . . Yes—now I remember him!" She did not say that he had been just old enough to fall in love with her, though that was the fact that helped her to recall him. "A tall boy, sixteen or seventeen. He can't have changed so much as to be unrecognizable."

"Exactly my point."

"Well, then, perhaps it really *is* Lykoan."

Menelaus, however, refused to believe it. Probably Euneus himself had been hoodwinked. Bards were notorious for confusing fact and fiction. At any rate, so long as the wine was the real thing, Menelaus didn't care. Euneus had better not try to fool him there!

When Lykaon heard that he was going to Sparta, he merely shrugged. When he heard for what purpose, he shrugged again. As usual he concealed a thought or two from Euneus. The news, illuminating in a lightning flash the end of his path, had in truth made his blood run backward in his heart.

Euneus—also as usual—felt pangs of anxiety. At such times he was prone to make deals. "Behave yourself on this trip," he said wheedlingly, "and I'll move the date of your manumission forward. On the day of our return, to be exact, you'll become a free man."

"Behave myself?"

"As a bard. I suggest, for instance, that you must not embroider the tale the way you did in Athens. These people were *there*. At least some were. They're not like the Athenians."

"The Muse inspired me," Lykaon said provokingly. "I myself would never have thought to connect Achilles' particular virtues with Athena's, much as I admire the goddess."

"In spite of what you think," Euneus said peevishly, for they both knew who the "Muse" had been, "it wasn't just good business, it was also common courtesy for you to do what other bards are doing in Athens. You weren't the first, after all, to suggest that Athena was the protector of Achilles. But since you've become such a stickler for facts, see that you stick to them in Sparta!"

Lykaon intended to. He was even grateful that the temptation of earlier freedom had been put in his way. Perhaps somewhere along the line he would have to fight down an impulse to save himself.

"Is he there?" Menelaus asked, behind his hand.

Helen, sitting beside him on a carved chair in the Court of Honor, scanned Euneus' entourage which the guards were just admitting. Wedding guests had been arriving all day, and she was a little blurry. But when her gaze met Lykaon's straight-on, "Yes," she said without hesitation, "it can't be anyone else."

Euneus brought him forward after the wine and medicinal mud. Menelaus retreated into royal woodenness, but Helen said with charming familiarity: "Lykaon, how handsome you've grown! Quite a change from the usual bard."

"From the usual prince, you might have said," Menelaus growled.

"Oh, that goes *without* saying," she replied amiably.

"Indeed, madam," said Lykaon, "what court these days doesn't have former royalty tending the children, keeping accounts, even advising on arms?"

Euneus saw that Menelaus' reserve would not last; he said roundly, "Not all conquered princes are as lucky as you, my boy. Some are—and deserve to be—sweating under the lash as they raise stone blocks into just such magnificent palaces as this."

"A son of Jason would never treat a son of Priam so," Lykaon said with a smile.

"Still," Menelaus put in, "he might set him to singing the praises of the son of Peleus."

"The praise of Achilles, sire, is a commodity, like my master's wine; or a labor, like hauling stones. I didn't invent it."

Menelaus hitched forward in his chair. Helen put a white hand on his arm and said lightly, "He only means, my lord, that bards aren't necessarily responsible for their songs, not that the praise of Achilles is an ignoble task."

"Just so, my lord! Thank you, my lady!" Euneus cried gratefully, and plucked Lykaon back.

He sent for him later in his quarters. "Have I mentioned your freedom?"

"Several times."

"The Trojan War is over. Don't let the sight of that red-headed fool Menelaus bring it all back."

"Am I not supposed to bring it back . . . with my song?"

"Not *per se*," said Euneus, pulling his beard nervously. "The old war spirit, yes, but not the old war. Menelaus is itching for a fresh adventure. Can't you see it? There are signs of it everywhere. Bronze ready for issue to the smiths. Tablets of operational strength from Spartan outposts. A dozen things." For he was a wonder around storerooms, archives, and prattling chief stewards. "And why," he asked only half aloud, "are there so many Dorians about? Everyone else keeps them at arm's-length. Is Menelaus working on an alliance? But against whom? His former allies? Perhaps he's trying to lull the Dorians . . . or is it to impress them?"

Since these questions were not about Menelaus' principles but only his intentions, they could not be answered. "Whatever it is," Euneus said meaningfully, "I don't care to be his victim. Let's do our job and put Sparta behind us. Did I mention your freedom? . . ."

"She can't wait," breathed Hermione. She and her betrothed stood in the shadows as an old woman led Lykaon to Helen's chambers.

"What does she expect to find out?" Neoptolemus wondered.

But Hermione, though she always suspected far-reaching conspiracy on the part of her elders, was never sure of the details. She usually had to answer as she did now: "I don't know, but *something's* going on."

Neoptolemus nodded thoughtfully. He had never made any effort to be like his father. On the contrary, his determination to go his own way had led him to positively cultivate a lack of physical prepossessingness. He was scrawny, beardless, he wore his hair short, went about unarmed, mumbled when he spoke. The very sight of him repelled Menelaus. Hermione, however, was unaccountably stricken with him and threatened to kill herself, go mad, or run away in men's clothing if forced to marry anyone else. She had an ally she didn't want in her mother. Helen privately took the view that they deserved each other, for Hermione refused to do so much as lengthen the too-round eyes in her too-round face, and the front of her dress was as likely as not to be spotted with wine. But principally Helen did not propose to turn a harmless eccentric into a dangerous lunatic as her sister had done. "No more Electras, please," she said to Menelaus. He was persuaded.

Neoptolemus now believed that he saw what was going on in Helen's chambers, or, more important, in her mind. "This bard is an imposter. She wants to let him know secretly that they'll play his game."

"They? Father too?"

"Naturally. I've never believed the story that he ordered Lemnian wine just for our wedding, and that Euneus 'volunteered' to bring a Trojan bard. Your father planned the whole thing. It's part of his effort to create a new militarism."

"Using *your* father as a symbol. . . ." Hermione was breathless with enormity of it.

"Not that he would object," Neoptolemus said bitterly.

"How sick it all is!"

Once again they were gripped with sudden passion for each other, and slipped off to commit the act that pleased them no less than it always did for making their coming wedding ceremony superogatory.

"Well, Lykaon," Helen said, "so we meet again."

That was so unworthy of her that she instantly understood and forgave his impudent grin. "Ah well," she smiled, "now that I'm older I find it more comforting to make fatuous remarks. It allows both parties some leeway. You know, Lykaon, my most casual relationships used to be so . . . emotional and direct. One wouldn't keep that up even if one could."

She waved him to an upholstered stool, then raised an arm to touch her hair. Her loose heavily-embroidered half-sleeve slid deliciously off the round white upper arm. Lykaon shifted his gaze to the wall behind her, but the brilliant frescoes of birds, beasts and plants only set her off. She had to be faced.

"I wish we were meeting under conditions more favorable to you," she said. "But perhaps you've noticed that your room isn't in the servants' quarters."

"I did notice, but thought maybe there were Trojans among your slaves who'd resent me. Dead birds don't sing."

"No, it's exactly as Euneus says: Achilles has transcended partisanship. The Trojans are quite proud to have been defeated by him. It would be another matter if you were here to praise Odysseus."

He didn't answer. She went on: "But I didn't bring you here to talk about Achilles. I want to hear about *you*. Everyone was sure you'd been killed."

"Hearing the story twice might bore you."

"I'm not asking you for the official version."

He looked into her eyes, saw the color shift, and doubted that he could trust her. It was tempting, though, to talk about himself. He aimed at a neutral tone. "No one in the War has a story separate from Achilles, least of all me. The War was hardly over before people reduced it to a demonstration of Achilles' heroism, a testing ground for *his* honor, a springboard for *his* fame. A man like that needs scope, a war like that gives it."

Helen made a little mouth. "Yes, even in Egypt, where Menelaus and I spent some time, the Trojan War might as well have been the Achillean War."

"Not many people want to hear how the Greeks and Trojans came to blows over a tax on ships—especially now that both sides have lost the sea lanes they fought over."

Helen smiled. "So the Phoenicians are the true victors?"

"Even the Phoenicians are fascinated by Achilles. I think Euneus first got the idea of training me as a bard from them," he mused. "They often used to put in at Lemnos. But it could have been from anyone he was doing business with. As soon as word got around that a veteran of the War was in his service, the questions would begin. Had I ever met Achilles? What was he really like?"

"And who could answer better than you?" said Helen, her smile more subtly encouraging.

"I'm talking too much," he thought, even as he said aloud, "It was Euneus who made it official, to use your word. The first time Achilles sold me to him, he tried to train me as a clerk. I was so inept that he was glad to let me be ransomed. Then when I met Achilles again and was left for dead, slavers picked me out of the reeds and took me straight back to Lemnos; it was always their first stop. Euneus didn't bat an eye when he saw me, for fear of running the price up. The slavers didn't know who I was, only that I was young and strong enough to recover. Euneus, though, saw a second ransom in prospect. He got me for a silver ring. As soon as the slavers left, I had the pleasure of telling him the painful news that Hector had been killed, that Troy would fall, that my father could no longer afford such luxuries as ransom."

"How chagrined he must have been!"

"Less than he would have been if he'd paid more. Even so, he was determined to get his money's worth, so back I went to the clay tablets. I told him to send me to the mud pits and be done with it. I had no talent for totting up jars of wine and lengths of cloth. But he went on trying for two whole years. I think his real purpose was to convince me that a love of trade was honorable—for a son of Jason, or Priam, or any other prince. I never disputed that, only my fitness for it."

"And then our enterprising friend discovered the market for Achilles, is that it?" she said with dazzling marksmanship.

"He called me in one day and pointed to an old man who'd been a professional bard. He was to help me put my experience into tolerable verse."

"You refused."

I said it would be infamous to celebrate the man who had done more than anyone else to destroy my city."

"Ah! But he had an answer."

"He said that Achilles had actually tried to stop the fighting before Troy fell, that he had been in love with my sister Polyxena and tried to arrange a truce."

"There *was* a story to that effect."

"Oh yes, and others too—all to the same effect: Achilles was not an ordinary enemy. It wouldn't be a disgrace to praise him."

"That, surely, wasn't what persuaded you?"

"No."

"What, then?"

He was silent a moment before he answered: "Freedom at the end of seven years." He smiled ironically. "Counting of course from the time when I could first perform creditably. That wasn't right away! The problem wasn't the lyre or the versifying, but the intractability of the experience. Who would think that being first sold into slavery and then flung nearly decapitated into a river would someday count as an enviable acquaintance with a man? But that's the way things worked out."

"Fate has a sense of humor," Helen said. "I've always thought so. Well then, you did arrive at a satisfactory Song of Achilles?"

"Yes, lady."

"And once you did—or now that you have—do you, bard-like, introduce variations for one reason or another?"

Her tone was casual but her eyes were changeable as the sea. He said cautiously, "Seldom, and then only in details. I have a few variations for particular places—Athens, for example, where the people claim to be the only true natives of the peninsula, more Greek than the rest of you."

"Indeed, they proved their difference by not going to the War," she said. But she was not interested in Athens. "Do you have a variation for us?" she asked suddenly.

"No, lady."

"There is a variation that's appropriate . . . if only you knew it."

"In Sparta I'm especially commanded not to take chances. Spartan taste in heroes is conservative, I hear."

"Besides, your freedom is at stake," she murmured; then shrugged prettily: "Oh well, someday someone will come along who'll—" she paused just perceptibly "—who'll be able to keep me awake during these Songs of Achilles."

He had a sudden impulse to trust her—at least so far as to say, "I promise you, lady, that my song will have you leaning forward in your chair . . . if I'm allowed to finish it."

She raised her brows quizzically but did not pretend to think the matter over too long. "I'm intrigued," she said, giving him her hand. "I shall certainly do all I can to see that you're not interrupted."

He could have fallen in love with her all over again. It disturbed him somehow, this impression that she now had other goals than that. Even more disturbing, the impression that he was nevertheless still included.

The palace had no banqueting hall. Menelaus preferred to entertain in the old-fashioned way, in the Throne Room itself.

It was small but any overflow could be accommodated in the adjoining Hall of Honor. A little vestibule for guards separated the two rooms and prevented them from being continuous even when both sets of sliding doors had been pushed back, an arrangement which was both awkward and useful, for a guest might with equal ease be snubbed accidentally or by design.

Menelaus was not, strictly speaking, concerned with which sort of snub had been given to Euneus—the fellow deserved a reminder that his mercantilism was too obvious in a prince. But the evening on which his bard was to perform hardly seemed the time to put him out with minor officials, second-string Dorians, and a passel of ladies-in-waiting and opportunistic young bachelors whose tightly cinched waists would not prevent them drinking a great deal and becoming indecent. Helen insisted that Euneus' isolation was all a harmless error, and had dealt with it in her own way. Even now Menelaus caught a glimpse of an attractive young widow toward whom Euneus was leaning attentively. Her husband, alas, had died not long ago, and her sighs were making the pendant of her necklace tumble and wink between her high smooth breasts.

Of more concern to Menelaus was the spectacle of Hermione and Neoptolemus huddling together on plain stools that left them lower than the other guests. He and Helen sat on decorated chairs of ordinary height but he had taken care to wear a tall gold diadem. Helen owned one to match it but had elected on this occasion to make a diadem of her own hair, eschewing the ringlets, curls and braids of the court ladies in favor of a simple lofty upsweep of natural gold. In addition she wore a gown, modestly cut, of finest white Egyptian linen, as far removed as might be from the multicolored flounces and ruffles, the exposed shoulders and bosoms of the other ladies. This last, however, was nothing new. Ever since their return from Troy, Menelaus had noticed Helen's growing fondness for white draperies. He had also noticed the court ladies' silent but unanimous resistance to her taste, where ordinarily the queen's fashions would have been aped. Since he had seen her naked and therefore seldom saw her clothed, he usually did not care how she dressed.

But he detected something that pleased him in this latest fancy of hers: political advantage. A queen could be imitated, a goddess could not. It was as if Helen meant to put herself, and thus the throne, beyond criticism.

For there had been talk when she went to Troy on a visit and pleaded first one excuse, then another for not coming home. Menelaus had never warned her that she would be trapped in a siege if she kept prolonging her stay in that doomed city. The omission was Agamemnon's idea—her presence would lull the Trojans into a false sense of security; they were too idealistic to suppose that a man would besiege a city in which so precious a wife was trapped.

Rumors flew, of course, about Helen and Prince Paris. Her trip to Troy had followed his to Sparta rather too closely. Menelaus shrugged off such talk. Two more natural targets for scandal could not be imagined. The only thing that really bothered him was the possibility that he might be thought of as storming Troy in the ridiculous guise of a cuckolded husband.

When he brought Helen home he was annoyed to find the innuendoes and smiles behind hands reviving—or continuing, and he was driven at last to tell her the truth: by allowing her to stay in Troy he had irreparably damaged her reputation. He offered to say so in public. But since that would only have converted loose common knowledge into hard-and-fast common knowledge, she would not permit it. Instead, extraordinarily intuitive or consciously clever as always, she began to dress in a manner that suggested the Moon, a wanderer perhaps but hardly unchaste. Ladies who said that her radiant fashions were perfect for *her* but wrong for anyone else, found themselves condemned out of their own mouths. Her critics were put in the galling position of having to consider that she was perhaps the perfect wife after all for showing no resentment of Menelaus' dangerous, even dishonorable use of her. He was the betrayer, not she, yet never in their marriage had she seemed more devoted to him or more oblivious to mortal opinion. Menelaus toyed with the conceit that the two of them were (or in time might be regarded as) the Sun and Moon. Oriental? Well, but these identifications, if not too literal, never did any harm.

His satisfaction with her would, indeed, have been complete had he been sure that the white gowns, the silver and iron ornaments, the shining coiffures were not simple vanity, a desire to be personally unique with no thought of political advantage, no idea of dramatizing the indissoluble and the symbolic in their marriage. With Helen there was always an opposite possibility. He did not dare ask.

Momentarily disgruntled by this turn in his thoughts, he fell upon Hermione. She had squatted on the floor like a slave while she ate, good! but while her bridegroom's father was being celebrated she and Neoptolemus *would* sit in chairs beside himself and Helen. His tone and his look brooked no disobedience; the young couple rose and waited sulkily while servants put their chairs in place.

Menelaus felt better. He turned to Helen and said gallantly, "Your new iron necklace, my dear, is not only becoming but clever, with Dorians in the room."

He realized too late that he was testing her. She replied graciously, "Thank you, my lord, for noticing. I was in some doubt."

"Doubt? As to whether it was becoming?"

"My lord?"

"That doubt could never be, of course!" he said hastily. "You meant doubt as to whether the Dorians would think we value their metal much or little—I mean, since we make ladies' things of it," he added compulsively.

Helen touched the necklace. "The Dorians would never know from the design, I suppose, that the necklace is Hittite."

"No, my love," he said, and raised her hand to his lips without exactly knowing why.

Instead of the vision of her white body that usually flashed through his mind when he touched her, he suddenly saw an ironclad Dorian warrior. He sat back troubled, and signalled the bard to enter. "Sing with feeling," he admonished Lykaon silently, "of Achilles' invincible bronze!"

Lykaon was garbed in an ankle-length smock embroidered around the neck and sleeves, girdled below with bands of blue, red and yellow fringe. Helen's gift. It was basically quite proper for a slave, yet Lykaon looked like nothing so much as a prince in disguise. He did not sit down nor, standing, did he remain in one spot; he moved about, carrying his lyre, directing his song now here, now there, occasionally using a gesture or change of posture to dramatize the words. It was a style that was something of a fashion in Athens where people were not hide-bound—or where they were always running after novelty—depending upon one's point of view. It struck Menelaus as undignified, but the younger courtiers found it exciting. Euneus had simply seen in it a useful way for Lykaon to disguise his inadequacies as a bard, which, to tell the truth, were many.

Now he struck his lyre and began: "Achilles is my theme! Help me, goddess, to answer truly, what was the son of Peleus really like?

"The feud with Agamemnon King of Men had ended. The death of Patroclus had brought Achilles back into battle, that and the mankiller's thirst for fame. As he buckled on his armor he made a frightful vow: 'Not one of all the sons of Priam will be alive tomorrow!'

"The Trojans, massing for battle on the plain, saw his shield and helmet flash fire as he strode among the Greeks. No mistaking that resplendent figure! Hector, slayer of Patroclus, moved among his men too, trying to ward off panic: 'Achilles is a mortal man and must die. As to the day, this could be it! Perhaps you, Imphition—or you, Demoleon—or you, Hippodamas, you will be the instrument of Fate. For myself, I pray the gods to let me be the man!'

"Soon all the plain rang with the clash of brazen arms. Achilles made straight for the center of the Trojan lines, hewing a path of destruction. Imphition . . . Demoleon . . . Hippodamas—who can tell the names of all that fought well and died? Among them, Polydamas, Priam's youngest son, spitted navel to backbone on Achilles' javelin.

"Before his murderous onslaught the Trojans broke ranks

and fled, some across the plain to the city, some toward the
River, where they plunged pell-mell into the current. Achilles
followed these; he stalked the bank, often leaping in to dye the
water red. The River pitied some and carried them downstream,
where they meant to scramble out and circle back to save their
friends. They should have known that Achilles, hungering for
death as fire hungers for brush, would be on hand to meet
them.

"The first to crawl out dripping, weaponless, without a helmet, was Lykaon, since Polydamas' death the youngest son of
Priam. Achilles stopped in his tracks—he thought he saw a
ghost! Twelve months before, in a night raid, he had captured
this very lad in Priam's orchard where, with five companions,
he was cutting saplings to make chariot rails. Before daylight
he had shipped Lykaon off to Lemnos as a slave. The price—
one hundred oxen—to be shipped back by night. The others
went to pirates for cash in hand. Prisoners taken in the dark—
profits not accounted for to Agamemnon."

Scattered guffaws, chiefly Dorian, broke out in appreciation
of Achilles' cunning, but Menelaus drew his brows together
lest anyone think he approved of his brother's being cheated.

"While Achilles was dealing with the pirates, he left Lykaon
in his tent, and Patroclus set out bread and wine. Because
Patroclus seemed as kind as reputation said he was, Lykaon
spoke: 'Persuade Achilles to let my father ransom my friends
and me.' Patroclus had his eyes on the door: 'Can Priam still
afford such luxuries?' 'Speak to him, my lord Patroclus! People
say he loves you better than his wife, better than his parents!'
'No,' said he, 'it is I who love, he who does the persuading and
prevailing. I would not oppose him though it led to my death.
I suffer him gladly; so should you.' Then Lykaon fell silent,
seeing that conversation between slaves was useless.

"On Lemnos King Euneus paid Achilles' price—then tempted
his displeasure. He let word get around of where Lykaon was.
He got as ransom—three hundred oxen."

There were more guffaws but mixed this time with grumbling

and coughing. Neoptolemus began to look interested. Helen scanned the faces of guests who were gradually crowding in from the Hall of Honor. She had hoped Euneus would be off some place admiring the little widow's pendant at closer range, but he suddenly bobbed up, turning his head and straining to hear.

"For eleven days Lykaon rejoiced in reunion with his family. On the twelfth he disobeyed his father and returned to battle. Then it was that he found himself on all fours on the river-bank, while Achilles' surprise turned to wrath: 'What's this—some trumped-up miracle? Aren't you the puppy I sent by ship to Lemnos? And have you returned by water, like a shade rising out of the West, to mock me? Foolhardy runaway!—for I know Euneus would never send or sell you back—if all the Trojans I've sold took a hint from you I'd soon be a laughing-stock. Someone should have warned you not to court disaster twice!'

"He cast his spear—and missed. Lykaon, crouching, seized the shaft quivering in the ground beside him, but could not dislodge it. With a fearful grimace Achilles drew his sword and moved in for the kill. Lykaon, armed only with words, grasped Achilles' sword arm with one hand, touched his knees with the other, and cried: 'Think now, son of Peleus, how your ship and spear have both miscarried! Men do not praise Achilles because he is a killer of men but because he is obedient to Fate!'

"He answered with a grim smile, 'That is surely the strangest plea for mercy that ever a man made or heard. What! do you think Fate wants you to live? You, or any man? Did death spare Patroclus? What you call Fate, my friend, is Luck, an altogether trivial force. Look at me: my size, my strength, a goddess for a mother, a kingdom for an inheritance. What luck! men say. And yet . . . some morning or some afternoon, I too—'

"He struck his shaggy breast, his eyes rolled up to the whites. 'Why linger, then—why hang back? I find my enemy—I make death my goal—here, under the walls of Troy. My willingness to die will be my fame. *That* is obedience to Fate! And you—

though Luck has lengthened your days a little—you too can choose. No more pleading, then, no more evasion. Choose the manner of it, choose a sovereign Fate—death in battle!'

"Lykaon dropped his hands and sat back on his heels. The two-edged blade circled in air and fell upon his neck—just here. Gushing blood, he stretched out his arms toward Death.

"Achilles dragged the body to the River, uttering a savage farewell: 'Instead of a mother to wash your wounds and a father to follow your bier, I give you to the River to roll out to sea! May fish pick your bones and seaweed be your shroud! The sons of Priam die! Not one shall live!'

"Lykaon heard his impious boast. Turned by the collarbone, Achilles' sword had torn, not severed life. He sank into the water with a prayer: 'Remember, River, the bulls and horses Priam sacrificed to Thee!' The River heard and left him on a sandbar in the reeds downstream. There wavelets lapped his wound, and stopped the bleeding. There, too, slavers, scavengers for the living dead, heard his groans. They took him back to Jason's son! The shrewd Euneus pretended not to recognize these damaged goods and got them for a song. But the gods had robbed him of his wits that day. He forgot to ask how Hector did! The shield of Troy had fallen. From that day forward Troy had no more ransoms for her sons."

By now Euneus had worked his way close. The laughter that Lykaon raised at his expense provoked him, but the insults to Achilles frightened him. Menelaus' brow was dark. Luckily no one was entirely sure of how to take Lykaon's ragged improvisations, and Euneus did not mean to let their doubts be resolved in his disfavor. "Accept this gift of song, Neoptolemus!" he cried in a jovial voice which cut Lykaon off. "Primitive art, as you see—unpolished and fanciful in detail but striving wholeheartedly to exalt the subject, your heroic father!"

To everyone's astonishment Neoptolemus stood up and said in a reedy piercing voice, "Since Fate let this man escape thrice from my father I do not expect the usual song. Let him continue."

"Continue?" Menelaus said blackly. "What more can he

say? He had brought us up-to-date, and not in a way that does much credit to Achilles, if you ask me. Your father was not a man to stop in the midst of battle and explain himself to cowards."

"Hear, hear!" someone shouted.

"He called Patroclus a slave!" shouted another.

"Shame!"

"Mere lack of polish!" cried Euneus. "Even the best bards—"

A voice more rasping than the others cut across Euneus' babble: "Come, Lykaon, you coward, tell these Greeks the truth!"

It was a serving-man with close-cropped hair and a short tunic which allowed him to dodge the guards that Helen instantly signalled. "Coward! When you begged Achilles for your life you didn't talk philosophy. I was there, crouching under the riverbank well within earshot. You begged Achilles not to blame you for what Hector had done to Patroclus. Hector, you said, was not even your brother, only a half-brother. Shameless disavowal to save your skin!" His shouts continued to carry back as the guards dragged him from the room. "You weren't sorry when pirates took you back to Lemnos. You didn't have to face King Priam there, or see that half a brother fall!"

A confused silence followed. Menelaus asked blusteringly, "Who was that fellow?"

"Not a Trojan, my lord," Helen said in a clear voice, putting her hand on his wrist. "A Carian, one of their allies, a breed noted for uncouth speech and half-formed ideas. We should have asked him to tell us how Amphimachus, one of their leaders, went to battle decked in jewels, like a woman!"

Laughter rose obediently, died away expectantly as she turned to Euneus: "You were saying, sir, that your bard lacks polish. Yet what has he done but tell the story so as to make Achilles a worthy conqueror? What honor would there be in hacking at the neck of a grovelling boy? What explanation for botching the job? Achilles, we know, was as eloquent as he was brave. Though the passage on the riverbank might offend a barbarous Carian, I thought it well-contrived to display Achilles' rhetoric, so civilized in its irony, so fearsome in its savagery."

Euneus, not knowing what else to do, bowed. Menelaus erased all expression from his face. Not so Hermione and Neoptolemus: they measured Helen with narrow eyes and pursed mouths. Smiling at them both she went on: "Anyway, Euneus, you heard Achilles' son say that he wants the song continued—that is, concluded"—for she felt the hair bristle on Menelaus' wrist. "In Sparta at least, we know the difference between a song that's ended and one that's broken off."

She removed her hand from Menelaus' wrist with a little pat. He asked grudgingly, "Is there a peroration, then, to Lykaon's Story? for though I don't know much about poetry, I can't call this Achilles' Song."

Lykaon picked at his lyre tunelessly, as if deep in thought. "Goddess," he resumed in a moment, "you who have wrenched my tale from its customary track, touching me with divine madness, making me tell some things as they were, others as they might have been—help me to conclude all fittingly. Say why men praise Achilles, Slayer of Men. Young, strong, handsome, highly placed he comes, the hero comes! Men love him as Patroclus did—unnaturally! His sword goes through their bodies on its way to self-destruction. Inspired by him they call it Fate. Achilles Barbarian! What-Must-Be has other faces than the one that turned you into stone and dust. Lykaon, Priam's son, survives to say it!"

Neoptolemus was on his feet ahead of everyone. He drew off a gold ring and said piercingly, "Take this with my thanks, bard!" Hermione set up a drumming on the arm of her chair by way of applause. The guests, one eye on Menelaus, reluctantly followed suit.

Menelaus bent his lips to Euneus' ear: "This will not go unpunished." Upon which words Euneus put his own interpretation: "He shall be flogged, sire, despite the fact that Achilles' son encouraged him."

Lykaon strode out but Euneus was gracefully intercepted by

Helen: "Since the song did not displease Achilles' son, it cannot displease the rest of us. My only question, son of Jason, is whether material such as this isn't better suited to the lyric than the lay." She turned her brilliant eyes upon a courtier who was known to compose verses. "Wasn't it rather a personal interpretation of events than a true narrative, Phyleus? What do you think?"

"In point of fact, madam," that flattered courtier replied, "the use of the third person struck me as an extremely forced attempt to create the illusion of objectivity. I think you may have hit upon the reason."

A rival of Phyleus objected to sterile categorizing of poetic types, and at once an animated discussion boiled up and spread around the room. Only the Dorians had nothing to say, covering their contempt for literary battles with heavy drinking.

Menelaus could read their minds but did not know his own. Was it a good thing or bad to show the Dorians that Sparta was sophisticated enough about heroes to hear them disparaged? He decided that on the whole it might be useful for them to underestimate Spartan character. They would learn to their sorrow that Spartans would always fight!

For a second time he raised Helen's hand to his lips, and this time got a more pleasing vision.

Lykaon's first visitors were Neoptolemus and Hermione. They looked eagerly for signs that he had been flogged, and upon being told that Euneus had never gone in for that sort of thing, they seemed disappointed. "Not that we think you *should* be whipped for your opinions," Neoptolemus said. "It's just that we hope you're *willing* to be."

Hermione leaned against her betrothed's shoulder. They stood looking at him—"worshipfully," he thought, would not be too strong a word. It gave him an idea.

"A flogging doesn't amount to anything," he said. "But to be silenced—that's something else."

"No, no, you must not be silenced!" they chorused. "You must go on telling the story in your own way."

"In a stone quarry? To fellow slaves?"

"Wherever you are!"

How dense they were! "Why not help me escape?"

Neoptolemus looked stern, Hermione drooped. He tried again: "Buy me yourselves, then, and set me free. Euneus, I'm sure, will sell cheap."

"Ah!" breathed Hermione, happy to be faced with the impossible. "Too late for that."

"Too late?"

Neoptolemus grasped Lykaon's wrist in farewell: "Beware of Helen!" Hermione repeated it in a burning whisper. But neither of them stayed to explain what they meant.

Helen sent for him three times. On the first she told him that Euneus had gone, leaving him in—or on—her hands. "Not that he lost money," she said, adding charmingly, "Of course I know nothing about business. I expect to be cheated."

When Lykaon asked if he were to be set free, she pouted. "Surely you don't expect not to serve me at all?"

He hadn't, and was more than a little curious to see what she had in mind.

On the second time she told him, lifting one hand to the back of her hair so that the golden tangle in her armpit glinted. "We want you to be our bard."

"We?"

"Well, Menelaus has a natural reluctance to encourage anything new, but in time he'll see the advantages. Anyway, *I* want you to stay, and he has agreed."

"I'm not a bard, lady."

"No," she smiled, "you won't be able to claim the born poet's privilege of divine madness. But that's no handicap. I prefer someone amenable to reason."

"So did Euneus."

"And you served him well . . . for nine years. But times change. One can't go on praising Achilles indiscriminately these days, anymore than one can tell stories of the gods in the old way. On the other hand, I don't think you'll get very far merely *dis*praising him and nothing else."

She had, of course, a suggestion for the something else. If he'd been born a bard she wouldn't dare to criticize, but since he hadn't been, well, his song had seemed—incomplete. It lacked . . . well, idealism.

She was not disturbed when he grinned broadly. "The fact is, Lykaon, men did fight and die—bravely—for ten long years. I agree with you that it's monstrous to personify their spirit in a brute like Achilles. But that still leaves a question. Why did they fight?"

"For what ideal reason, you mean."

"Yes, dear Lykaon."

All the same he could hardly believe his ears when, after giving him a day or two to think it over, she sent for him a third time and proposed as the ideal reason—herself! Or, to be more exact, proposed the redemption of Love and Domestic Honor, symbolized in Menelaus' rescue of herself.

He couldn't get past the word "rescue."

"From Paris," she said patiently. "I *was* the seduced, you know, not the seducer."

He tried to put it together. "Paris seduced you, and Menelaus beseiged Troy to get you back?"

"Yes."

"Wouldn't Menelaus object to having Helen linked with Paris officially, so to speak, and perhaps forever? You know how these things gain currency."

"Oh well," she answered easily, "the world doesn't expect much from women. One might even say that I was exactly *like* Love and Honor—frail—in need of protection—in need of redemption by a strong male arm."

"You could have left Troy at any time!"

"Not at all. No one knows better than Menelaus that I was detained against my will. I know him—he'll be enchanted with the whole idea, especially when he sees how useful it can be in this new adventure of his."

"Then there is a new adventure?"

"Isn't there always?" she said carelessly. His silence gave her a sobering thought: "I hope, Lykaon, that you're only anti-

Achilles and not anti-war. One oughtn't to say it or believe it, but war is inevitable, isn't it?"

"If it is, Achilles is a better explanation of it than you are, lady."

"Oh, *Achilles!*" she exclaimed in a rare burst of anger. "Men like that are special cases—abnormal. They make the whole thing so . . . unbelievable. What about all the others, all those soldiers on both sides of the walls of Troy who didn't want to die but took one look at Helen and said, 'It was worth it!' "

"No one in Troy ever said that."

"Yes, Hector said it—when he saw Helen in his wife and son—what were their names?"

"I think now that Hector was in love with dying too," he said musingly. "We had to listen often enough—Andromache included—while he made those same iron connections that Achilles made. Find your enemy and call him Fate! Die fighting! Life?— just Luck, a suspect quality, not basic. These notions, Lady, aren't partisan. When I praised Achilles, I praised Hector. If I dispraise one, I dispraise the other."

"Ah, now I see how you've reconciled your conscience all these years. I'm glad your view of Hector isn't entirely hindsight. Lies are meant for others, not oneself."

He searched her tone for irony, but she was—astoundingly— sincere. He said, "Some hindsights are worth waiting for. I've never had an easy conscience. I've always felt that I was be- traying Hector."

She swept easily to the conclusion: "But now you simply in- clude him with Achilles. Very well. I don't object."

He warned her off: "The story has no hero."

She corrected him: "The story has no idealism. Listen to me: men must have a good opinion of what they're doing. Soon former enemies will be uniting against the Dorians. Achilles, praised or dispraised, is no longer enough. Helen is needed. Why should all these deaths be meaningless? There must and will be Helen!"

"Times change, you said. What comes after Helen?"

She gave him her hand, her eyes were a single brilliant blue.

"Unfortunately, dear boy, neither now nor later can any case be made for praise of Lykaon, if that's your question. I don't know why. It's the way things are. Mere survival is just . . . nothing."

So there it was again, this time as beautiful as Helen. The famous white hand, as he put his lips to it, sent a shudder of remembrance through him. He heard the bright sword slicing through the air: "Choose Helen—or silence."

Neoptolemus and Hermione, palm clutched in damp palm, looked from the body to Helen and back again at the dagger between the shoulder blades. They had been first on the scene, Helen and Menelaus second.

"We told him to beware," Hermione murmured, not quite inaudibly.

"Of what, miss?" Helen asked sharply.

"Trojans, no doubt," said Menelaus.

To please her, and himself, he ordered all of them put to death. He rather regretted Lykaon's murder. For the first time, after the banquet, he had been told authoritatively—that is, by Helen—that his wife had been seduced in Troy. But he had already faced that possibility and only needed a new light for others to see it in. Helen told him he was to figure prominently in a forthcoming part of Lykaon's song. When he asked in what light he was to figure, she smiled faintly. "As an idealist." When he looked alarmed she added reassuringly, "To balance Achilles, the self-serving hero."

"Is that what he was driving at?"

"He had already taken the first step."

To a man the Trojans confessed to the crime. Which only proved that one of them really was guilty. They died cursing all cowards. They might be slaves but they did not believe in insignificant fates.

Helen composed herself and waited. Once in the story she would be hard to dislodge.

F.

John Herrmann

from *Northwest Review*

F., the young German, drove his garbage truck while intently watching the traffic from behind gold-rimmed dark glasses, his bone-white spike nose protruding from between the round lenses as though it had been neatly trimmed thin by two expert ax blows. His nostrils were in fact deformed, were nearly nonexistent, and the tight passages were normally plugged—delightfully so, since F. had for several years been reduced to collecting the garbage from a once elegant neighborhood in which he had lived with his parents before circumstances had forced them to abandon their home. F. had other deformities and had had torturous operations on his eyes but remained dreadfully walleyed and so wore dark glasses to hide his affliction. Otherwise F. enjoyed good health, was bull strong and could lift the empty ash cans easily though many equalled his own body weight.

To afford a tolerable existence for his wife and children, so that they might wear decent clothing and so that his children might be able to take their place in the community along with its other children, etc., F. took advantage of his wife's expert baking ability and put her to work baking bread during the day, and at night after he had washed and eaten and changed into a business suit, he would load into a panel truck and deliver personally to many of the same houses from which he collected waste during the day. It often amazed F. that the occupants of these houses did not recognize him and he explained it away as being the fault of the nature of night.

His garbage truck was his own invention. It operated inexpensively on diesel oil but its uniqueness lay in a single lever that when thrown would activate steel "lips" at the rear of the truck that would slowly part and await the contents of a garbage can, the weight of which would start huge jaws moving together, and F. had only to replace the can and get back into the cab and trip the lever again before driving on. The second lever position caused steel teeth to tear at the refuse while F. drove on toward his next stop, setting the lever on "position off" when he felt there had been sufficient time to "chew" the material into a very small load. Though his job might have annoyed some, F. took great pride in his invention; on weekends when some families cleaned house and clipped front lawns, F. washed down and hand dried his white "sanitary wagon," and at the close of each month he took a half day off his route and spent it inside the machine filing each glistening tooth to a needle's point. So efficient was his disposal process that many neighboring communities sent him official city contracts to collect for them. But F. continued to perform his duties for his own interest, taking the profits and losses directly, and each year he returned many legal agreements to their creators, all of them unsigned.

His dark lenses were necessary to filter the harsh sunlight which so bothers the walleyed. F. felt little discomfort except during particularly clear mornings when he had to drive from his shack at the edge of town eastward into the first fresh rays of the day. He felt a moment's relief now though, as he turned off on to a dirt side road which would lead him to the alley behind all the houses of the first block.

He parked the truck in back of the first house and threw the lever and waiting a moment, listening to the garrrrund-garrrund groan of the rear jaw motor as it spread its steel lips to reveal the morning-cold, ice-sharp layers of teeth deep within. When the groaning clicked off, F. dismounted and took the lids off of both cans, one for wet garbage, the other for inflammable materials. F. rooted through the can of papers and cardboard, his bent frame hinged low, appearing half submerged. A passerby would have seen only the short legs standing on slightly raised, heavy double-thick polished boot heels, old but well cared for, remnants from his aristocratic days when he wore a different pair of polished boots every day of the week. F. emerged from the inflammable materials can satisfied that the householders had complied with his rule and had not mixed the wet with the other refuse. Then he emptied both cans into the same set of waiting jaws, smiling as he recalled the argument he had with the owner of the second house on this block about the separation regulation.

—All I can tell you, F. tried to explain, is the rule is necessary to our mutual conveniences.

—Rubbish is rubbish, the man had argued. By definition it is rejected, useless material worth nothing to anyone.

—I make my meager living serving your need to be rid of this filth. You must comply with this simple request to compensate in part for my miserable lot.

And seeing that F. was indeed a pathetic case—partially blind, obviously existing without the normal pleasures because of his olfactory defect, dressed always in the same thickly stained rubber apron about which hundreds of flies darted and tossed when he moved, settled to feast when he was still—the owner of the cans nodded in defeat and from then on complied automatically with the senseless regulation.

F. drove to the second set of cans as the teeth ground the first load of waste into a grayish paste. Unseen, a rubber "tongue" passed back and forth between "bites," compressing the broken fragments into a single unit so that it could be further diminished in size and consistency.

The two cans at the next stop were as thoroughly investigated as the first set had been. In the wet can F. found a strip of gauze drenched in part with a thick red fluid, a piece of burned steak and bone on which small life wriggled furiously, a portion of an orange candle, a bag of blackish potatoes, a strip of silk, wet and stained yellow, a fly-ridden portion of some unrecognizable creamed vegetable, a broken hairbrush covered with syrup, a smeared gob of colorless hair stuck to its back. . . . When he set the empty can back in place he noted half a cantaloupe covered with cigar ashes still stuck to the bottom of the can and he pulled it free, threw it in the truck then emptied the paper can and continued on his route.

As he drove toward the next house he watched the swarm of flies through the rearview mirror as they followed him instinctively, some darting and beating against the truck's shell as though in a rage at being kept from what was rightfully theirs. A short-haired mongrel dog suddenly sprang at the truck's front wheel from beneath a hedge. It barked continually at what it could not understand, and when F. dismounted the dog snarled furiously until F. was compelled to reach into the cab for the ready tire iron. He checked the nearby windows then approached the mongrel and beat him over the head several times until the dog lay limp in the dust, his eyes open, staring sightless at a piece of his tongue which lay in the dust near him in a bead of blood. F. quickly picked up the dead animal and threw him far back into the truck's jaws and watched as the limp weight started the teeth downward. The lips contracted from the open, oval position back toward the closed, thin grin. Before F. serviced the next house he scraped his boot on the slowly closing lower jaw. The dog, in dying, had defecated and F. had stepped in it. He finished wiping the boot with the edge of a paper plate.

He mounted the truck once again. One might expect that by now F. would be cursing the conditions of his life. But as he drove on he smiled to himself again: it was, after all, the bread business which was flourishing, because his wife was indeed as expert in the trade as the world had need of. The orders were increasing and many requests were now coming from out-of-town. He had already hired men who were eager to make deliveries and share in the profits, and they learned the simple ways quickly, thoroughly, from F.'s example. It became apparent

F.

to F. that very soon both businesses would be managed and carried out at a thriving pace by these trainees while he and his family could rebuild their aristocracy, overseeing the necessary affairs from a respectable distance.

He drove on, smiling because his miseries were temporary. He made his collections faster and faster, and as he did, the truck's hidden teeth gnawed and tore and ground today's rejected, useless, worthless waste and formed it into the paste of tomorrow's bread.

The Monopoly Story

Gerald Locklin

from *TransPacific*

"three," i say. "one two three. baltic. i'll buy it."
  "BALTIC!" exclaims inga. "baltic is worthless."
  "oh, i don't know," joan says.
  "well, you're the banker," hengest chortles.
  "and i collect two hundred dollars for passing go."
  "well, you're the banker," hengest chortles.
  "it is the dawning of the age of aquarius," i add.
  "what?" says hengest.
  "it is the dawning of the age of aquarius."
  "oh, mel," says joan, "how wonderful!"
  "what?" i say.
  "i didn't realize you were interested in astrology."
  "i'm not," i say.
  "how wonderful," she says.
  "it is the dawning of the age of aquarius," she says.
  "what does that mean for me?"
  "it means you're going to be in the forefront of the revolution."
  "oh," i say, "how wonderful."
  "ventnor," says inga, "i'll buy it."

"now just a minute, little lady," says hengest. "it seems to me we might be able to negotiate a mutually beneficial transaction. indiana and illinois for ventnor, then you'll be able to build."

"he'll be able to build also, inga," joan warns her.

"yes," i warn her. "you'd better not let him talk you into it, inga. besides, he has money and you don't."

"i'll throw in the water works."

joan says, "utilities aren't any good. you can't build on utilities."

"utilities are some good, inga," hengest assures her.

"oh, dear," says inga, "what to do, what to do."

"going . . . going . . ."

"okay," says inga.

inga passes the deed of ventnor to hengest, who reciprocates with the deeds for indiana, illinois, and water works.

"you're not angry are you dear?" says inga to me.

"no, dear," say i, "it would certainly be silly of me to let a little thing like a game upset me. i do feel, however, that you made an error in trading with hengest. only time, of course, will tell."

"well, mel," says hengest, "while you're recovering from the shock of that little transaction, i think i'll take a little trip to the bedroom."

"sure," i say.

"excuse me," says inga, "but i have to go to the bedroom also."

"of course," i say.

"don't rush," says joan. "mel and i will just smoke a joint while you're gone."

when hengest and inga are gone, i say to joan, "your husband is certainly an excellent player of monopoly."

"yes," joan replies, "he is also very young and muscular."

"i imagine he's also good at other games."

"yes," says joan, "he is intelligent and manages to win without giving the impression of being aggressive."

"therefore, he is also very . . ."

". . . well liked."

"i understand your husband owns almost as much property in real life as he always seems to end up with in monopoly."

"oh yes, hengest is quite shrewd in his investments."

"well, well," i say. "well, well."

"let's talk about me now," i say.

"alright," joan says.

"i'm not very good at monopoly, as no doubt you must have noticed."

"of course, mel," joan agrees. "hengest and i have often discussed you and our conclusion is that you will never be worth a damn."

"it is, however, the dawning of the age of aquarius."

"what is it you do out at the plant, mel?"

"i'm an existential engineer."

"how wonderful."

"i invented the existential microscope."

"hengest and i have often said you're going to go a long nowhere."

"i count the existential electrons."

"how interesting, and now, mel, why don't we stop talking about you and just enjoy this joint."

when inga and hengest return from the bedroom, i say, "well, well, gone long?"

"relatively," hengest chortles.

"have a good time?"

"oh yes," inga assures me.

"what were you doing?" i smilingly ask.

"we were playing a game," inga explains.

"oh, any game i know?"

"not really," inga further explains.

"hengest certainly is wonderful at games," i shake my head in admiration.

"yes," inga agrees. "you know, joan, your husband certainly is wonderful at games."

"i know," joan nods enthusiastically.

"well," hengest says, rubbing his palms together, "back to the wars."

"ten," says joan. "one two three four five six seven eight nine ten. st. charles place. i'll buy it."

"i already own it," says inga, "you owe me . . ."

"here," says hengest, handing me a large wad of money. "i want hotels on boardwalk and park place."

"certainly," i say. i count out the money and present hengest with a hotel for boardwalk and a hotel for park place. then joan picks up the dice from in front of inga and hands them to me, scratching my palms in the process. i roll the dice.

"four. chance."

i select a card from the top of the chance

"go directly to boardwalk. do not pass go."

"well, mel," hengest chortles, "looks like that just about cooks your goose."

"poor, mel," says inga, "poor dumb mel."

"poor goose," says joan.

"dumb shit," chortles hengest.

"poor goose," says joan. "hengest," says joan, "you know i think the poor goose deserves a little trip to the bedroom."

"okay," says hengest. "you just run along to the bedroom with the dumb shit while i take a look at the property i'm getting from him."

"come along, mel," says joan.

"okay," i say. "excuse me, inga, excuse me hengest."

in the bedroom joan says, "well, here we are," and pulls off her blouse.

"yes," i say smiling genially.

"hurry up and take your clothes off."

"okay," i say. i hurriedly remove my clothes and stand there naked in the middle of the room.

joan sits on the edge of the bed removing her stockings. when all her clothes are off, she rolls back on the bed and says, "come here now, mel."

"are we going to play the game?" i ask.

"yes," joan says.

"fine," i say and join her on the bed.

when we return, hengest says, "hi. how was it?"

"wonderful," i say.

"about as bad as that sort of thing can be," joan says.

"that's about what i expected," hengest says.

"i want to compliment you on joan," i say. "she's a very valuable property."

"i want to express my sympathy to you, inga," joan says.

"no, i'm not at all surprised," hengest says. "you know, mel, joan and i have often enough discussed you and we reached the conclusion that you'd never be worth a damn."

"that's very perceptive of you, hengest," i grin, shaking my head in admiration. "it's taken me a long time, let me assure you, to reach that very same conclusion."

"what is it you do out at the plant anyway, mel?"

"i'm an existential engineer. i invented the existential microscope."

"isn't worth a flying fig, is it?"

"no, hengest, you're absolutely right."

"well, joan and mel, while you were gone i took all of inga's property."

"yes," said inga, who by now has moved over to sit on hengest's lap where she is occupied with unbuttoning his shirt in order to reach inside and tweak his nipple with her chill little hand—"yes, i landed on marvin gardens."

"i think i'll surrender up all my property too," joan suddenly announces. "all i have left anyway is the reading railroad."

"well, hengest," i say, slapping the table for emphasis and shaking my head in appreciation, "it looks as if you've won again."

"yes indeed," says joan, "and i for one think you have earned a little trip to the bedroom."

"sure has," i agree.

"come along, girls," hengest says, lifting inga from his lap, "the three of us will just run along for a little victory celebration and mel can just sit here and tell himself a story."

"fine," i say.

"mel just loves to tell himself stories," inga says.

"do you have a good story to tell yourself, mel?"

"yes, joan," i reply. "i've been saving a dandy for a special occasion and i guess tonight qualifies. now you kids just run along to the bedroom and enjoy yourselves."

while they are gone i light up a joint and tell myself the story of the sweater woman. in this story i am in an old-folks bar down in the old part of the city and i have sat down to have a beer next to a woman in a powder-blue heavy-knit sweater with an eagle embroidered on the back. the woman is in her fifties but has a big bosom. she turns to me and says, "hi, young fellow, what's your name?"

"mel," i say.

"i'm mamie," she says.

"hi mamie," i say, "it's very nice to meet you."

"you see that scrawny little sonuvabitch of a scotchman down the end of the bar?"

"the one with the crooked arm?"

"that's my husband."

"oh."

"i guess you wouldn't think to look at him that he's the world's champion arm-wrestler?"

"no, i wouldn't."

"been married to the little runt for thirty years and never seen him put down. know what his secret is?"

"no, i don't."

"his secret is that he's had to do everything with his one arm since the other one got smashed up on the waterfront. wouldn't guess it to look at him, but the muscles in his good arm are like steel cables."

"i see."

"he's defending his championship this afternoon. in fact, here comes the challenger now."

through the door comes a product of the era of vitamins and minerals, six-foot-seven and a lean two-hundred-fifty pounds. his forearms are the radii of wharf piles.

"poor kid," says mamie, "they're all like that nowadays, so beautiful and full of confidence. but watch what happens."

the kid and the old man take their places facing each other

across a vinyl table. the bartender comes forth as starter and referee. "go," he says.

the kid slams the old guy's wrist half-through the table.

"impossible," says mamie. "his elbows must have slipped."

they set it up again and the bartender says, "go!"

this time the kid slams the old man's arm so hard that he winces and rubs himself.

"stop him," i say to mamie; "stop him before he doesn't have a good arm left."

"he'll never stop," she says, fierce tears coursing down her cheeks. "he's too proud to give in, the crazy old fool."

her husband gets up and reaches to shake the young kid's hand. "youth must be served," he says, "i think i'll quit while i've still got one good arm left."

later, however, at the bar, his drunken shame has turned to hostility.

"who's the bum?" he says, shrugging a shoulder towards me. "who's the young bum you're sucking up to now?"

"arnold," she says, "you shut your filthy mouth or i will take this young bum home with me instead of you."

"you would," says arnold to her. "you really would." to me he says, "what's your name, young bum?"

"my name is mel."

"whattaya do for a living? college kid, i bet?"

"no sir, i work out at the plant."

"yeah?" he says, interested, his reverse snobbery thawing somewhat. "whattaya do at the plant?"

"i'm an existential engineer. i invented the existential microscope."

"yeah? no kidding? whattaya do with it?"

"i count the existential electrons."

"no kidding! you hear the young gentleman, mamie?"

"pshaw, i could've told you mel was well educated."

"well, mamie" i say, "i feel that no one ever really *finishes* his education. i still take an occasional refresher course at the university."

"say, i bet you could answer my question."

"what is that, mamie?"

"well, i've been thinking of taking a course at the university, but i'm not sure if they offer just what i want."

"what's that, mamie?"

"spelling."

"spelling?"

"yes, spelling. you see i make us quite a few extra dollars knitting sweaters, but lots of times people want a little something embroidered on the back or over the pocket, some little bit of wisdom, and sometimes . . ."

". . . you make spelling errors. i see. but i'm sorry i don't really know if they teach spelling at the university. you see i spent my seven years there in the existential sciences."

"oh, i'm sorry. i'm just a foolish old woman."

"no you aren't, mamie. on the contrary, you are the salt of the earth. you are the real thing, mamie, the stuff without which sociology, for instance, could not survive."

"isn't he sweet, arnold . . . you know . . . i think i'm going to knit mel a sweater!"

"mamie, really, i couldn't accept . . ."

"arnold, run out to the car and bring in *your* sweater."

"but mamie . . ."

"hurry up. i want mel to see the sort of sweater i'm going to knit him."

"mamie, i swear you're going to have me in tears."

arnold returns with his sweater. it is powder-blue and heavy knit and has an eagle embroidered on the back . . .

"well," says hengest when they have returned from the bedroom, "i guess we'll be running along now."

"be sure to drop in again," i say.

"we will," he chortles; "we'll be dropping by in the morning to bring inga back."

"oh," i say, turning to inga, "have hengest and joan invited you to spend the night with them? what a nice chance for you to get out of the house."

"yes," says inga, "and they have even offered to drop me off in the morning in time for me to get you up for work by kicking you in the kidneys."

"hengest and joan," i say with deep feeling, "all i have to say is that i certainly do feel deeply about you."

"bye-bye, mel," says joan, "don't trip over your shadow walking before you."

"bye-bye, mel," says hengest, "don't get goosed by your shadow walking behind you."

"bye-bye, mel," says inga. "if you masturbate in the sink please remember to rinse it out."

i clear the table and leave the dishes stacked neatly on the washboard. i put the monopoly set away in the closet. i remember to turn down the heat and to make sure all the doors are locked. i set the alarm clock.

i go in and wake up our little girl, mickey, so i can say goodnight to her, so i can kiss her good-night.

"what's new, old pal," i say to her.

"not much," she says, my two-and-a-half-year-old colloquial daughter.

"are your grends all asleep?" i ask her.

"yes, doddy," she says, and shows me her monkey and her lion and her $.59 doll.

"what're you going to do when you get up?" i ask her.

"i'm going to have gun," she says.

"you're a funny old girl," i say.

"you gunny old doddy," she says.

i tuck her in and go to tell myself a bedtime story.

friday night at the project and tenuous relationships reaching to long island.

Peter Lord

from *Duel*

sue got out of the volks and ran up the steps in the front door of the project. she punched the wall button the round lite went on and she waited maybe half a minute before the elevator doors opened. inside she punched another button and the doors slid shut. in the 9th floor corridor camera #4352B fixed on the closed elevator door then picked up a left profile close up as she stepped out onto the by-the-gross maroon carpeting. she went into 917 and past her mother who sat reading/watching the Daily News/Hollywood Palace in the black vinyl corner chair by the window facing north to 22nd. please don't ask me any questions tonite mother she said on the way into her bedroom where she savagely poked her Peter Fonda motorcycle pinups with the butt of her tear gas pistol. her mother burped to the left and turned to page 27.

bill sat outside in the volks fingering the latest in a series of lite green pimples and wondering why the hell sue had jumped out of the car without saying goodbye or anything. camera #3841 (outdoor) zoomed in as he trickled the rite index finger down the rite cheek thru his button down collar and down his ribs to his new madras belt. he became aroused and felt around under his zipper until making contact. patrolman jeff monroe new on the force had little or no experience with perverts and therefore quite naturally assumed that bill was working out in a highly perverted fashion. after all wasnt his gaze locked on the hole in the center of the blinking Mr. DoNut sign down the street? so very carefully patrolman jeff slipped out of his unmarked car and hand-and-kneed it across the street to the drivers door of the volks. #3841 (out-door) lowered and boom microphone #AJ035 swung out overhead to pick up the essentials. patrolman jeff eased his hat/eye/nose/up to the window level just in time to catch bill in the act of whipping out the old stick. DROP IT he shouted thru the closed volks window and pulled out his well oiled and factory fresh repeating colt. well bill was so startled that he did just that but the fact was that all his underground chafing before hand had really set the thick juices in motion so that when patrolman jeff let out his Manually perfect yell he dropped it alrite but it fell onto his lap and lay there spitting at the dashboard. #3841 (outdoor) rolled on while #AJ035 edged closer in order to distinguish the various vocal inflections.

sue had decided to go to the john and adlib for awhile with her new all purpose Maybelline make up kit. her mother turned to page 61 yawned then got up and changed the channel to a Perry Mason rerun. sue dabbed and etched for maybe ten minutes with the blue eyeliner then switched her efforts to the Summer Rose blush on. bill had really pissed her off tonite with his casual talk about janet her best friend that she had introduced him to only last week. why the hell should she sit there all nite and listen to those stupidly obvious fucking questions about whether or not janet had a steady (which she didn't) and whether or not maybe some nite bill could set up janet with his friend frank (who really was a grade A prick and always grabbed her ass on the 167 home from work). the sound tape crouched in the U-trap transposed this subconscious dialogue into verbal patterns for future use should the final edit contain the overhead shot from camera #2649K hidden behind the twin overhead Westinghouse 60 watts. in this case the screen mite possibly split in order to show sue in the can pouting at the mirror and at the same time pick up bill who was torn between a desire to keep his hands on the roof of the volks like patrolman jeff had told him to do while also wanting to tuck himself in just in case anyone should happen by that he mite know and get the wrong impression about the whole thing.

patrolman jeff took bill to the station after radioing his position and asking for additional help upon finding a worn Boy Scouts of America (B.S.A.) membership card (life) in bill's breast pocket Lord Buxton. those scouts were taught all types of subversive activities such as self defence and liteing fires without matches not to mention caressing the elderly regardless of sex at any given busy intersection. this interior dialogue was also broken down into verbal patterns for possible future use by mobile microphone #AK046 concealed with the testicles of a hovering plastic/feather sparrow. bill sat beside patrolman jeff in the unmarked car while reinforcement constable o.j. rafferty drove carefully thru red lites on his way to the precinct house. bill had politely asked permission to tuck himself in during the trip but patrolman jeff had decided that this was evidence so out it stayed. constable rafferty shot narrow arcs of spit across the front seat and out the rite hand side window.

sue went to bed after a thick application of Clearasil and Nivea and couldn't understand why her titely rolled head kept sliding off the pillow. camera #6328D (periphial-left top door-frame) faded out slowly the final shot consisting of sue lying nude under the aqua electric blanket sucking her thumb. her mother snored high and to the rite covered by the Daily News and grey chip dip by her left elbow on the end table.

harold was on his way home on the 108 after a bad nite of losing pool followed by downing 6 rapid Pabst then throwing up in an alley behind 50th and Lexington. he rolled/swayed in his seat and camera #4172P located on top of the drivers blue serge had registered his complete range of facial expressions. A grey homosexual got on at 38th and looked him over finally deciding against an approach when harold unleashed a loud dripping fart that curled forward in layers. he entered 414 after a slite nauseous feeling on the elevator just in time to see his father apply the finishing whacks to a thorough beating of his mother. he ran into the bathroom and turned on the lite which unfortunately was delayed-reaction neon so he missed the toilet with his vomit. a close up of liquid pizza and beer nuts on the tiled floor from toilet-base camera #7284G. his mother sobbed for awhile on the sofa then wiped her nose on the sleeve of her house dress and picked up where she'd left off in True Confessions. his father swore litely and left to visit marty and maybe play some dime-limit poker if any of the boys happened to be there.

sue dreamt of low cut dresses and caviar on rye sandwiches strate out of Suzie Knickerbocker jet set parties in Acapulcan villas while bill tried to explain his behaviour to desk sergeant maxwell higgins (married-5 kids) at the 12th precinct. no luck and they penis-printed him (rolling not-so-gently counterclockwise) and threw him in the tank with about 25 other drunks and exposure artists after booking him on a 119 (morals) count. sue's mother fell out of her chair shortly before the N.B.C. sign of Sermonette and decided to have another Schlitz before bed. camera #8143K was stuck in the key hole of 623 where a puerto rican couple made an illegal type of love involving use of the tongue on the living room carpet. camera #11027FR (from another studio) poked thru the hallway carpet and filmed camera #8143K for future use in a slowly compiling invasion of privacy suit. harold was almost asleep when his head started to spin so he got up and stuck his head out the window.

out on long island cars of community vigilantes in squeeze-me-madge-baby-i-just-enlisted uniforms carrying Sears-Roebuck shotguns tooled down unlined streets looking for left-over looters from the previous days riot. alyson who had once known someone who had known someone who had lived in the project checked to make certain her diaphragm was in the bottom of her purse before kissing alan goodnite with a slite squeeze in the lower groin. she padded quietly into the house and slipped by her parents door which was slitely open. she changed into a sheer 45-dollar christmas-present-from-daddy nitegown then headed downstairs to the refrigerator to pick up something to eat and finish the short story in 17 Magazine. 2 and ½ levels above her parents turned over in unison in pastel twin beds. alan really had a big cock and it seemed to her that it was larger in the back seat of the car than anywhere else including sandra's house where they had been last weekend while her parents were in Connecticut.

rachel turned on with some sweet tasting hash sprinkled liberally over a bowl of rice crispies and cream (15%). in the living room the 2 kids she babysat screamed obscenities across the latest game from Parker Bros. she had never heard of the project and said so when the Life correspondent had asked her for a typical Long Island Female High School Student view on this shameful waste of the American taxpayers money. she hallucinated a 2500-piece 3-D jigsaw (half completed) then sat back on the tubed aluminum chair with a Dr. Peppers. she knew alyson but not well enough to call her a friend which she probably wouldn't anyway because shed heard that alyson was lite on the drop for just about anyone while rachel prided herself on her selectivity and screwed only for major heads who usually tossed an ounce or two in her direction immediately afterwards.

bill finally got to sleep after making the mistake of pulling out an almost full pack of Camels which instantly disappeared into a crowd of shaking outstretched hands.

patrolman jeff monroe received a pat on the epaulettes from lt. blake then headed back to the project (minus constable rafferty) to continue his stake-out of the suspected call girl/boy ring on the 5th floor of 21348 w. 20th. he stopped off for an all dressed hamburger and glass of milk on the way and killed time by winking at the counter girl in the soup stained blouse and red hair just hours out of the bottle. mobile camera #3449T situated in a broken Cherry Blossom box caught patrolman jeff in the can having a quick spurting piss then focused on socially redeeming graffiti such as I HATE JEWS ADELE AND SOFT BROWNIES/MOBY DICK IS A SOCIAL DISEASE/and/EAT SHIT. A MILLION FLYS CAN'T BE WRONG. he was glad he'd never joined the boy scouts and shined his badge with a pale yellow Scott Towel before sauntering out to pick up his order. he left an extra nickel for the counter girl who smiled at him and wished she could have 2 minutes alone with his nuts and a rusty Gillette blade.

all cameras (with the exception of camera #11027FR-from another studio) went back to the East Village in the same taxi driven by a hump-back japanese anarchist named neo moto badge #3326. the microphones took busses and transferred several times keeping in shape by recording the hum of the diesel engines below the rubber floor. the 2 groups met at approximately 3.36 a.m. outside a coldwater on barrow and discussed who was to be nominated as unique character of the nite. all agreed on the choice of bill with alyson and her mail order diaphragm a distant second.

rachel put the kids to bed rite after Huntz Hall shot Lassie then returned to her jigsaw. the parents returned drunk and 43-year-old mr. johnson attempted a wet kiss/feel while driving her home which she avoided by leaving the car following a sharp elbow to the solar plexus. she sat on her front steps and completed the jigsaw before going to bed.

alyson finished the story and threw out the chicken bones then crept upstairs to her room.

sue slept and dreamt of lying buried in the warm Riviera sand beside bill.

harold rolled over and was sick on the edge of the bed.

The Anniversary

William Minor

from *Colorado Quarterly*

Tonight, Jammie did not want to think of the house. He did not want to admit that it was one of those that everyone, including the owners, makes fun of. He did not want to confess that his street reminded him of a line of freight cars. That even this impression wasn't quite right because freight cars, some intended for cattle, others to house oil or fruit, are not so identical. And he didn't wish to think of his neighbors: of wives who had forgotten to thaw the chickens they were to serve for dinner, of small daughters carting martinis to young men slumped in a Father's Chair (listening to *Ebb Tide,* the squeal of gulls, staring blankly at paintings of surf and rocks and spray). Jammie didn't want to be aware of *them,* the others. Tonight he wished only to think of Lorna. And so he bent to her, lifting the lighter with great pride.

It was a marvelous thing, this lighter, transparent, made completely of glass so that you could see what was going on inside, even though nothing went on inside. The fluid sat there, as placid as the waters of a lake. But Jammie prized it, highly, for Lorna had given it to him a year ago, on their fifth anniversary. He struck fire now, raising the lighter to the candle so that each of his wife's features lit up . . . almost as if he were setting them aflame. First rose sheen spread to her cheeks, and then the brilliant lips, artfully limned. (She had a tray with thirty-six colors in the bathroom; he had given this to her on their fourth anniversary.) Light seemed to purl at her teeth, nostrils, nose, the small innocent eyes, and, last, her hair, held tightly in place at the crown by the silver brace he had given her on their third anniversary. How proud he was. How lucky he had been to win her, and *keep* her these six years!

He snapped the lighter shut and stepped to the stereo, turning to smile at Lorna, although he could see only the erect shadow in candlelight and the soft glow at its face. He began to search for the dials. The cabinet was so long that he frequently forgot where they were. He struggled with a record, disrobing it of the tight plastic girdle, then switched on the turntable and placed the record upon it. He set the needle on the fifth band and strolled back to the table, pleased when the trumpet began to accompany his walk with "I Married an Angel." Lorna emerged from candlelight and he could see that she was smiling. He bent to kiss her.

"Happy anniversary, Poopsie," he said. That was his other name for her, although he never uttered it in public.

The couple ate silently, Lorna lifting her fork to her lips with such easy grace that Jammie half suspected there was no food there. Yet when she drew the fork away her mouth glistened with a light film. She smiled from time to time. Then Jammie stood to uncork the champagne bottle (Gene Bresnik at the liquor store had promised that this was his best) and kissed her as he poured the glasses. Too long, for hers ran over and the cold prancing liquid ran down the back of his hand, into his cuff. Lorna wiped her fingers and the stem of her glass with a linen napkin, and then handed the cloth to Jammie so that he might take care of himself. They raised their glasses.

"To sixty more," he said, grinning widely.

Lorna smiled.

"Well, go ahead," he said enthusiastically. "Open your gift."

The Anniversary

As Lorna began to unwrap the elaborate package Jammie thought, "Six years. That's not such a long time really. But with a girl like Lorna!" How lucky he had been to win and keep her. The music moved him. "I Married an Angel." Well, there was no doubt about it, he had. He was grateful that they had grown up together in a time that kept its faith in the word *forever*. Their songs had been filled with it. How he enjoyed letting their titles ramble through his mind: "Forever and Ever," "Till the End of Time," "Love is Here to Stay." Fidelity. Intimacy. Eternal commitment, eternal moonlight. How lucky they were to be able to turn this lush knowledge into deed. Even the voice of their favorite crooner, soft and low, had been flushed with the accents of eternity. Jammie thought of the many times he and Lorna had danced to him in darkened rooms, the walls luminous with the names of lovers, the phonograph stacked high with old seventy-eights, floor sleek with wax on which they mimicked the box step learned together at Mrs. Brown's Dancing School.

He recalled the ridiculous contests in which he and other boys had competed, for the sake of their "Girls," to see just who could drink the most Orange Crush and eat the largest number of glazed doughnuts. And he remembered the time he caused a stir because, thinking Lorna no longer loved him, he had broken a seventy-eight record over the back of a chair. (You could hardly do that with the records they made today, which suggested a truth about the time: you could warp things now or bend them out of shape, but never wholly keep or break them.)

"Hhmmmm. . . ."

Lorna was pleased with her gift. Jammie had given her, this year, an automatic back scratcher: a long silver thing with a plastic hand at its tip. He had thought she would like it and apparently she did. She didn't say thanks, but she pressed its small button, arched her back, and let the plastic hand play against the submissive flesh.

Now it was his turn. (This exchange of gifts had begun simply, inconspicuously enough, but had, through Jammie's increased devotion, been raised to the height of ritual.) A rectangular carton sat before him. It was covered with bright yellow wrapping, which he tore eagerly, curious to see what Lorna had given him. To his surprise it was a bottle of creme de cacao.

"Well! Well, thanks Poopsie," he said, trying his best to conceal the disappointment. Funny, she knew he didn't like liqueurs.

Lorna had finished her meal. She grazed her lips with the edge of her napkin, smiled, and sipped the last of her champagne. Then, to his further surprise on this the night of their anniversary, she reached across the table, took possession of the bottle she had given him, uncorked it, poured herself a shot and left the room.

Jammie was stunned. Yet he knew, feared, what was coming next. He knew when he heard the click of the automatic channel selector (the Space Commander Three Hundred he had given her on their last anniversary), knew when he heard it move from "mute" to "full volume" that he would find her in the living room, seated on the new divan, sipping her (his?) creme de cacao, wearing sunglasses while she watched color TV.

Jammie slouched in his chair, staring at the rings of grease that had begun to form in the hollow of their plates. How strange, the way a room shuts down when someone you care for goes out of it. He picked up the back scratcher and tried it out. Pretty nice. It had been a fair gift, he thought. The little plastic hand nibbled at his scalp. The sensation reminded him, sadly, of the tingle of Lorna's kiss and, easily lost when left alone and stuck in that permiglue of sentiment, Jammie recalled the afternoon, eight years ago, when she had been Senior Queen.

He had been picked, along with seven other football players, to carry her float to the stadium for Field Day. It was a grand show: crowds flanked the street as the entire Senior Class marched by, Jammie at the head of the procession. A hot day. His muscles bunched, then seemed to flower beneath his tee shirt. He was proud of himself, but prouder yet of Lorna, who was simply dressed and therefore all the more outstanding. She wore a clean white blouse, that dipped in a semicircle above her breasts, and a flatteringly small skirt. Her hair was crowned with a wreath of roses. He couldn't see her once he had shouldered the float, but the eyes of the crowd, its warm applause, told him all he needed to know. How proud he was. *His* girl.

The players carried the float for nearly a mile, but Jammie was not a bit tired, having placed so high a value upon the burden he bore that it had ceased to be one. However, one player was—Mort Ficklin, a stupid tackle. As they were about to enter the stadium the float ran against a tree and Mort, impatient and fatigued, dipped his end and down came Lorna. She must have fallen at least six feet. Jammie kicked aside the confused, jabbering players (Mort was exclaiming, "Why the hell don't *you guys* watch where you're goin'?") and was by her in a flash. Her cheek was bruised and there was a mean red gash on her stomach, her blouse having been ripped apart, revealing also the full young breasts cupped in small pink pockets. Jammie closed his eyes and, removing his own sweaty tee shirt, covered the embarrassed girl with it. The look she gave him when he opened his eyes confirmed the act's full magnitude, and their love.

Creme de cacao?

What do some people do when they can no longer worship? Confused, Jammie began to toy absently with the ring of grease in his own plate. Then he wiped his fingers on a linen napkin. *Creme de cacao?* True, he was proud of his collection of after-dinner drinks, but for Lorna's sake, not his own. Next to the projector and the movies there was, perhaps, nothing of which he was so proud. Except, of course, Lorna.

He was a beer man himself but, longing to see people have a good time, he had gone, shortly after they moved into the new house, to Gene Bresnik at the liquor store and asked that he stock him with at least one of everything. Gene sold him the Basic $100 Bar, plus a cabinet that you could wheel around. When Gene suggested that Lorna might like liqueurs Jammie bought a complete set. He felt a bit silly driving home, the bottles clattering in the back seat (all the drinks looked and sounded the same to him), but Lorna was thrilled.

This hadn't been the case with the fancy spice rack he had bought her two months before (even though she was not a very good cook). The apothecary jars were still empty, aside from those she had filled with pepper and salt. However, she took to the liqueurs right away. That very evening she asked the Van Drutens to come by (Joe and Connie, old high school friends), and, at Lorna's insistence, Jammie had brought out *all* the after-dinner drinks and placed them on the new glass-topped table where, seated about this transparent circle, the two couples drank liqueurs from small green cordials until the separate tastes were indistinguishable, they themselves insensible.

Jammie didn't like to remember such things. Now, seated at the abandoned table, watching the flicker of the candles which, a few minutes before, had given him such pleasure, he had to admit he felt quite blue. Then, strolling across the room, returning to Lorna in stereo time, he had felt like one of those men of unbelievably good looks born to grace the pages of *The New Yorker,* born to be a complement, to bend and light the cigarettes of unbelievably beautiful women. *Now,* he had to admit, he felt like one of those less imposing models who wear undershorts in a Sears catalogue.

What had happened? Lorna, he knew, was in the living room, sipping creme de cacao, wearing sunglasses while she watched color TV. She had begun this practice lately, in spite of the fact that she knew it upset him. He had frequently been left to clean up the dishes. It hurt him to listen to the confused jabber of television while he was scraping and rinsing the plates. It hurt him to picture Lorna, seated, watching her favorite programs from behind a wall of dark impenetrable glass. Thank goodness the children ate first and were sent to bed, or he would perhaps be left to take care of them also. However, he tried to be understanding. Lorna put in a rough day, what with the new house to clean, showers to attend (her old friends were grabbing up husbands at a fearful rate), and kids to take care of. She deserved whatever portion of rest she could find. But did she have to wear sunglasses? It seemed to separate them somehow.

In life, Jammie had not accomplished much by anybody's high standards. His job as land site estimator brought him as close as he would ever come to gratifying a youthful passion for geology. The job was now so routine that he could no longer remember just what he wanted when he wanted *out*. His athletic ambitions had been sublimated to a Sunday afternoon interest in the Green Bay Packers, and his love of children (he had once been a camp counselor) compromised by the fact that his own got on his nerves.

When he was honest with himself, which was seldom, he realized that he had but one accomplishment: Lorna. And that was nothing to sneeze at. A third of his friends seemed to consider their wives as something behind whose back you tell a dirty joke. Another third walked through the world in dark suits that hid the guilt of divorce, while others squatted in a seamy room and tossed their house keys to the center of an unpaid carpet. Friends? Once perhaps, but now acquaintances. He had nothing but Lorna.

Leaving behind the burning candles, the grease-incrusted scraps of food, and his own empty glass, he went into the living room. There she was: seated just as he had pictured her, sunglasses, channel selector, creme de cacao and all. Lately they had begun to squabble over a preference for red or green in the picture (just as they had over new checks when, in the presence of the bank clerk, Lorna had *insisted* on Wine Cellini). However, Jammie decided that tonight Lorna should have her way and, stepping to the TV, he deliberately set more green (her choice) and stood back with a feeling of well-being, of near oblation. After all, it was *her* anniversary.

Lorna smiled, the sunglasses rising on her nose. She was seated on the divan, her legs tucked beneath her buttocks, her hips circumscribing a lovely arch, one hand languid within her lap, the other fondling the glass, her full breasts protrusive, head erect. How perfect she was. And yet, she was wearing *them,* the silver pair with very dark lenses. Jammie's heart sank. He took a seat across from her, their eyes meeting in the apex of a V, the lines of sight centered on the television set. Lorna sipped her creme de cacao.

On the screen a comedian appeared. His face was too green, but Jammie did not change it. The comedian began to tell jokes about Superman, policemen, and Abraham Lincoln. Jammie did not think they were especially funny, but Lorna laughed. The man was a good-looking man, in spite of his green face, and fairly young.

"He looks like Jack Gilroy," Lorna said.

The sound of her voice took Jammie by surprise.

"Who?"

"Him," she said, pointing to the TV, her voice floating out from beneath the sunglasses.

The comedian. Well, yes, he did look like Jack Gilroy. Jack Gilroy! Could Lorna have mentioned a more forbidden name on this, the night of their anniversary? Watching the comedian, the most unfavorable, the most culpable thoughts ran through Jammie's mind. He recalled, although not so much remembering now as drumming up a nightmare, the second party in the new house. He and Lorna had moved the stereo out to the garage for dancing. They had set up the ping-pong table for booze and ice; and swept and cleaned. A large crowd came. They all drank too much. Jack and Lorna . . . but Jammie could not bear to think about it. Besides he had smooched a little himself. With Dusty Gimpel's wife. Some light stuff. Sticky face, as his mate of the moment had called it. After all, he was only human. But Lorna . . . that was something else. Things had worked out. The incident was forgotten. Nearly. . . .

Yes, the comedian did look very much like Jack Gilroy. So much so that Jammie had a sudden urge to turn the set off. Why must Lorna mention Jack's name on *their* anniversary? It was the first thing she had said all night. Jammie looked at her. Damn those sunglasses.

The couple watched television, he bitterly, she silently, for another hour. In his pocket, Jammie opened and snapped shut the lighter, closed his fist on it, then forgot it. The comedian was replaced by a female singer whose hair was such a sickly green that Jammie was forced to go to the screen and change it. Fortunately, Lorna did not protest. Jammie adjusted the dials, nullifying the effect of her hair with red. Taking his seat he saw that she now looked quite old and gray, haggard in fact, slightly vermilion, as if her face had been lost in the pages of a book, a long forgotten pressed flower. The woman sang a song which declared that one man had her heart while she had another's name.

Jammie hoped that Lorna couldn't hear the song. She hadn't stirred since the mention of Jack's name, but continued to sit erect, one hand limp within her lap, her cheeks and mouth invariable, sedentary beneath the dark sunglasses. The swing of her hip was sharp against the divan, like the edge of the moon. Was he really *jealous* of Jack Gilroy? The whole mess had been cleared up long ago. Jammie and Lorna both agreed that people aren't themselves when they've had too much to drink. They agreed that, in such a state, people do and say things they don't mean. They agreed that the friends they had invited to the party, especially the single men and dates (like Jack), had probably been a bad influence on them. Jammie and Lorna agreed on all of these things, so why was he disturbed about Jack, over the mere mention of his name?

He felt ashamed. He had a sudden desire to go to Lorna, to sit beside her, to take her in his arms and . . . and now he knew that things were slipping away from him, for the only word he could think of was *crush*. Crush her? It was a horrible thought, but it was there, there in his head, first green and then red, like the picture on TV and just as real. Yes, he did wish to . . . displace? wrinkle? *crush* Lorna somehow. With love of course. It was the violence of the desire and not its name that disconcerted him. Lorna sat, as perfect as an advertisement. Why was she so distant from him? And even at the table, where she had been no more than four feet away?

Was there a chance that he'd trumped the whole thing up, that Lorna wasn't *distant,* that he had begun to imagine things? Suspicion, jealousy, anger, the works. Was he simply afraid of her? This thought struck him as nonsensical and, in order to dispel it, he got up from his seat and went to her. However, he did not crush her, or even sit by her side. He knelt, at her feet. Lorna remained erect and still.

"Poopsie," he began. Then he cleared his throat. The whole thing was ridiculous. He felt as if he were proposing.

"Poopsie," he continued. When she did not stir, he stared at her. When he reached up and raised the silver sunglasses he saw that she was asleep. Her faintly green lids were shut tight.

Jammie frowned and stood up. Anniversary, hell!

He was back in the kitchen again, looking with loathing at the candlelight, the rings of grease in the dishes, the empty glass. He picked up the back scratcher and listened to its minute whir, then set it down with disgust. He poured himself a drink of creme de cacao. He hated the stuff, but after all it was his. Then he opened the door to the basement and descended a flight of creaking wooden stairs. The rumpus room was cold and clammy, the dehumidifier running, not too successfully, in a distant corner. The feeling of dampness clung to his shirt and trousers like fog. The large iron box purred, perched atop the rack he had built for it just below the ceiling, its large rubber hose protruding from the front, an elephant's trunk, curving slowly to the tin bucket which caught water at the floor. Jammie rubbed the muscles in his arm, not from the cold really, but discomfort and shame. He felt as if he had gone swimming before the season opened, as if he had been unwillingly wrapped in a used dishrag. Yet he knew his purpose. Something had gone wrong and Jammie sought, in the only source he knew, for the clues to What and Where and Why.

He had come to the basement, he knew, for the projector. It and the films he had been shooting for six years were his prize possessions, and he went directly to the cabinet for them now. The projector was a beauty: a Super Automatic, equipped with a knob for fine focus, a *Slow Motion* and *Still* switch, plus an Auto-Thread device that, once the film had been introduced to the mouth of a special unit, made it possible for him to avoid the burdensome task of threading. Jammie picked up the projector as if it were a baby. He set it up and pulled down the screen he had attached to the far wall. Next he took out his plastic tray of films, all carefully labeled according to date and subject matter. He removed one, *The Wedding June, '56,* placed it on the reel, turned out the overhead light, and flicked the projector switch. A series of dots began to sputter before his eyes.

Jammie's father appeared. He was smiling meekly while his hands attempted to decide which pockets they should occupy. He wore the urinous yellow tuxedo that Jammie had borrowed from a musician friend. Jammie's father was a butcher, and he looked it. His demeanor was that of a man who is uncomfortable unless he is near a piece of dead meat. Lorna's father referred to him as "our favorite butcher," and this in spite of his wife's outspoken preference for shopping at the new supermarket.

His father's discomfort on the screen reminded Jammie of the quarrel which had preceded the wedding. Lorna's mother demanded that champagne be served at the reception, while Jammie's father desired beer. The families had finally settled for a punch but, unfortunately, on the night of the reception thunder showers drove the guests in from the patio, and the punch was consumed at an extraordinary rate. The two fathers had driven off to replenish the supply, but in separate cars: one in search of champagne, the other for beer. It spoiled the wedding somehow.

Watching now, Jammie saw himself appear. He too was wearing a borrowed tux, though his not quite so yellow. His mother had taken these shots and seemed to have trouble locating a subject in the viewer. Following a prolonged study of Jammie's shoes, the two men, father and son, linked arms and, smiling at each other in gross disharmony, stepped past a sign that read, "The Church is a Hospital for Sinners, not a Showcase for Saints," and entered a prominent stone building. The overly powdered face of Lorna's mother appeared, a woman swishing back and forth with all of the poise and none of the endowments of a Hollywood starlet, mincing for a few painful minutes; then she too disappeared within the church. The bride was next, with her maids of honor. She was beautiful, like many brides.

Flip, flip, flip. The movie was over and the tag end of the film began to spin and snap on the reel. Jammie rewound it and returned it to the appropriate yellow carton. With some fear he took from the tray *Friends 1961*. Well, he had come for this, hadn't he? However, as if to warn him, the film caught in the mouth of the threader. He heard a grinding noise, a crackling sound, the mashing of cellulose, swore, flicked on the overhead light, and spent the next ten minutes cleaning out the complex network of spools and gears. He oiled the machine, gave it a trial run, and then turned out the light. At his back the dehumidifier purred like a strange animal. Jammie's nerves were on edge.

He flicked the switch, and the projector's whir drowned out the dehumidifier. Dots splattered, and then the face of a friend (or former friend), freckles, Shuttle Riley. A barbecue, at his house. Shuttle stepped up to a rotating spit where his wife was inspecting a mound of sizzling meat. Then Lorna appeared, sedate and smiling behind sunglasses. The Benjamins, notorious gadabouts, Collie and Ethel. Collie was a much lauded lawyer who worked like a dog for five days, drank like a pig on the weekend, and was something of an animal either way. It was rumored that the Benjamins had parties to which everyone came nude. Lorna had once greatly disturbed him by saying she would like to go. (The idea filled him with loathing. To think of *sharing* the sight of Lorna. A round of pleasure, sensual, uncommitted, short and narcotic as a cocktail, a shot of eternity in order to kill time. How he hated the word *tradesies*.) Jammie no longer saw the Benjamins. Nor Shuttle Riley, nor Harold Overand, who now appeared on the screen, a bachelor who watched all of their troubles with delight, fed on them, swore he would never marry, but clung to the company of couples and purposely stirred dissension within the institution he sought to avoid.

Friends? Jammie was about to shut the film off when a disarming face appeared. This, then, was why he had come to the basement. The whole mess had been recorded, and Jammie had done the job himself. He flicked the *Still* switch and stared at the face of Jack Gilroy. He set the machine on *Slow Motion.* . . .

Jack, carrying two sacks of booze, one beneath each arm, meandered across the freshly swept garage floor and placed the liquor on the ping-pong table, which had been covered with cheesecloth and was already piled high with bottles and sacks of ice. The party. The Benjamins and Van Drutens arrived, then Harold Overand, the latter dateless. The camera skipped ahead to other guests. Someone began to dance: arms and legs and slices of hair and clothing, the camera tilting precariously. Already drunk? And then (had he really done such a foolish thing?) Jammie stripped down to his shorts for the start of his race around the block with Dusty Gimpel's wife (and, thank goodness, no further). Dusty himself had taken these shots, joking that it was all in the family.

Next, Jammie was dancing, pants replaced. Joe Van Druten was arm wrestling with his wife Connie on the floor while Collie Benjamin danced with Jack Mattigan, Jack's pants rolled up above the knee while he dipped his hand, flaccidly, and pretended a leer and a lisp. This was followed by a swirl of couples, so strangely paired that Jammie could not even think of them in terms of their original alliances. And Lorna. Lorna without sunglasses, beaming, radiant, seated on Jack Gilroy's lap, her skirt shimmied far above the stocking line. The kiss seemed endless. Jammie groaned, experiencing that pain, that helplessness, that same sense of impotence and nausea which had come to him as a kid when, on Saturday afternoons in a darkened theater, he had inched his way to a bewitching and besweatered Lorna, arriving only to find her eyes locked, her feelings already wedded to some overlong and obscene kiss between two people

on the screen. He had not been able, then, to take her away
from it. He could not, then, create something, a love, which
could rival the super-existence she had witnessed. And here it
was again, only this time Jammie's eyes were locked, wedded to
the screen. And he was watching Lorna. She was a participant,
no spectator. That distant kiss, and Jack's hand sliding . . .
Jammie felt sick. He set the film back and ran it forward. He
watched it *Still* and he watched it in *Slow Motion*. Jack's hand,
sliding. . . .

Jammie snapped off the projector. He sat in the dark for a few
minutes, listening to the whir of the dehumidifier, then turned
the switch back on. He watched the film seven or eight times
and then put the projector away, having first dusted the lens,
inspected the Auto-Thread device, checked the fan which cooled
the hot bulb. He went upstairs.

In the kitchen the dishes had been rinsed and stacked. The
empty champagne bottle lay on its side in the trash bin. Jammie
had not touched the creme de cacao he had carried to the basement, and he now poured it down the drain. The living room
was dark and silent. Lorna's sunglasses lay on a table beside the
divan, along with the pad she kept for lists of good commercials.
She had gone to bed.

Jammie tiptoed down the hall, past the kids' room, and
opened the door to his own. The room glowed faintly with blue.
He could hear Lorna's soft somnolent breathing. Going to the
bed he pulled back the covers. She wore nothing, but herself,
perfect, beautiful, distant, and . . . cold. In the faint light her
skin was flushed with amber, as if (once his eyes were accus-
tomed to the light) an invisible fire glowed in some distant
corner of the room. She slept on her side, one leg thrown across
the other in such a manner that her hip inscribed a soft naked
curve. Her hair, let down, fell loosely at her shoulders, her
breasts pressed against the smooth skin of her arms. Unthinking,
she varied her pose with an innocence that struck him as child-
like, again drawing her leg across the one on which she lay, as if
to shield the unphotographable. That was the horror of it. She
was as pretty as a *picture*. Try as he might Jammie could not

dispel the thought. He saw her as some kind of *Playmate of the Month*. No one was supposed to take those girls seriously, and yet the whole nation did. (One man in Jammie's office had collected the pictures for years. They were mounted on a bulletin board in his basement, in a special room which, because of his wife, he kept under lock and key.) Lorna's skin was lustrous, as glossy as a page. There was something inaccessible about her.

When she shivered and drew her arms about herself so tightly that her breasts were pushed up close to her chin, Jammie dropped the covers he held in his hand. He put on his pajamas and crawled into bed. As usual Lorna had the electric blanket set at "8." Jammie preferred "2," but did not change it. Nor did he touch her. He lay still, helpless and confused. He longed to pass into the movie of a sleep, but couldn't.

Jammie tossed first to the left and then to the right. He stopped, for he didn't wish to disturb Lorna. What should he do? In the room's dark he thought, I was born for reverence, born to give it. Loving Lorna was *all;* it was everything to him. He had always admired the necessity of rank (on teams, in the services, in the office), and eight years ago, as he knelt before his Senior Queen and offered her his scant tee shirt, he had realized fully his position on the ladder. It was low, but for Jammie enough, enough to be able to look *up,* up to Lorna.

This sense of distance had worked wonders in his soul, had actually made him feel *good*. For eight years he had entertained one, and only one, conception of himself; he was Lorna's *man* (as the songs said, the old ones they used to dance to, the songs that spoke of *forever*). He felt he had increased her worth through worship. He had never exactly thought about it this way of course; things simply had been that way. His reverence had made him original, given him a purpose in life. *Increasing her worth through* . . . her worth? He had once known her worth, but now? Now he didn't.

That was the problem. Why, there were times now when he doubted that she even existed. The distance was too great; it no longer encouraged him. It was almost as if she were . . . *dead*. Jammie shuddered. Good God, no. He couldn't bear to think that. He was surrounded by death: in the tract, at work, in his former friends. Everywhere, but no, not in Lorna. He had once visited a construction site on a routine checkout. The place had been the scene of an accident, his firm being sued for faulty evaluation because a bulldozer, caught in sliding ground, had mangled one of the construction crew. Standing on the site, Jammie had noticed strands of flesh caught in the teeth of the huge machine. The man's helmet, red tin and caked with tar, sat but a few feet from the bulldozer: so small and yet so singular an object. There was a dent in it about the size of a softball. Jammie couldn't stand the thought of death.

He rolled out of bed. Lorna was sleeping, warm and safe beneath the covers, and Jammie left her. Passing through the kitchen he headed straight for the basement. In that cold damp room he gathered up his films and the projector and returned to the bedroom. There he silently shifted a chest of drawers away from the far wall, leaving it free and white. He returned to the bed and set up the projector, on the bookcase headboard above a sleeping Lorna.

He crawled in beside her, flicked the switch, and waited for Jack Gilroy. When the face appeared Jammie snapped it to *Still* and began to nudge Lorna. She sat up, rubbing her eyes, and drew the covers above her breasts. Jammie slipped his arm about her shoulder, nestling his head against hers, smiling, drifting back to those times, eight years ago, when he had stolen to her side in dark theaters. He flicked the *Run* switch with his free hand and the party commenced on the far wall. When Lorna appeared on Jack's lap she sighed and cuddled up to Jammie who, responding, let the film run. He showed it *Slow Motion* and he showed it *Still*.

Lorna began to stroke the hairs on his chest, the two of them entangled, lost on a Saturday afternoon, content in a childhood theater forever. When *the kiss* appeared, shimmering on the bare white wall, their eyes were wedded to it and they held each other tightly.

"Are you happy, Poopsie?" Jammie asked.

"Yes, dear," she said.

"Happy Anniversary."

They looked at each other, leaned back against the head-board, and began to laugh, slowly at first, then freely.

This year's performance had been even better than the last, than the one a year ago when Jammie, humiliated, crushed by the gift of that silly, idiotic lighter, had gone to the basement to watch his films while Lorna, wearing sunglasses for the first time, had retired to the living room to watch TV. Now, as then, he had brought her back to life with the film of the party and she, well, she had pulled him through another year.

Kick

Thomas W. Molyneux

from Shenandoah

He had returned to the city yesterday, Sunday, arrived at his apartment about noon, unpacked, done some situps, and then watched the world figure skating championships from Switzerland on television. When he thought about them today, he smiled, remembering how fine he had felt seeing Peggy Fleming bend to have the gold medal hung round her neck. Then, he had thought that he never now could be world champion at anything, that already the time was past when he might have begun to become best.

Today being his first day back, he had left work early, at four-thirty, wanting some exercise. But vaguely he had wanted to avoid the camaraderie and responsibilities of the New York Athletic Club, where the firm had a membership for him, and so had taken the subway to Sixth Avenue in Greenwich Village, where he still maintained a membership in a small gymnasium he had used when he first came to New York.

His name was Jared Walker. He was a big boy, over six foot, heavy in the shoulders, powerful in a padded clubbing way. His yellow blonde hair lay short and damp across his forehead. He wore a gabardine suit, custom made, he said, because it was impossible to get ready made suits to fit his high shoulders, but really he enjoyed the slight pinch at the waist, enjoyed standing out just slightly from the crowd when he could be sure of doing so in good taste. He was twenty-eight years old, soon twenty-nine, and he expected that next year the firm would offer him a junior partnership.

He came up from the subway into the sharper sounds and more sudden movements of the dimming October day. His eyelids hung nearly closed, so that passersby no doubt thought him tired after the weekend. When he felt the pain open and pulse along his shin, he took two steps more before he stopped. The sting still reached out, a sharp crack settled and nauseating along the bone of his shin. He looked to the building beside him, as though he might have bumped into that; but its side was a person's width away. Turning, he saw the people against the piercing plastic pastel signs and the traffic snapping away from him up Sixth Avenue and he looked across the constant downward set of their faces for some explanation. Then, sensing someone staring behind him, he turned and saw the boy going away from him. The boy moved slowly, seemed to linger. With each step he rolled onto the ball of his foot and hovered there before swooping down and stepping ahead. He looked back over his shoulder, his damp mouth cocked grimly above his upturned dark collar. Already knowing, Jared found the thin boy's eyes. As he did, he thought the boy lingered still longer at the peak of one step. While Jared watched, the boy looked away and walked on. Jared took a quick step forward as though to follow him. As he did, he stepped flat into a woman. He looked down to excuse himself. But already she had pushed around him and was moving on. "Hey," she had said.

In the distance he saw the boy's narrow black jacketed back canting through the pedestrians. But what anyhow could he have done, there? Finally, he turned, and, looking before him as though the boy might recur, walked on to the gymnasium.

The fluorescent lights lined bare along the gym's ceiling and reflected silver from the room's three mirrored walls. In the sudden still clarity of the room, Jared halted. Two men in skimpy bathing suits stood talking by the weights. One wore construction gloves so that his hands would not callous. Jared went into the locker room to change. Sitting on the gray bench before his locker, his shirt unbuttoned, he crossed his left leg over his right and saw on the pantleg the smudged glossy darker brown mark of dirt and smeared shoe polish. Newly he knew, surely now, that the boy had kicked him. He stood and pulled off his pants and sat again. Along the edge of his shin he saw the bruise, already gone glossy blue in one small place, and around that the beads of pale red where the kick had broken the skin. He thought how hard the boy had kicked him. But what anyhow could he have done? It was different for the skinny boy in the chino pants and short corduroy jacket. But what could he, Jared, have done there, then?

He pulled on some sweat clothes, went into the bright main room and worked out alone. Around him he heard the slight conversations punctuated by the puffs of the others and by his own caught, hucking breath. He watched for a while the man with the construction gloves who stood sideways to the mirror to do curls. When the man finished with his right arm, he turned around so as to watch the left. Jared did some final chinups, used the sunlamp, showered and dressed. He felt a little dizzy, as though he had done too much, though he had worked out slowly and methodically, and he sat for a second on the bench before knotting his tie, sensing the close movements around him. A radio played show music from the fifties.

When Jared came out of the gym, the streetlights were lighted and the early night had closed greyly on the sky. Beneath his shirt his body felt damp and he knew he should have waited before dressing to let all the sweat be dried.

At Sixteenth Street he turned right and then at Park South, left. He heard ahead of him the tlick of shoe cleats rapping in quick cocky steps against the sidewalk. Looking up he saw the boy a half block from him pass too quickly under a streetlight, regain too quickly the anonymity of silhouette. Once a foot dragged and a cleat grated, like fingernails on a blackboard, so that Jared felt a thin tremor pass in himself. With each step the approaching form rose onto the ball of his foot, coming forward in prolonged lurches. His collar, like Jared's, was up.

The tlicks of the figure's steps clicked off his motion against the continuing and anonymous background noise: tlick; tlick; tlick. The figure's hands were in his chino pockets and, coming nearer, he seemed to pop onto his toes as he rolled forward. His face, even close, was hung with dim shadow, dark on dark, and so obscured. As they came abreast, the figure popped forward and up and Jared's hand, already cupped, flung back and balled. Jared's right leg dragged back and he flexed some at the knees. Then he realized that the figure had passed. He heard the sudden and distinct tlick of the figure's heels and, after a time, another and then, deliberately, another. Jared turned round, aware of his still-balled fist, his still-cocked forearm. He watched the figure recede directly from him with its smooth patterned lurch.

The other figure had passed out of sight when Jared turned back and started again toward his apartment. Ahead of him, far along the avenue, he saw the hazed height of the buildings which were the city for him, sure and weathered like a natural landscape, towering and careless as that too. He thought about walking on into their dominion. When he had first come to the city and been sometimes broke, he had done that: walked up Park past the Ritz and the Waldorf, stopping to look in the store windows; walked across and along Broadway, studying the photographs of the dance hall girls until, sometimes, a pimp would approach him and he would say no and walk on, stopping also to look at the movie advertisements and into the souvenir store windows, knowing that everything was available; walked up Broadway and across 59th, down Fifth for a bit, past Tiffany's and by Rockefeller Center where people took him for a native. But he did not want any pimp approaching him tonight. He did not want to pass among the slower more prosperous people whose daughters he might marry or to see the photographs with the black bands across the breasts.

In his apartment a single light lit the living room. Jared turned on the kitchen and bathroom lights and two more table lamps, fully in the living room. His walls were white and the four neat lithographs on the opposite wall were light and framed in thin dull black wood. The heavy armoire his father had made stood alone against one wall. Except for it the furniture was the third set he had had in the apartment. He had bought the first set of furniture even before he met Sally, and already by the time he did meet her had begun to replace it. He had already got the armoire from his father.

Four years ago when he had met her he had been out of law school just five months. Though he was handsome and had been in the city two months, he knew few girls. He had located the village gym in the yellow pages and he worked out regularly there, going after to Julius' bar for a beer. Often he stayed for supper, eating a hamburger and drinking slowly at the bar. There he had met a few men his own age—interns from St. Alice's, some acting students, one or two whose work he didn't know—and through them, at occasional parties, some girls—nurses mostly, but too some stewardesses, an occasional salesgirl. But he did not date much, had had only two or three dates during the two months, because he found it impossible to date without spending thirty or forty dollars. He took his few dates to places he had read about in men's magazines, to the Stork Club and to Trader Vic's, Toots Shor's and Basin Street.

Still sometimes the posed faces of girls he had watched then but had not met recurred to him: the model daubing her lips as she stepped from the Horn and Hardart's on Lexington Avenue whose widened eyes had mocked his looking and whom he had later recognized dancing sleekly across a full page of *Look Magazine* in her Maidenform; the tanned slouched girl with the dry laugh, whose smiling photograph planning the April in Paris Ball Charley Samp had shown him in the *Times* the day she had come into the office during his first week. The faces lay occasional and haphazard in his mind—sometimes not faces even: the gracile back of the long blond haired girl wearing a bright yellow sweater and faded blue jeans running up the library steps—with the same self-conscious sentimental regret that he had felt at home during vacation when in his room and in the attic he had seen the furniture and prints he bought when he first moved to the city. He had been surprised, flipping through the thick stack of reproductions, at how accurately he recalled the names: Pissarro, Gris, Degas. Manet he still confused with Monet. He had laughed half aloud at the tattered bulky briefcase, which Sally had replaced with his black attaché case.

He sat on the floor, intending to do some situps, but his kicked leg struck the floor and a quick pain spread again from the bruise.

The boy came toward him, rising on his toes and swooping forward, his mouth cocked arrogantly. His foot kicked out, slashed into Jared's skin, smearing blood and shoe polish widening on the pantsleg; he laughed bitterly, passing on, while Jared only stood, big, his big hands clasping on nothing, looking around at the getting away boy.

Jared stood very still in the center of the room listening. He stepped to the window, looked out at the fire escape, leaned out to look up, let down the clanking blinds. It all outside seemed tighter and quicker than he ever could be. He watched the horizontal pattern of the drawn blinds. He crossed and dialled her number.

"May I speak to Sally, please?" he said.

"She's out."

"What?"

"She's out. Not in. Is there a message?"

"Are you her roommate?"

"No, I'm her friend. I'm staying the night. Who's this?"

"Could you tell her Mr. Walker called?"

"Want her to call you?" the girl asked.

"No need. Just tell her I called, please?" He hung up and, after a while, went to bed.

The next day, in conscious repetition of Monday's pattern, Jared left the office at four-thirty, took the subway to Sixth Avenue, walked past the women's detention house and turned left at the corner. He wore an old thin tweed suit which he had owned in law school. He was looking for the boy who had kicked him. He walked slowly; his neck bowed, but his eyes looked ahead, hooded by the controlled drooping of his lids. His hands rested high in his pockets. He passed Julius' and continued in the same dogged, tired manner to the Eighth Avenue corner. There he halted, looked about him, then turned and walked on the same side of the street back to the subway entrance.

The boy loomed sudden, his arms arcing in loops behind him. When Jared looked up the boy kicked him in the shins, laughed loud. People were stopped to watch, but while the smaller boy walked leisurely from him, Jared could only stand. He saw himself reflected somewhere. Then while he still stood, the people went away, talking in small groups.

Jared had stopped and braced his feet. He saw a man pass him watching candidly. Carefully, doggedly, he walked once more to the Eighth Avenue corner and once more back to the subway entrance. He wondered that he could have been here this long and seen no one familiar. He turned again and walked into the wind to his gymnasium.

There he worked out more vigorously than he had the day before. Sitting after on the locker room bench, he looked up to nod to several men. He showered, used the sunlamp, dressed and walked home.

The apartment elevator was in use, so Jared walked the two flights of stairs. From the stairhead he heard the phone ringing. He loped along the hall, held the receiver from him, covered, while his breath broke in chops from his dry chest until after a second he said, "Hello."

There came no answer for a second. He stepped back and flicked on the foyer light.

"Hello," said he again.

"Who is this?" she said.

"Who is this?" he said.

"Jared?"

"Yes. Who's calling."

"I'm sorry. I must have dialled the wrong number."

"Who is it?"

"It's Sally," she said.

They were both quiet for a second. Sally repeated then: "I'm sorry."

Jared said, "I called you last night."

"I know," she said.

"How have you been?"

"Well. Good." She laughed. "I can never get it straight since you made me think about it. I live alone here now."

"I got to wondering last night."

"It would be nice to see you," she said.

When he paused, she continued, "You could come out if you want. I've got some scotch and we could have a couple of drinks.

"Why don't you come in?"

"No," she said.

Her voice on the phone was quick and near seeming; hearing it, Jared thought of her hair, dyed wheat, streaked, cut short, and without curl. He tried to hear how she said the s's, tried to make her speak in paragraphs, because he liked the voice's recall and for the other reason too: wondering had she been already drinking. When he had hung up he thought to himself how silly it would be to go. In words he thought how difficult it had been before to stop seeing her, how there would be nothing to say now after a year and a half, how he did not want to marry her, how she drank.

He left the many bright lights of the apartment lighted as he went out and downstairs to flag a taxi.

After he gave the cabby Sally's address, he nestled into the seat corner and watched dimly and tiredly out the window. They went up Third Avenue, slipping flat through the traffic on the broad street. Ahead, lights stroked thinly into the dark. Nearer, they opened and dimmed, thickly limning passed pedestrians; they seemed, the ones anyhow he watched, brisk and single.

The little bar where he had met Sally was on Third. Jared sat up in the seat and looked out, trying to remember was Malachi's on his right or left. "You walk through once with your hands at your sides and you know who's wearing a girdle. I tell you, kid, it's the best place to meet them. That's what they're there for." Who had told him about Malachi's? He wondered was it still popular.

She had been drunk the night he met her; so she said anyhow later. The weekend thrum loud in the bar forced them to bend to each other and shout to be heard. He watched her lorn face, the hair short and strict around it, the small scar like a peeled scab in the fullness beneath her eye and from her calm look he sensed the quiet of the narrow, fought for space between them. Leaning to her so that he could see only the plane of her cheek, he said, "I'm Jared, Jared Walker."

"You already said that," she said close to his ear. "Remember, I said it was a good name?"

He bucked back then to see her laugh, the expression short and sharp, sure in her face in the way he never came to understand. Then a sudden lurch from behind caught him off guard and he stumbled against her. Her arms clamped at his sides and he felt her slight body push without detail into his, ease free.

"Let's go someplace else," he said.

"I know you did it on purpose," she said, with a quick laugh.

"I didn't."

"Now, now," still laughing.

He poured the last of his beer into his glass and stepped near her while two couples pushed by toward the door. He laid his hand loosely on her hip, feeling in his palm the dry smooth slippery texture of her sweater. She dropped her glass at his feet. It clattered there between them and he watched it catch and lose the little light on the shadowed floor. She dropped her arm across her front then and cupped his hand. Her foot darted forward to roll the glass and she looked up at him and winked, laughed. She lifted his hand from her hip, squeezed it quickly, and let it fall.

They went out then through the place and by the blazered bouncer, turned right and walked down Third. In the night bleakness, the carlights snapping by them, shutting gone, her face was changeling. Her eyes were deep pocketed, as though from too many parties he thought. She spoke in a quick voice, stopping abruptly to puck her lips, continuing, and her voice in the simplest statement seemed to question. She was a secretary. On weekends sometimes she modeled for catalogues: shoes, nylons, gloves, bras once.

Jared said, "I thought that place was only for new girls in town. How come you go?"

"Free beer," she said. "Good kind of guys. Like you."

"It is a good place," he said.

"Yeah. Whoopeedoo."

They turned onto 57th Street, crossed to the downtown side. Across the street the closed opulent small stores held their quiet lights. Someone had told him JFK had bought at Frank Brothers.

At the edge of the park in front of the Plaza they took a hansom. Inside the must smell was still like settled dust. The cab lurched twice as the horse started and then settled to a steady dugadug like bicycle wheels over cobblestones as it turned into the park. Sally had pushed close to him and his arm lay along the slight slope of her back. Her hair wisped at his eyes, and close to her, aware of the slight dampness of her skin, he smelled the faded perfume on her, a close smell amid the must.

They kissed and then she turned her face down, pressing her head to his chest. For a time the dugadug of the cab persisted around them, isolating them from the far thin streaks of city noise. She tilted her head and the darkness of her eyes cocked mocking up to him and he saw the short groove of scar beneath her eye.

"Am I tight?" she said.

She kissed him again quickly then and repressed her head to him.

Looking ahead he said, "We could go to my place."

She leant free, smiled in the quick way she always did so that he could not say what she meant. "No," she said.

They got out of the cab and crossed to the fountain. Fifth Avenue, lighted, lay away ahead of them. The Plaza and before it the constant white bright fountain seemed permanent and distant as though caught in a photograph for a postcard, as perhaps St. Mark's or Trafalgar or any of the many travelogue squares he had never seen might have looked, the lights sharp and clean.

Leaving her at the door of her apartment, he went out again into the night, loud but far around him. The wind was slow, pushed softly. He crossed to Park Avenue and walked down that. The sudden clearness of the glass buildings, the blue sheen shading, sure and manmade, straight, simple, stilling the night, their night, caught him, made him feel young; at once inconsequent and splendid. The buildings, he thought, were of the same wispy blue as the searchlight beams which had dropped back and forth on night skies in his childhood to advertise supermarket openings, which before, his father said, had swept the sky during World War II watching for air raids.

Ahead of him a formally dressed couple strode from the Waldorf and he watched the man stop obtrusively to tip the doorman, the doorman look at the bill before balling his fist. Through the cab's rear window he saw the man lay his arm across the girl's shoulder and her face turn to him.

He thought again of the girl he had left and for a moment he could not remember her name. It came to him finally, the name only first, then too the eyes, wary within their pockets, promising depravity, and he thought that he had failed and all around him other men were succeeding. He thought that another man—that other man who had come out of the Waldorf—would have succeeded with Sally that night, as he was succeeding with the richer girl. After a while he had begun to run so that the city bobbed to him and the cold air cut sudden in his throat.

As though far from him Jared felt the taxi lurch and he settled again against its seat.

"You drunk buddy?" said the cabby. "We're here."

"No, just tired." He paid the meter, tipped and thanked the driver. He slammed the door and stood for a second at the curb while the cab jerked away, throwing up the dry grit of the street. Then he turned, went into the foyer and rang Sally's bell. The foyer was chill. Outside a wind shuffled, bucking occasionally against the outside door. After a second he rang the bell again.

"C'mon," he said.

He looked again at Sally's number, then rang three random upstairs apartments. The door buzzed and he entered. As it pushed closed behind it buzzed again.

He walked to Sally's apartment and knocked. A light shone under her door. He knocked again. He pressed his eye against the eyepiece, thinking to surprise Sally who was surprising him. After a minute he stopped that and tried to listen for some motion in the apartment.

Then he stepped away from the door. "She could have left a note," he said half aloud and went to sit on the steps to wait for Sally's return.

From above he heard someone call: "Who's there? Anyone there?"

"Just me," he called after a second.

"Who's me?" asked the voice.

"Jared Walker," he called, "forgot my key."

He rooted in his pockets, found paper but no pen. He crumpled the paper. He wasn't going without seeing Sally anyhow.

He went down the hall and knocked again. Softly, a record played inside. He could not recall whether it had played when he had knocked before. He bashed at the door. His hands, self aware from the striking, felt long and futile at his sides, and he felt bulky and somehow too washed, too surely shaven there. After a second he reached up, opened his collar and pulled his tie loose.

He knew that when she did come he would be surly. He would resolve not to be, but she would shrug and smile in the quick way he had never understood, and could never satisfactorily recall, and he would be surly. It would not matter whether she were drunk. The shrug, if she were, and the smile would be slower, would seem to taunt more deliberately. But drunk or sober she would affect not to care and then he would be surly.

"We're too much alike," she would say laughingly.

"We're nothing alike."

"Okay."

But they were alike. That was the strange thing. He was from the small town on Cape Cod and she from New York; he had gone to college and to Harvard Law School and she—except for a course in the novel at the New School after they met—only to high school. But they were alike.

No, they were not alike. Because she would have married him when he first asked her and he would not marry her then. The firm had just taken the NYAC membership for him and with some of the other bachelors he had met there he had begun going around to the charity balls and with a few models and even to coming out parties for college girls who laughingly said they'd been out too long already. At the Waldorf he danced with the girl Charley Samp had shown him in the *Times* and at the end of the dance she had thanked him in a dry deep voice, curt as her laugh, and walked away.

Then for no reason, after three months, he had called Sally again and asked to see her and she had said yes—the one word, sure as the smile or as her no the first night in the hansom, as though she had known what she would say long before he asked. He had taken her at the end of the evening to ride in the hansoms again, still a little surprised that she had come out with him at all, and she had let him kiss her, but when he asked her to come back to his apartment, she had said, "No."

For a month after that he had alternately dated her and a model who stood primly windblown on a sandhill, made tranquil by Modess on the inside cover of—he supposed among others—*Look Magazine.* Then he had laughed aloud at an important friend of the model's and insulted him, and after that had dated Sally exclusively. When she was with him she was slow spoken, seemed withdrawn and waiting, as though she had another answer surely ready and bided lingering for him to ask whatever question it matched, and he told himself that that was what she was waiting for. A month later he asked her a second time to marry him. She smiled. "No," she said.

So they were not alike, because when she had been ready he had not, and when he had, she had not.

"Then why do we go out?" he had said.

"You ask me."

"But you don't have to go."

"I like to."

"But then there's no reason to go out."

"You ask me."

But it had taken another month before he stopped seeing her finally. And now here he was, knowing better, to see her again, and when she came back or opened the door he would be surly because he did not know why he was there and he thought that she did.

"Dammit, Sally, I know you're in there," he called aloud now. He heard his voice then, as another's in the bare chill corridor, and subsided. "Sally," he whispered into the corner of the door and jamb. He tried the knob.

He heard the snap of the door behind him opening, and he straightened suddenly.

"Why don't you let somebody sleep," the woman's voice said.

"She said she'd be here," said Jared.

"Well she ain't," said the woman.

Jared took a step toward her. The door jerked back, bucked snapping against the chain, hesitated, slammed forward, puffing the air before it.

Jared said, "Wait a minute. Let me talk to you."

"I got to sleep. My husband works shifts and I got to get up when he gets home."

Jared turned back then and tried Sally's knob again.

"Sally," he whispered.

"Wait a minute lady," Jared said after a minute to the closed and already settled door, "I'm not hurting anything," he said.

The door snapped open again and the angry woman's head darted briefly visible. "You better get now. I called the cops. My old man would have said to. I called the cops and they're coming." Immediately she shut the door.

"Lady," he said. And after a second: "Lady, open the door a second. You can keep the chain up. Just open it and look at me. I'm not doing anything wrong. She said she'd be here."

"Well she ain't."

"But I'm just waiting. If you'll just look at me, you can see I'm not doing anything wrong. I've never been in trouble."

"You don't get, you will be now. I called the cops and they're coming."

He pulled his pockets out, letting his keys and change clink to the ground.

"Look," he said. "I don't have any weapon."

"Get away. I tell you," she said through the door. "The cops are on their way."

The boy had kicked him and he had done nothing. He had stood feeling bulky and awkward while the boy strutted canting through the unknowing crowd. He had done nothing.

The door buzzed into the quiet. Looking the length of the corridor, seeing its sheer bare walls converge to the door and the runner of blue carpet also point there, Jared saw, bleak and deliberate as an old dream, the door open and the two policemen enter. One of them slapped his nightstick like a pendulum tick, tick into his palm as he came along the corridor.

"Hello, sir," Jared said, extending his hand.

"What's going on, buddy?" said the policeman with the nightstick.

"Nothing that I've seen," said Jared

"We got a call," said the policeman with the nightstick. "What's your business here?"

"I'm waiting for the young lady who lives here. She invited me out and must have stepped out to get eggs or ice or something."

"At 12:30?"

"Is it that late?" said Jared.

"You can't wait here, buddy."

"I've got to. The young lady's expecting me."

The second policeman said, "Why don't you just forget about her, buddy? It'll still be good tomorrow. It don't go stale."

"I've got to wait," said Jared. "I can't let her down. She's expecting me."

The policeman stepped forward and lightly lay his hand on Jared's forearm. Jared stepped away from it.

Then the door opposite snapped open and the woman's face appeared in the narrow column. She had taken her curlers out and removed her nightcap.

"He won't let anybody sleep, officer," she said.

"You the lady that called?"

"My old man'll be home soon and wanting dinner and who knows what else and this one keeping me awake."

"You the one that called, lady?"

"I said I was, dint I?"

"No," said Jared.

"He's shouting and asking why she called and yelling. Why, way she drinks, she could just as likely be passed out cold in there the whole time. I've seen it. Heard her phone ring for hours and that victrola, hours at once and she too drunk to hear. Why my old man comes home he'll lace hell out of him."

"All right, lady. We'll take care of it. You can go back to bed now."

"No point in that now. My old man'll be home any minute. I wouldn't have called only he wouldn't let me sleep even a minute." The woman closed the door with a quiet push of air.

"All right, buddy, let's go outside," said the policeman.

"I said I'd be here. I've got to wait."

"Last time, I said. You want to go in?"

Again the policeman touched Jared's elbow. Like that, Jared in front, they went down the corridor toward the door.

They were outside then, the chill sharp against them, fluttering their pantslegs. The policeman with the nightstick flicked it abstractedly into his palm. Twice he gave Jared directions to the subway.

The boy loomed like a sudden bird before him, swooping, lashing lacerations across his leg, streaked on, laughing loudly and lewdly and leering back across his hunched thin shoulder.

Jared turned, but only saw himself, fit and futile, his hands dangling long at his sides. When he turned again, the boy was just a small speck taunting in the distance. He disappeared into an anonymous doorway. Jared looked down then and saw, spurting through his pants, his rushing blood.

He began walking along the curb, balancing. Once he tottered into the street. Twice he stepped across onto the pavement proper. He tensed his arms, crooked at the elbow, his fingers opened and cracked tensely. Like that, along the curb, he walked the length of the street.

When he was nearly to the corner, he heard from across the street the faint caught chuckle. He walked a few steps on, then heard the chuckle again and toppled into the street. Balancing, he saw the boy across from him. The boy walked slowly, watched Jared frankly. He was lighted between a streetlamp and an apartment entrance. He wore a bow tie and dark suit. Under his arm he clasped a briefcase. As Jared crossed the street toward him he slowed. Approaching, Jared saw the boy, pale like himself, tall and flat, neatly dressed, exact under the night light, and he thought of himself when he had first come to the city and taped random reproductions at jaunty angles on the walls of his apartment and taken stewardesses to Trader Vic's and thought he recognized Tuesday Weld there.

When he came opposite the boy, Jared stopped in the street. The boy continued walking, looking ahead, away from Jared now.

"Hey," Jared said.

The boy continued, his walk now slowed still more, stiff.

"Hey, you," Jared said.

The boy stopped and turned. Jared crouched his knees, cocked his fists in a rigid parody of a photograph of a bare knuckle boxer. "Put up your dukes. Let's fight." He flicked his nose with his left fist, nodded his head. A short breath like a laugh escaped him. "Humph." "C'mon," he said, "let's fight."

Without speaking, the boy turned away and continued down the street.

"Hey, hey college boy," Jared said. "College boy, I'm talking to you. I want to fight you."

Jared scurried ahead of the boy, blocked his path on the pavement, assuming the same rigid photographic stance. For a quick second, the boy halted before him.

"Let's go," said Jared.

"I don't want to fight you," the boy said. He angled a little to Jared's right and brushed past him, the briefcase thick and awkward under his arm. Jared turned and scurried again in front of the boy, assuming the stance, blocking the boy's path once more. The boy halted.

"Pretty tacky briefcase," Jared said. "Let's fight, college boy."

"I don't want to fight you," said the boy.

For a second they were quiet, so that Jared heard his own breath chopping from him as though he had run a long way. The boy before him was about his size, perhaps a little smaller, dim shadowed now on the blear street. Finally Jared said, "Then go the other way."

"What?" said the boy.

"You heard me. Go the other way. Walk back the way you came. If you want to pass me, you've got to fight me."

Jared had relaxed his stance. Now he snapped into it again. He flicked once at his nose. He bobbed his head. The noise, like a laugh, like a question, broke from him again: "Humph." He lolled out a teasing jab at the boy's arm.

The boy walked again slowly and deliberately at angle past Jared. Again Jared scurried past him to block his path.

"This is getting monotonous," the boy said.

"I'll tell you what," Jared said. "If you won't fight, you can run. You can just run, and if I don't catch you by the time I count ten, I'll let you go. But if I catch you, I'm gonna whup hell out of you."

"Look," the boy said. "It's late, I'm tired. I have no fight with you. Just let me by."

"What's the matter, college boy. Chicken aren't you? Bow tie dilly."

Then quickly the boy drove his shoulder into Jared's stomach, driving him back so suddenly that Jared saw, past the boy's haunches, his briefcase dropping like a shadow. It hit the sidewalk on its edge and flopped hollowly onto its side, and Jared could hear the huck huck huck of his startled breath chopping from him before he began to hit at the boy's bent back. He cracked against the wall and he heard that noise too before he felt its pain. He tried to turn, feeling the breath which would not come deep and locked in his belly, pulling there. But already the boy was turning him. Already the boy was behind him and had locked his forearm across Jared's windpipe and pulled him back so that his back bowed.

"Look mister," the boy said near to Jared's ear. "I don't have any fight with you. If I let you go, will you just go on?"

Jared felt the pressure on his windpipe loosen and he clawed suddenly at the boy's arm and tried to turn into the boy. But immediately the forearm clamped again. He felt the thud of the boy's knee into his back. He was being pulled back, down, and then he hit flat onto the pavement. The boy bent close over him, holding his wrists loosely.

"Now look, mister," said the boy. "I'm not going to run and I'm not going to walk the other way. And I don't know what the hell your gripe is, but I don't have any fight with you."

The boy's face was rounded and taut and a light from the building beside them sloped down it, lighting it with dramatic highlights as in a ballet photograph. The building above loomed powerfully and beyond that, past the boy's strained face, the sky was lurid and luminescent. But the boy's voice was caught and pleading and what he was saying was all wrong.

Jared snapped at the boy's bent near face with one flung forearm. But he felt the boy's grip tighten on his wrist. The boy hit him full in the face, once, twice, again, the fist romping down into the trapped face so that immediately Jared tasted the blood wet in his mouth and felt the tears start uncontrollably in his eyes. The noise broke from him, sudden and surprised: "Oww." He lay still then. His eyes were closed and he felt the taunting slow jerking movement of the tear down his cheek. His tongue found the opened place on his lip. He could hear the boy's slow scuffled steps, hear him brush at his clothes, pick up and whisk off his briefcase.

"Oww," Jared said again, more quietly now, the sound twisting somehow from him against his will.

He heard the boy say "Sorry" and then the footsteps go away from him.

Voyeur

William Moore

from *Literary Review*

I watch them arrive at the cottage on the beach. An eager, exuberant explorer, the man races from door to door. "You see! You see! It's fine," he keeps shouting. "Fine!"

The wife inspects things more cautiously, notices the rickety beds, the dirty stove, the questionable water supply. At last she joins the man on the beach in front of the cottage and, responding to his enthusiasm, kisses him. He embraces her. Arms locked, their hands move sensually on each other's body.

He releases his arms and stoops down to remove his shoes. "Let's do it in the water," he says.

The woman glances carefully up and down the beach without seeing me. "But suppose," she says, "someone comes."

"No one will come," the man declares, removing his pants. "There's no one here." He drops his shorts, revealing his sensual excitement.

"O great Minos!" the wife says affectionately. She removes her shirt and brassier. He seizes her. She breaks away to step out of her remaining clothes.

With a roar, the man dashes wildly down the beach to charge

the waves. The water is cold, and the man is breathless when his head reappears above the surface.

The woman walks uncertainly to the water's edge. "Cold?"

He shakes his head. "Invigorating," he gasps.

The woman tries the water gingerly with her foot. "Cold."

"Come on! It's great—when you get used to it!" The man shivers as he wades toward her.

The wife points. "Not cold?"

The man glances ruefully at himself. "Don't slander the gander."

Their mood has changed. The wife gazes up and down the beach, not seeing me. "It's too desolate out here. Let's go into the cottage."

Inside the cottage they copulate familiarly and routinely on one of the old stained mattresses, the bed springs discordant beneath them.

The next afternoon I see the little boy and the aunt arrive at the cottage. From the beach where he and his wife are lying on the sand, the man summons the boy and the aunt with his arm. The aunt is provoked by the prospect of walking across the sand, but the boy pulls her with him in his eagerness to reach his parents.

The man becomes a whirling dervish of welcome, seizes the boy and overwhelms him with shouted enthusiasm for the beach, the cottage, the ocean, the waves. "We'll ride the waves— just like big fishes." To the man's irritation, the boy is startled by the water talk and retreats to the aunt.

"He's too young," the aunt says firmly. The boy burrows his head in the folds of her dress.

The man shouts furiously: "Will you let me raise my own son!" He reaches for the boy, snaps him free from the aunt's grasp and runs with him into the water. The boy screams in fear, his legs kicking and arms flailing. The aunt shrieks, and the wife calls angrily to her husband.

The cold water and the boy's terror sap the man's determination. He carries the boy back to the two women. "Here," he says to the aunt, but the wife seizes the child and clasps him to her. The child cries loudly in punitive anger. Rising, the aunt turns away and strides across the sand toward the cottage. The man kicks a shower of sand after her.

"You promised!" the wife cries. "You promised there wouldn't be any fighting up here."

"Fight? Who's fighting? I JUST WANT A BOY FOR A SON—NOT A SNIVELING LITTLE LADY!"

"You promised," the wife repeats. "You promised you wouldn't start that up here. You scared him yourself. How can you blame her for that?"

The man's anger dissipates. "I know. Cripes, aren't we even going to have a good vacation?" He kicks at the sand again.

I see the man's mother arrive the next day. "Hello darlings," she calls to them where they sit on the beach. The little boy runs to her. The grandmother runs back with him. She is panting.

The aunt says: "You ought not to run like that."

"At my age—you mean," the grandmother gasps. She brushes her cheek against her daughter-in-law's. "Hello, darling." She plops down on the sand, unsteady in the vigor of her actions.

Her son kisses her. "Are you all right?"

"Yes." She smoothes her skirt. "Well, what do you think of this place?"

"Great!" her son replies.

"The water seems awfully cold," his wife says.

"But good when you get used to it—as I remember," the mother-in-law declares. She smiles at her grandson. "Well, boy, how do you like this beach?"

The boy looks sullenly at his father. "I don't like it."

"Don't like it? Why it's a wonderful beach for a boy."

"I don't like it." The boy buries his head in his aunt's lap. The grandmother turns to her son. The father shrugs his shoulders.

"It's time for his nap," the wife says to the aunt.

"Can't he nap right here on the beach?" the grandmother asks.

"In the sun?" The aunt is incredulous.

Voyeur

The mother kisses the boy. "Have a good nap," she says. She herds the boy and the aunt off toward the cottage.

The grandmother glances at her son, her eyebrows raised and her mouth formed in a moue. Then she calls after the aunt: "Wait! I'll go with you. You can show me where to put my things.

Lying on the sand, husband and wife watch the threesome move toward the cottage, the aunt clinging to the boy, the boy holding his grandmother's hand. When the husband rolls over to face the ocean, the wife sits up, gather her knees under her chin.

"I don't think I can stand it," she says.

"Suffering mackerel!" the husband cries. "If I can stand it— have stood that desexed monster all these years—you can stand it! For creep's sake!"

The wife's expression is earnest. "I don't want to be unfair, unsympathetic, unkind, nor start a fight—BUT I REALLY CAN'T LIVE WITH YOUR MOTHER!"

"But I can live with your sister! ALL OUR CRABBY LIFE!"

The wife rises and steps off the blanket. Silently she watches the somersaulting waves. Finally she turns back to him. "It sounds equal, I know, but it isn't. I have lived with that de-sexed monster, as *you* call her, all my life. She raised me, fed me, clothed me, educated me, bartered her life for mine. Where can she go now? What can she do? She has no skills except in the home. Do we have the money to support her separately?"

The man groans and buries his head in the blanket.

"Your mother—your mother comes to you because she's out of husbands and lovers. She can support herself as an old woman anywhere."

The man, unboxed jack-in-the-box, bounds to his feet. "Great fish eyes! You're something. Put the old out to pasture. Terrific! Let them die at the hut on the edge of the clearing. Alone!" He waves his arms in frustration. "She's got no one but us and she thinks she's DYING!"

"Is she?" his wife asks.

"Dying?"

"Is she?"

"I don't know. I said she thinks she is—or may—or might—or will. How the great salt crud do I know?"

The wife smiles without humor. "Yet you want to be your mother's keeper."

"I can't turn away from my own mother." He grimaces in sardonic defeat. "She won't let me."

"O shit, WHY are there always these complications in our life," the wife says. "Why can't we just live our own lives?"

That evening there is trouble when the grandmother invites the boy to sleep with her. He happily accepts, but his mother insists that he sleep in his own bed in his aunt's room. He has a tantrum and scratches the aunt as she carries him off to their room.

The next day I watch the lines of struggle solidify. The grandmother rises early and walks back and forth along the beach, always well in sight of the cottage. After an hour she is joined by her son. "Shouldn't you at least be resting?" he asks.

She searches his eyes for feeling behind the words. Disappointed, she shows her disaffection by a quick forward stride. As he moves briskly to fall into step beside her, she says: "It's a matter of simple alternatives. Exorcism has been effective or it hasn't."

"You make the operation sound like black magic."

"That's the way it seems to me. Medicine is only a science when practiced on others. They die or survive by scientific principle. One never does oneself."

They walk on quietly until they are far from the cottage. Finally, she turns, and they begin to retrace their footsteps. "You have talked about me to your wife." The words do not form a question. "And she does not want to take me in."

His attempt to laugh is awkward. "Take you in? That sounds like charity. Or fraud. You're the one who's offering help—who made this possible." He waves his hand at the deserted beach.

"You're talking about money. I'm talking about something else. Or is it the aunt who doesn't want me?"

His facade splinters. "Wanting is not the question," he says in anguish. "Three women in one household! How is that possible?"

His mother stops walking to look into his face. "So it is you who does not want me."

"Why must you dramatize everything? No. It's not a question of wanting or not wanting. It's a problem of living! I'm surprised that you *do* want it." His eyes have been avoiding her but now he brings them up to hers in accusation. "You have always been an independent person.

She nods in acceptance as though the charge were praise. "You're my son," she says, and your son is my only grandson. I don't want to live this last part of my life in isolation from my flesh and blood."

"Isolation!" he exclaims. "There would be no isolation if you were in the same city. We could visit you. You could visit us."

"I want to be a part of your life, of my grandson's life. I don't want to die among strangers."

"How is that possible, mother, if we're nearby?"

"I can't force you to take me in, but I can force you to recognize what you do if you send me away."

"What are *you* trying to do?" He seizes her arm roughly. "Break up my marriage?" She frees her arm, walks away from him. In a moment he is running after her, calling: "Mother! Mother!" She stops. Sobbing, he throws himself on the sand at her feet. He clasps his arms about her legs, and she strokes his hair. After a while, he says: "Of course you don't have to leave us."

In the cottage, the aunt talks to the wife as the child draws ships on a pad. "I suppose he wants me to go now that *she's* here."

"No one wants you to go," says the wife.

"She wants to ruin the child the way she ruined *him*." The aunt walks over to the child and hugs him. "I won't let her, if I have to kill her."

"Sssh." The mother indicates the child.

The aunt leaves the child and looks out the window at the

beach. "There they are," she says. "They look more like lovers than mother and son." The wife hurries over to the window to see her husband kneeling on the sand, his arms about his mother who is stroking his hair. She turns from the window, her face flushed.

"You see," the aunt tells the wife, "she wants her precious boy all to herself."

That afternoon I watch them create two blanket camps twenty yards apart on the beach. Husband and grandmother garrison one; wife and aunt, the other. The boy wanders from blanket to blanket as grandmother and aunt vie for his attention. The parents enlist themselves in the struggle only to prevent lasting defeat for their camp. The husband and his mother strike their blanket first, and the grandmother tries to lure the boy back to the cottage with her. The boy finds their blandishments an amusing chance to tease, finally runs off to the cottage by himself.

The adults spend the next morning in household routines of formal courtesy. I watch the boy play moodily on the beach, searching for shells, making forms of sand, glancing often at the cottage. Picking up wet sand for his building, he elaborately avoids the waves.

In the afternoon, I see the grandmother arrive on the beach armed with a gaily colored ball. Soon afterwards her son joins her. Mother, aunt and boy come out on the beach together. The aunt spreads their blanket out on the sand at greater distance from the others than the day before, but the boy sees the ball and victory goes to the grandmother. The boy plays with the ball most of the afternoon while mother and aunt sit stiffly on their blanket. At last the boy falls asleep and the father carries him to the cottage.

The aunt lingers on the beach. "I'll come soon," she tells the mother, "but I want to bring in some shells for him." I see her wait until the mother is in the cottage. Then she walks over to where the boy's ball rolled after he last played with it. She looks up and down the beach, does not see me, picks up the ball and, concealing it in her arms from the cottage, carries it down to the water's edge. After a glance back at the cottage, she hurls the ball out into the water with an awkward, surprisingly powerful, spinsterish throw. Immediately afterwards she hurries across the sand to the cottage.

The husband and wife shouting in their room can be heard all over the beach. The grandmother joins the fray as the aunt rushes into the room to defend the mother. The boy, awakened, follows her and looks on in stunned horror.

"Take that child away!" shouts the grandmother to the aunt who slaps her face. The husband shoves the aunt away from his mother and the aunt trips on a chair and falls to the floor. The wife begins to pummel her husband, and his mother tries to protect him. They are all yelling. The boy puts his hands over his ears and runs sobbing from the room, out onto the beach, down to the water. He throws himself down on the sand.

The boy lies on the sand until a wave comes very close to him. I see him stand up slowly, staring at the wave tongues as they lick the sand. He lifts his eyes and sees the ball, buffeted by the surf a constant fifteen feet from the moving edge of the water. A little cry of dismay breaks from him. He takes a tentative step toward the ball, retreats, steps again. The waves keep up their teasing, moving the ball in and out, in and out, again and again. He grows bolder and steps out into the breaking water until it reaches his knees. He takes a further step, and a huge roller tumbles him head over heels. He regains his feet only to be caught by the undertow. Then he is out beyond the ball.

At the cottage, the adults have separated. The wife is looking for the boy. She comes out on the beach to call him. Her calls to alert the others of his disappearance. Cries for the boy resound across the sand. The mother is the first to identify the small object bubbling along on the tops of the waves.

I see husband, aunt and mother-in-law follow her in a mad race over the beach to the water. The wife plunges into the waves well in advance of her husband, loses her footing and becomes entangled in her skirt. Her husband reaches her, and with a frantic, despairing glance out to the boy, seizes her and drags her back toward the beach. She struggles to free herself, screaming for him to save the child. The husband shoves her out of the water onto the beach and plunges back into the surf. The aunt takes hold of the wife, prevents her from following him. The grandmother, both hands clasped to her chest, stands nearby, shivering.

I watch the panic of the father's struggle against the waves. They tease him with the boy as they did the boy with the ball. He misuses his strength in savage, desperate effort, realizes the error and tries to husband his strength.

The mother begins to scream and fights wildly to free herself from the aunt. The aunt's grip loosens and the mother jumps into the waves.

The grandmother falls to the sand, clutching her heart, gasping for breath. The aunt releases a long agonizing wail for help, looking in frenzy up and down the beach. She sees me and comes running toward me.

"O god!" she cries. "We need help!"

But I, I, of course, am not there.

Unmailed, Unwritten Letters

Joyce Carol Oates

from *Hudson Review*

DEAR MOTHER AND FATHER,

The weather is lovely here. It rained yesterday. Today the sky is blue. The trees are changing colors, it is October 20, I have got to buy some new clothes sometime soon, we've changed dentists, doctors, everything is lovely here and I hope the same with you. Greg is working hard as usual. The doctor we took Father to see, that time he hurt his back visiting here, has died and so we must change doctors. Dentists also. I want to change dentists because I can't stand to go back to the same dentist anymore. He is too much of a fixed point, a reference point. It is such a chore, changing doctors and dentists.

Why are you so far away in the Southwest? Is there something about the Southwest that lures old people? Do they see images there, shapes in the desert? Holy shapes? Why are you not closer to me, or farther away? In an emergency it would take hours or days for you to get to me. I think of the two of you in the Southwest, I see the highways going off into space and wonder at your courage, so late in life, to take on space. Father had all he could do to manage that big house of yours, and the lawn. Even with workers to help him it was terrifying, all that space, because he owned it. Maybe that was why it terrified him, because he owned it. Out in the Southwest I assume that no one owns anything. Do people even live there? Some people live there, I know. But I think of the Southwest as an optical illusion, sunshine and sand and a mountainous (mountainous?) horizon, with highways perfectly divided by their white center lines, leading off to Mars or the moon, unhurried. And there are animals, the designs of animals, mashed into the highways! The shape of a dog, a dog's pelty shadow, mashed into the hot, hot road—in mid-flight, so to speak, mid-leap, run over again and again by big trucks and retired people seeing America. That vastness would terrify me. I think of you and I think of protoplasm being drawn off into space, out there, out in the West, with no human limits to keep it safe.

Dear Marsha Katz,

Thank you for the flowers, white flowers, but why that delicate hint of death, all that fragrance wasted on someone like myself who is certain to go on living? Why are you pursuing me? Why in secrecy? (I see all the letters you write to your father, don't forget; and you never mention me in them.) Even if your father were my lover, which is not true and cannot be verified, why should you pursue me? Why did you sign the card with the flowers *Trixie?* I don't know anyone named Trixie! How could I know anyone named Trixie? It is a dog's name, a high school cheerleader's name, an aunt's name . . . why do you play these games, why do you pursue me?

Only ten years old, and too young for evil thoughts—do you look in your precocious heart and see only grit, the remains of things, a crippled shadow of a child? Do you see in all this the defeat of your Daughterliness? Do you understand that a Daughter, like a Mistress, must be feminine or all is lost, must keep up the struggle with the demonic touch of matter-of-fact irony that loses us all our men . . . ? I think you have lost, yes. A ten-year-old cannot compete with a thirty-year-old. Send me all the flowers you want. I pick them apart one by one, getting bits of petals under my fingernails, I throw them out before my husband gets home.

Nor did I eat that box of candies you sent. Signed "Uncle Bumble"!

Are you beginning to feel terror at having lost? Your father and I are not lovers, we hardly see each other any more, since last Wednesday and today is Monday, still you've lost because I gather he plans on continuing the divorce proceedings, long distance, and what exactly can a child do about that . . . ? I see all the letters you write him. No secrets. Your Cape Cod sequence was especially charming. I like what you did with that kitten, the kitten that is found dead on the beach! Ah, you clever little girl, even with your I.Q. of uncharted heights, you couldn't quite conceal from your father and me your attempt to make him think 1) the kitten suggests a little girl, namely you 2) its death suggests your pending, possible death, if Father does not return. Ah, how we laughed over that! . . . Well, no, we didn't laugh, he did not laugh, perhaps he did not even understand the trick you were playing . . . your father can be a careless, abrupt man, but things stick in his mind, you know that and so you write of a little white kitten, alive one day and dead the next, so you send me flowers for a funeral parlor, you keep me in your thoughts constantly so that I can feel a tug all the way here in Detroit, all the way from Boston, and I hate it, I hate that invisible pulling, tugging, that witch's touch of yours. . . .

Dear Greg,

We met about this time years ago. It makes me dizzy, it frightens me, to think of that meeting. Did so much happen, and yet nothing? Miscarriages, three or four, one loses count, and eight or nine sweet bumbling years—why do I use the word *bumbling*, it isn't a word I would ever use—and yet there is nothing there, if I go to your closet and open the door your clothes tell me as much as you do. You are a good man. A faithful husband. A subdued and excellent husband. The way you handled my parents alone would show how good you are, how excellent. . . . My friend X, the one with the daughter said to be a genius and the wife no one has ever seen, X couldn't handle my parents, couldn't put up with my father's talk about principles, the Principles of an Orderly Universe, which he sincerely believes in though he is an intelligent man. . . . X couldn't handle anything, anyone. He loses patience. He is vulgar. He watches himself swerve out of control but can't stop. Once, returning to his car, we found a ticket on the windshield. He snatched it and tore it up, very angry, and then when he saw my surprise he thought to make a joke of it—pretending to be tearing it with his teeth, a joke. And he is weak, angry men are weak. He lets me close doors on him. His face seems to crack, with sorrow, but he lets me walk away, why is he so careless and weak . . . ?

But I am thinking of us, our first meeting. An overheated apartment, graduate school . . . a girl in dark stockings, myself, frightened and eager, trying to be charming in a voice that didn't carry, a man in a baggy sweater, gentle, intelligent, a little perplexed, the two of us gravitating together, fearful of love and fearful of not loving, of not being loved. . . . So we met. The evening falls away, years fall away. I count only three miscarriages, really. The fourth a sentimental miscalculation.

My darling,

I am out somewhere, I see a telephone booth on a corner, the air is windy and too balmy for October. I won't go in the phone booth. Crushed papers, a beer bottle, a close violent stench. . . . I walk past it, not thinking of you. I am out of the house so that you can't call me and so that I need not think of you. Do you talk to your wife every night, still? Does she weep into your ear? How many nights have you lain together, you and that woman now halfway across the country, in Boston, weeping into a telephone? Have you forgotten all those nights?

Last night I dreamt about you mashed into a highway. More than dead. I had to wake Greg up, I couldn't stop trembling, I wanted to tell him of the waste, the waste of joy and love, your being mashed soundlessly into a road and pounded into a shape no one would recognize as yours. . . . Your face was gone. What will happen to me when your face is gone from this world?

I parked the car down here so that I could go shopping at Saks but I've been walking, I'm almost lost. The streets are dirty. A tin can lies on the sidewalk, near a vacant lot. Campbell's Tomato Soup. I am dressed in the suit you like, though it is a little baggy on me, it would be a surprise for someone driving past to see a lady in such a suit bend to pick up a tin can. . . . I pick the can up. The edge is jagged and rusty. No insects inside. Why would insects be inside, why bother with an empty can? Idly I press the edge of the lid against my wrist, it isn't sharp, it makes only a fine white line on my skin, not sharp enough to penetrate the skin.

Dear Greg,

I hear you walking downstairs. You are going outside, out into the back yard. I am tempted, heart pounding, to run to the window and spy on you. But everything is tepid, the universe is dense with molecules, I can't get up. My legs won't move. You said last night, "The Mayor told me to shut up in front of Arthur Grant. He told me to shut up." You were amused and hurt at the same time, while I was furious, wishing you were . . . were someone else, someone who wouldn't be amused and hurt, a good man, a subdued man, but someone else who would tell that bastard to go to hell. I am a wife, jealous for her husband.

Three years you've spent working for the Mayor, His Honor, dodging reporters downtown. Luncheons, sudden trips, press conferences, conferences with committees from angry parts of Detroit, all of Detroit angry, white and black, bustling, ominous. Three years. Now he tells you to shut up. All the lies you told for him, not knowing how to lie with dignity, he tells you to shut up, my body suffers as if on the brink of some terrible final expulsion of our love, some blood-smear of a baby. When a marriage ends who is left to understand it? No witnesses. No young girl in black stockings, no young man, all those witnesses gone, grown up, moved on, lost.

Too many people know you now, your private life is dwindling. You are dragged back again and again to hearings, commission meetings, secret meetings, desperate meetings, television interviews, interviews with kids from college newspapers. Everyone has a right to know everything! *What Detroit Has Done to Combat Slums. What Detroit Has Done to Prevent Riots* updated to *What Detroit Has Done to Prevent a Recurrence of the 1967 Riot.* You people are rewriting history as fast as history happens. I love you, I suffer for you, I lie here in a paralysis of love, sorrow, density, idleness, lost in my love for you, my shame for having betrayed you. . . . Why should slums be combatted? Once I wept to see photographs of kids playing in garbage heaps, now I weep at crazy sudden visions of my lover's body become only a body, I have no tears left for anyone else, for anything else. Driving in the city I have a sudden vision of my lover dragged along by a stranger's car, his body somehow caught up under the bumper or the fender of a car and dragged along, bleeding wildly in the street. . . .

My dear husband, betraying you was the most serious act of my life. Far more serious than marrying you. I knew my lover better when he finally became my lover than I knew you when you became my husband. I know him better, now, than I know you. You and I have lived together for eight years. Smooth coins, coins worn smooth by constant handling. . . . I am a woman trapped in love, in the terror of love. Paralysis of love. Like a great tortoise, trapped in a heavy death-like shell, a mask of the body pressing the body down to earth. . . . I went for a week without seeing him, an experiment. The experiment failed. No husband can keep his wife's love. So you walk out in the back yard, admiring the leaves, the sky, the flagstone terrace, you are a man whom betrayal would destroy and yet your wife betrayed you, deliberately.

To the Editor:

Anonymously and shyly I want to ask—why are white men so weak, so feeble? The other day I left a friend at his hotel and walked quickly, alone, to my car, and the eyes of black men around me moved onto me with a strange hot perception, seeing everything. They knew, seeing me, what I was. Tension rose through the cracks in the sidewalk. Where are white men who are strong, who see women in this way? The molecules in the air of Detroit are humming. I wish I could take a knife and cut out an important piece of my body, my insides, and hold it up . . . on a street corner, an offering. Then will they let me alone? The black men jostle one another on street corners, out of work and not wanting work, content to stare at me, knowing everything in me, not surprised. My lover, a white man, remains back at the hotel, his head in his hands because I have walked out, but he won't run after me, he won't follow me. *They* follow me. One of them bumped into me, pretending it was an accident. I want to cut up my body, I can't live in this body.

Next door to us a boy is out in his driveway, sitting down, playing a drum. Beating on a drum. Is he crazy? A white boy of about sixteen pounding on a drum. He wants to bring the city down with that drum and I don't blame him. I understand that vicious throbbing.

Dear Marsha Katz,

Thank you for the baby clothes. Keep sending me things, test your imagination. I feel that you are drowning. I sense a tightness in your chest, your throat. Are your eyes leaden with defeat, you ten-year-old wonder? How many lives do children relive at the moment of death?

Dear Mother and Father,

The temperature today is   . Yesterday at this time,   . Greg has been very busy as usual with   ,   ,   . This weekend we must see the   's, whom you have met. How is the weather there? How is your vacation? Thank you for the postcard from   . I had not thought lawns would be green there.

. . . The Mayor will ask all his aides for resignations, signed. Some he will accept and others reject. A kingly man, plump and divorced. Why can't I tell you about my husband's job,

about my life, about anything real? Scandals fall on the head
of my husband's boss, reading the paper is torture, yet my
husband comes home and talks seriously about the future,
about improvements, as if no chaos is waiting. No picketing
ADC mothers, no stampede to buy guns, no strangled black
babies found in public parks. In the midst of this my husband is clean and untouched, innocent, good. He has dedicated
his life to helping others. I love him but cannot stop betraying
him, again and again, having reclaimed my life as my own to
throw away, to destroy, to lose. My life is my own. I keep on
living.

My darling,

It is one-thirty and if you don't call by two, maybe you won't
call, I know that you have a seminar from two to four, maybe
you won't call today and everything will end. My heart pounds
bitterly, in fear, in anticipation? Your daughter sent me some
baby clothes, postmarked Boston, I understand her hatred, but
one thing: how much did you tell your wife about me? About
my wanting children? You told her you no longer loved her
and couldn't live with her, that you loved another woman who
could not marry you, but . . . did you tell her this other
woman had no children? And what else?

I will get my revenge on you.

I walk through the house in a dream, in a daze. I am sinking
slowly through the floor of this expensive house, a married
woman in a body grown light as a shell, empty as a shell. My
body has no other life in it, only its own. What you discharge
in me is not life but despair. I can remember my body having
life, holding it. It seemed a trick, a feat that couldn't possibly
work: like trying to retain liquid up a reed, turning the reed
upside down. The doctor said, "Babies are no trouble. Nothing." But the liquid ran out. All liquid runs out of me. That
first week, meeting with you at the Statler, everything ran out
of me like blood. I alarmed you, you with your nervous sense
of fate, your fear of getting cancer, of having a nervous breakdown, I caused you to say stammering *But what if you get*

pregnant? I am not pregnant but I feel a strange tingling of life, a tickling, life at a distance, as if the spirit of your daughter is somehow in me, lodged in me. She sucks at my insides with her pinched jealous lips, wanting blood. My body seeks to discharge her, magically.

My dear husband,

I wanted to test being alone. I went downtown to the library, the old library. I walked past the hotel where he and I have met, my lover and I, but we were not meeting today and I was alone, testing myself as a woman alone, a human being alone. The library was filled with old men. Over seventy, dressed in black, with white shirts. Black and white: a reading room of old men, dressed in black and white.

I sat alone at a table. Some of the old men glanced at me. In a dream I began to leaf through a magazine, thinking *Now I am leafing through a magazine; this is expected.* Why can't I be transformed to something else—to a mask, a shell, a statue? I glance around shyly, trying to gauge the nature of the story I am in. Is it tragic or only sad? The actors in this play all seem to be wearing masks, even I am wearing a mask, I am never naked. My nakedness, with my lover, is a kind of mask—something he sees, something I can't quite believe in. Women who are loved are in perpetual motion, dancing. We dance and men follow to the brink of madness and death, but what of us, the dancers?—when the dancing ends we stand back upon our heels, back upon our heels, dazed and hurt. Beneath the golden cloth on our thighs is flesh and flesh hurts. Men are not interested in the body, which feels pain, but in the rhythm of the body as it goes about its dance, the body of a woman who cannot stop dancing.

A confession. In Ann Arbor last April, at the symposium, I fell in love with a man. The visiting professor from Boston University—a man with black-rimmed glasses, Jewish, dark-eyed, dark-haired, nervous and arrogant and restless. Drumming his fingers. Smoking too much. (And you, my husband, were sane enough to give up smoking five years ago.) A student stood up in the first row and shouted out something and it was he, my lover, the man who would become my lover, who stood up in turn and shouted something back . . . it all happened so fast, astounding everyone, even the kid who reported for the campus newspaper didn't catch the exchange. How many men could handle a situation like that, being wilder and more profane than a heckler? . . . He was in the group at the party afterward, your friend Bryan's house. All of you talked at once, excited and angry over the outcome of the symposium, nervous at the sense of agitation in the air, the danger, and he and I wandered to the hostess's table, where food was set out. We made pigs of ourselves, eating. He picked out the shrimp and I demurely picked out tiny flakes of dough with miniature asparagus in them. Didn't you notice us? Didn't you notice this dark-browed man with the glasses that kept slipping down his nose, with the untidy black hair? We talked. We ate. I could see in his bony knuckles a hunger that would never be satisfied. And I, though I think I am starving slowly to death now, I leapt upon the food as if it were a way of getting at him, of drawing him into me. We talked. We wandered around the house. He looked out a window, drawing a curtain aside, at the early spring snow-fall, falling gently outside, and he said that he didn't know why he had come to this part of the country, he was frightened of travelling, of strangers. He said that he was very tired. He seduced me with the slump of his shoulders. And when he turned back to me we entered another stage of the evening, having grown nervous and brittle with each other, the two of us, suddenly conscious of being together. My eyes grew hot and searing. I said carelessly that he must come over to Detroit sometime, we could have lunch, and he said at once, "I'd like that very much . . ." and then paused. Silence.

Later, in the hotel, in the cheap room he rented, he confessed to me that seeing my face had been an experience for him—did he believe in love at first sight, after all? something so childish? It had been some kind of love, anyway. We talked about our lives, about his wife, about my husband, and then he swung onto another subject, talking about his daughter for forty-five

minutes. . . . A genius, a ten-year-old prodigy. I am brought
low, astounded. I want to cry out to him, *But what about me!
Don't stop thinking about me!* At the age of six his daughter
was writing poems, tidy little poems, like Blake's. *Like Blake's?
Yes.* At the age of eight she was publishing those poems.

No, I don't want to marry him. I'm not going to marry him.
What we do to each other is too violent, I don't want it brought
into marriage and domesticated, nor do I want him to see me
at unflattering times of the day . . . getting up at three in the
morning to be sick, a habit of mine. He drinks too much. He
reads about the connection between smoking and death, and
turns the page of the newspaper quickly. Superstitious, stubborn. In April he had a sore throat, that was why he spoke so
hoarsely on the program . . . but a month later he was no
better: "I'm afraid of doctors," he said. This is a brilliant man,
the father of a brilliant child? We meet nowhere, at an unimagi-
native point X, in a hotel room, in the anonymous drafts of air
from blowers that never stop blowing, the two of us yearning
to be one, in this foreign dimension where anything is possible.
Only later, hurrying to my car, do I feel resentment and fury
at him . . . why doesn't he buy me anything, why doesn't he
get a room for us, something permanent? And hatred for him
rises in me in long shuddering surges, overwhelming me. I
don't want to marry him. Let me admit the worst—anxious not
to fall in love with him, I think of not loving him at the very
moment he enters me, I think of him already boarding a plane
and disappearing from my life, with relief, I think with pity of
human beings and this sickness of theirs, this desire for unity.
Why this desire for unity, why? We walk out afterward, into the
sunshine or into the smog. Obviously we are lovers. Once I
saw O'Leary, from the Highway Commission, he nodded and
said a brisk hello to me, ignored my friend, obviously we are
lovers, anyone could tell. We walked out in the daylight, looking for you. That day, feverish and aching, we were going to
tell you everything. He was going to tell his wife everything.
But nothing happened . . . we ended up in a cocktail lounge,
we calmed down. The air conditioning calmed us. On the

street we passed a Negro holding out pamphlets to other Negroes but drawing them back when whites passed. I saw the headline—*Muslin Killed in Miami Beach by Fascist Police*. A well-dressed Negro woman turned down a pamphlet with a toothy amused smile—none of that junk for her! My lover didn't even notice.

Because he is not my husband I don't worry about him. I worry about my own husband, whom I own. I don't own this man. I am thirty and he is forty-one, to him I am young, what a laugh, I don't worry about his coughing, his drinking (sometimes over the telephone I can hear ice cubes tinkling in a glass—he drinks to get the courage to call me), his loss of weight, his professional standing. He didn't return to his job in Boston, but stayed on here. A strange move. The department at Michigan considered it a coup to get him, this disintegrating, arrogant man, they were willing to pay him well, a man who has already made enemies there. No, I don't worry about him.

On a television program he was moody and verbose, moody and silent by turns. Smokes too much. Someone asked him about the effect of something on something—Vietnam on the presidential election, I think—and he missed subtleties, he sounded distant, vague. Has lost passion for the truth. He has lost his passion for politics, discovering in himself a passion for me. It isn't my fault. On the street he doesn't notice things, he smiles slowly at me, complimenting me, someone brushes against him and he doesn't notice, what am I doing to this man? Lying in his arms I am inspired to hurt him. I say that we will have to give this up, these meetings; too much risk, shame. What about my husband, what about his wife? (A deliberate insult—I know he doesn't love his wife.) I can see at once that I've hurt him, his face shows everything, and as soon as this registers in both of us I am stunned with the injustice of what I've done to him, I must erase it, cancel it out, undo it, I caress his body in desperation. . . . Again and again. A pattern. What do I know about caressing the bodies of men? I've known only two men in my life. My husband and his successor. I have never wanted to love anyone, the strain and risk are too great, yet I have

fallen in love for the second time in my life and this time the
sensation is terrifying, bitter, violent. It ends the first cycle,
supplants all that love, erases all that affection—destroys everything. I stand back dazed, flat on my heels, the dance being
over. I will not move on into another marriage. I will die
slowly in this marriage rather than come to life in another.

Dear Mrs. Katz,

I received your letter of October 25 and I can only say

I don't know how to begin this letter except to tell you

Your letter is here on my desk. I've read it over again and
again all morning. Is it true, yes, that I have made the acquaintance of a man who is evidently your husband, though he has
not spoken of you. We met through mutual friends in Ann
Arbor and Detroit. Your informant at the University is obviously trying to upset you, for her own reasons. I assume it is a
woman—who else would write you such a letter? I know nothing
of your personal affairs. Your husband and I have only met a
few times, socially. What do you want from me?

And your daughter, tell your daughter to let me alone!

Thank you both for thinking of me. I wish I could be equal
to your hatred. But the other day an old associate of my husband's, a bitch of a man, ran into me in the Fisher lobby and
said, "What's happened to you—you look terrible! You've lost
weight!" He pinched the waist of my dress, drawing it out to
show how it hung loose on me, he kept marvelling over how
thin I am, not releasing me. A balding, pink-faced son of a
bitch, who has made himself rich by being on the board of
supervisors for a county north of here, stuffing himself at the
trough. I know all about him. A sub-politician, never elected.
But I trust the eyes of these sub-men, their hot keen perception.
Nothing escapes them. "One month ago," he said, "you were a
beautiful woman." Nothing in my life has hurt me as much as
that remark, *One month ago you were a beautiful woman.* . . .

Were you ever beautiful? He says not. So he used you, he used
you up. That isn't my fault. You say in your letter—thank you
for typing it, by the way—that I could never understand your
husband, his background of mental instability, his weaknesses,

his penchant (your word) for blaming other people for his own faults. Why tell me this? He isn't going to be my husband. I have a husband. Why should I betray my husband for yours, your nervous guilty hypochondriac husband? The first evening we met, believe it or not, he told me about his *hurts*— people who've hurt him deeply! "The higher you go in a career the more people take after you, wanting to bring you down," he told me. And listen: "The worst hurt of my life was when my first book came out, and an old professor of mine, a man I had idolized at Columbia, reviewed it. He began by saying *Bombarded as we are by prophecies in the guise of serious historical research* . . . and my heart was broken." We were at a party but apart from the other people, we ate, he drank, we played a game with each other that made my pulse leap, and certainly my pulse leaped to hear a man, a stranger, speak of his heart being broken—where I come from men don't talk like that! I told him a *hurt* of my own, which I've never told anyone before: "The first time my mother saw my husband, she took me aside and said *Can't you tell him to stand up straighter?* and my heart was broken. . . ."

And so, with those words, I had already committed adultery, betraying my husband to a stranger.

Does he call you every night? I am jealous of those telephone calls. What if he changes his mind and returns to you, what then? When he went to the Chicago convention I'm sure he telephoned you constantly (he telephoned me only three times, the bastard) and joked to you about his fear of going out into the street. "Jesus, what if somebody smashes in my head, there goes my next book!" he said over the phone, but he wasn't kidding me. I began to cry, imagining him beaten up, bloody, far away from me. Why does he joke like that? Does he joke like that with you?

Dear Mother and Father,

My husband Greg is busy with   . Doing well. Not fired. Pressure on, pressure off. Played golf with   . I went to a new doctor yesterday, a woman. I had made an appointment to go to a man but lost my courage, didn't show up. Better a woman. She examined me, she looked at me critically and said, "Why are you trying to starve yourself?" *To keep myself from feeling love, from feeling lust, from feeling anything at all.* I told her I didn't know I was starving myself. I had no appetite. Food sickened me . . . how could I eat? She gave me a vitamin shot that burned me, like fire. Things good for you burn like fire, shot up into you, no escape. You would not like my lover, you would take me aside and say *Jews are very brilliant and talented, yes, but. . . .*

I am surviving at half-tempo. A crippled waltz tempo. It is only my faith in the flimsiness of love that keeps me going—I know this will end. I've been waiting for it to end since April, having faith. Love can't last. Even lust can't last. I loved my husband and now I do not love him, we never sleep together, that's through. Since he isn't likely to tell you that, I will. He would never even think about it.

Lloyd Burt came to see my husband the other day, downtown. Eleven in the morning and already drunk. His kid had been stopped in Grosse Pointe, speeding. The girl with him knocked out on pills. *He* had no pills on him, luckily. Do you remember Lloyd? Do you remember any of us? I am your daughter. Do you regret having had a daughter? I do not regret having no children, not now. Children, more children, children upon children, protoplasm upon protoplasm. . . . Once I thought I couldn't bear to live without having children, now I can't bear to live at all, I must be the wife of a man I can't have, I don't even want children from him, I sit here in my room with my head and body aching with a lust that has become metaphysical and skeptical and bitter, living on month after month, cells dividing and heating endlessly. I don't regret having no children. I don't thank you for having me. No gratitude in me, nothing. No, I feel no gratitude. I can't feel gratitude.

My dear husband,

I want to tell you everything. I am in a motel room, I've just taken a bath. How can I keep a straight face telling you this?

Sat in the bath tub for an hour, not awake, not asleep, the water was very hot. . . .

I seem to want to tell you something else, about Sally Rodgers. I am light-headed, don't be impatient. I met Sally at the airport this afternoon, she was going to New York, and she saw me with a man, a stranger to her, the man who is the topic of this letter, the crucial reason for this letter. . . . Sally came right up to me and started talking, exclaiming about her bad fortune, her car had been stolen last week! then when she and a friend took her boat out of the yacht club and docked it at a restaurant on the Detroit River, she forgot to take the keys out and someone stole her boat! twenty-thousand dollars' worth of boat, a parting gift from her ex-husband, pirated away down-river. She wore silver eyelids, silver stockings, attracting attention not from men but from small children, who stared. My friend, my lover, did not approve of her—her clanking jewelry made his eye twitch.

I am twenty miles from Detroit. In Detroit the multiplication of things is too brutal, I think it broke me down. Weak, thin, selfish, a wreck, I have become oblivious to the deaths of other people (Robert Kennedy was murdered since I became this man's mistress, but I had no time to think of him—I put the thought of his death aside, to think of later. No time now.) Leaving him and walking in Detroit, downtown, on those days we met to make love, I began to understand what love is. Holding a man between my thighs, my knees, in my arms, one single man out of all this multiplication of men, this confusion, this din of human beings. So it is we choose someone. Someone chooses us. I admit that if he did not love me so much I couldn't love him. It would pass. But a woman has no choice, let a man love her and she must love him, if the man is strong enough. I stopped loving you, I am a criminal. . . . I see myself sinking again and again beneath his body, those heavy shoulders with tufts of dark hair on them, again and again pressing my mouth against his, wanting something from him, betraying you, giving myself up to that throbbing that arises out of my heartbeat and builds to madness and then subsides again, slowly, to become my ordinary heartbeat again, the heartbeat of an ordinary body from which divinity has fled.

Flesh with an insatiable soul. . . .

You would hear in a few weeks, through your innumerable far-flung cronies, that my lover's daughter almost died of aspirin poison, a ten-year-old girl with an I.Q. of about 200. But she didn't die. She took aspirin because her father was leaving her, divorcing her mother. The only gratitude I can feel is for her not having died. . . . My lover, whom you hardly know (he's the man of whom you said that evening "He certainly can talk!") telephoned me to give me this news, weeping over the phone. A man weeping. A man weeping turns a woman's heart to stone. I told him I would drive out at once, I'd take him to the airport. He had to catch the first plane home and would be on stand-by, at the airport. So I drove to Ann Arbor to get him. I felt that we were already married and that passion had raced through us and left us, years ago, as soon as I saw him lumbering to the car, a man who has lost weight in the last few months but who carries himself a little clumsily, out of absent-mindedness. He wore a dark suit, rumpled. His necktie pulled away from his throat. A father distraught over his daughter belongs to mythology. . . .

Like married people, like conspirators, like characters in a difficult scene hurrying their lines, uncertain of the meaning of lines. . . . "It's very thoughtful of you to do this," he said, and I said, "What else can I do for you? Make telephone calls? Anything?" *Should I go along with you?* So I drive him to the airport. I let him out at the curb, he hesitates, not wanting to go without me, he says, "But aren't you coming in . . . ?" and I see fear in his face, I tell him yes, yes, but I must park the car. This man, so abrupt and insulting in his profession, a master of whining rhetoric, stares at me in bewilderment as if he cannot remember why I have brought him here to let him out at the United Airlines terminal, why I am eager to drive away. "I can't park here," I tell him sanely, "I'll get a ticket." He respects all minor law; he nods and backs away. It takes me ten minutes to find a parking place. All this time I am sweating in the late October heat, thinking that his daughter is going to win after all, has already won. Shouldn't I just drive home and leave him, put an end to it? A bottle of aspirin was all it took. The tears I might almost shed are not tears of shame or regret but tears of anger—that child has taken my lover from me. That child! I don't cry, I don't allow myself to cry, I drive all the way through a parking lot without finding a place and say to the girl at the booth, who puts her hand out expecting a dime, "But I couldn't find a place! I've driven right through! This isn't fair!" Seeing my hysteria she relents, opens the gate, lets me through. *Once a beautiful woman,* she is thinking. I try another parking lot.

Inside the terminal a moment of panic—what if he has already left? Then he hurries to me. I take his arm. He squeezes my hand. Both of us very nervous, agitated. "They told me I can probably make the two-fifteen, can you wait with me?" he says. His face, now so pale, is a handsome man's face gone out of control; a pity to look upon it. In a rush I feel my old love for him, hopeless. I begin to cry. Silently, almost without tears. A girl in a very short skirt passes us with a smile—lovers, at their age! "You're not to blame," he says, very nervous, "she's just a child and didn't know what she was doing—please don't blame yourself! It's my fault—" But a child tried to commit suicide, shouldn't someone cry? I am to blame. She is hurting me across the country. I have tried to expel her from life and she, the baby, the embryo, stirs with a will of her own and chooses death calmly. . . . "But she's going to recover," I say to him for the twentieth time, "isn't she? You're sure of that?" He reassures me. We walk.

The airport is a small city. Outside the plate glass airplanes rise and sink without effort. Great sucking vacuums of power, enormous wings, windows brilliant with sunlight. We look on unamazed. To us these airplanes are unspectacular. We walk around the little city, walking fast and then slowing down, wandering, holding hands. It is during one of those strange lucky moments that lovers have—he lighting a cigarette—that Sally comes up to us. We are not holding hands at that moment.

She talks, bright with attention for my friend, she herself being divorced and not equipped to live without a man, he smiles nervously, ignoring her, watching people hurry by with their luggage. She leaves. We glance at each other, understanding each other. Nothing to say. *My darling!* . . .

Time does not move quickly. I am sweating again, I hope he won't notice, he is staring at me in that way . . . that way that frightens me. I am not equal to your love, I want to tell him. Not equal, not strong enough. I am ashamed. Better for us to say goodbye. A child's corpse between us? A few hundred miles away, in Boston, are a woman and a child I have wronged, quite intentionally; aren't these people real? But he stares at me, the magazine covers on a newsstand blur and wink, I feel that everything is becoming a dream and I must get out of here, must escape from him, before it is too late. . . . "I should leave," I tell him. He seems not to hear. He is sick. Not sick, frightened. He shows too much. He takes my hand, caresses it, pleading in silence. A terrible sensation of desire rises in me, surprising me. I don't want to feel desire for him! I don't want to feel it for anyone, I don't want to feel anything at all! I don't want to be drawn to an act of love, or even to think about it, I want freedom, I want the smooth sterility of coins worn out from friendly handling rubbing together, I want to say goodbye to love at the age of thirty, not being strong enough for it. A woman in the act of love feels no joy but only terror, a parody of labor, giving birth. Torture. Heartbeat racing at 160, 180 beats a minute, where is joy in this, what is this deception, this joke, isn't the body itself a joke?

He leads me somewhere, along a corridor. Doesn't know where he is going. People head toward us, with suitcases. A soldier on leave from Vietnam, we don't notice, a Negro woman weeping over another soldier, obviously her son, my lover does not see. A man brushes against me and with exaggerated fear I jump to my lover's side . . . but the man keeps on walking, it is nothing. My lover strokes my damp hand. "You won't . . . you're not thinking of. . . . What are you thinking of?" he whispers. Everything is open in him, everything. He is not ashamed of the words he says, of his fear, his pleading. No irony in him, this ironic man. And I can hear myself saying that we must put an end to this, it's driving us both crazy and there is no future, nothing ahead of us, but I don't say these words or anything like them. We walk along. I am stunned. I feel a heavy, ugly desire for him, for his body. I want him as I've wanted him many times before, when our lives seemed simpler, when we were both deluded about what we were doing . . . both of us thought, in the beginning, that no one would care if we fell in love . . . not my husband, not his family. I don't know why. Now I want to say goodbye to him but nothing comes out, nothing. I am still crying a little. It is not a weapon of mine—it is an admission of defeat. I am not a woman who cries well. Crying is a confession of failure, a giving in. I tell him no, I am not thinking of anything, only of him. I love him. I am not thinking of anything else.

We find ourselves by Gate 10. What meaning has Gate 10 to us? People are lingering by it, obviously a plane has just taken off, a stewardess is shuffling papers together, everything is normal. I sense normality and am drawn to it. We wander on. We come to a doorway, a door held open by a large block of wood. Where does that lead to? A stairway. The stairway is evidently not open. We can see that it leads up to another level, a kind of runway, and though it is not open he takes my hand and leads me to the stairs. In a delirium I follow him, why not? The airport is so crowded that we are alone and anonymous. He kicks the block of wood away, wisely. We are alone. On this stairway—which smells of disinfectant and yet is not very clean—my lover embraces me eagerly, wildly, he kisses me, kisses my damp cheeks, rubs his face against mine. I half-fall, half-sit on the stairs. He begins to groan, or to weep. He presses his face against me, against my breasts, my body. It is like wartime—a battle is going on outside, in the corridor. Hundreds of people! A world of people jostling one another! Here, in a dim stairway, clutching each other, we are oblivious to their deaths. But I want to be good! What have I wanted in my life, except to be good? To lead a simple, good, intelligent life? He kisses my knees, my thighs, my stomach. I embrace him against me. Everything has gone wild, I am seared with the desire to be unfaithful to a husband who no longer exists, nothing else matters except this act of unfaithfulness, I feel that I am a character in a story, a plot, who has not understood until now exactly what is going to happen to her. Selfish, eager, we come together and do not breathe, we are good friends and anxious to help each other, I am particularly anxious to help him, my soul is sweated out of me in those two or three minutes that we cling together, in love. Then, moving from me, so quickly exhausted, he puts his hands to his face and seems to weep, without tears, while I feel my eyelids closing slowly upon the mangled length of my body. . . .

This is a confession but part of it is blacked out. Minutes pass in silence, mysteriously. It is those few minutes that pass after we make love that are most mysterious to me, uncanny. And then we cling to each other again, like people too weak to stand by ourselves; we are sick in our limbs but warm with affection, very good friends, the kind of friends who tell each other only good news. He helps me to my feet. We laugh. Laughter weakens me, he has to hold me, I put my arms firmly around his neck and we kiss, I am ready to give up all my life for him, just to hold him like this. My body is all flesh. There is nothing empty about us, only a close space, what appears to be a stairway in some public place. . . . He draws my hair back from my face, he stares at me. It is obvious that he loves me.

When we return to the public corridor no one had missed us. It is strangely late, after three. This is a surprise, I am really surprised, but my lover is more businesslike and simply asks at the desk—the next plane? to Boston? what chance of his getting on? His skin is almost ruddy, with pleasure. I can see what pleasure does to a man. But now I must say goodbye, I must leave. He holds my hand. I linger. We talk seriously and quietly in the middle of the great crowded floor about his plans—he will stay in Boston as long as he must, until things are settled; he will see his lawyer; he will talk it over, *talk it over*, with his wife and his daughter, he will not leave until they understand why he has to leave. . . . I want to cry out at him, *Should you come back?* but I can't say anything. Everything in me is a curving to submission, in spite of what you, my husband, have always thought.

Finally . . . he boards a plane at four. I watch him leave. He looks back at me, I wave, the plane taxis out the runway and rises . . . no accident, no violent ending. There is nothing violent about us, everything is natural and gentle. Walking along the long corridor I bump into someone, a woman my own age. I am suddenly dizzy. She says, "Are you all right?" I turn away, ashamed. I am on fire! My body is on fire! I feel his semen stirring in my loins, that rush of heat that always makes me pause, staring into the sky or at a wall, at something blank to mirror the blankness in my mind . . . stunned I feel myself so heavily a body, so lethargic with the aftermath of passion. How did I hope to turn myself into a statue, into the constancy of a soul? No hope. The throbbing in my loins has not yet resolved itself into the throbbing of my heart. A woman does not forget so quickly, nothing lets her forget. I am transparent with heat. I walk on, feeling my heart pound weakly, feeling the moisture between my legs, wondering if I will ever get home. My vision seems blotched. The air—air-conditioning—is humming, unreal. It is not alien to me but a part of my own confusion, a long expulsion of my own breath. What do I look like, making love? Is my face distorted, am I ugly? Does he see me? Does he judge? Or does he see nothing but beauty, transported in love as I am, helpless?

I can't find the car. Which parking lot? The sun is burning. A man watches me, studies me. I walk fast to show that I know what I'm doing. And if the car is missing, stolen . . . ? I search through my purse, noting how the lining is soiled, ripped. Fifty thousand dollars in the bank and no children and I can't get around to buying a new purse, everything is soiled, ripped, worn-out . . . the keys are missing . . . only wadded tissue, a sweetish smell, liquid stiffening on the tissue . . . everything hypnotizes me. . . . I find the keys, my vision swims. I will never get home.

My knees are trembling. There is an ocean of cars here at Metropolitan Airport. Families stride happily to cars, get in, drive away. I wander around, staring. I must find my husband's car in order to get home. . . . I check in my purse again, panicked. No, I haven't lost the keys. I take the keys out of my purse to look at them. The key to the ignition, to the trunk, to the front door of the house. All there. I look around slyly and see, or think I see, a man watching me. He moves behind a car. He is walking away. My body still throbs from the love of another man, I can't concentrate on a stranger, I lose interest and forget what I am afraid of. . . .

The heat gets worse. Thirty, forty, forty-five minutes pass. . . . I have given up looking for the car. . . . I am not lost, I am still heading home in my imagination, but I have given up looking for the car. I turn terror into logic. I ascend the stairway to the wire-guarded overpass that leads back to the terminal, walking sensibly, and keep on walking until I come to one of the airport motels. A small city, this motel, the bizarre made domestic. I ask them for a room. A single. Why not? Before I can go home I must bathe, I must get the odor of this man out of me, I must clean myself. I take a room, I close the door to the room behind me, alone, I go to the bathroom and run a tubful of water. . . .

And if he doesn't call me from Boston then all is finished, at an end. What good luck, to be free again and alone, the way I am alone in this marvelous empty motel room! the way I am alone in this bathtub, cleansing myself of him, of every cell of him!

My darling,

You have made me so happy. . . .

The Naked Man

Bill Rodriguez

from *Minnesota Review*

Tried again today to write about the naked man. Psyched myself up feverishly before I touched the keys—though maybe it was just staring out the cracked window at the death-colored grays and browns of the city in the rain that kept the mood reverberating, or maybe some sound was still in my ears from Carol's crying last night—at any rate, my head was humming like after I first found out about it Friday morning. I had to change my sopping shirt when I was through. Didn't even read it this afternoon. Just tore it into postage-stamp pieces, carried them down the hall cupped in my hands like some bloody witness and flushed the foetus down the toilet. Really thought I could work it into the book, or at least a story this time. Not recollected after sufficient tranquility. Then too, it's like attempting to build a human being when you just have the entrails heaped before you. Was stupid to destroy that draft, Karl. Stupid. But no real loss since it's still clawing about inside your head. Damn it to hell, but it is.

That sorry spade queen down the hall slinked up to my open door again earlier this morning when he heard my typewriter. To borrow some instant coffee and sigh and survey my shirtless and sweating body. Old unrequited courtly love must have been a drag. Thought the pro fags around here all had to hang kimonos. This sweetheart's resorted to a more novel gift-wrapping (dealing in such a competitive market): a saffron and orange sari, to let bulge his modest pudendum. All squeaks and smiles. Exchanged friendlies, directed him to the cupboard. Carol slept over and was staring up from the bed in the corner with just a sheet over her. Wonder how he'd cope at a Melina Mercouri movie: he left the floor an inch when he caught Mary Poppins over there, as though she were coming at him with a bear trap between her legs. Twitched to the cupboard and out the door without looking at me. Carol really amazed me: bugged at my letting him in with her like that. Couldn't dig what I found so funny about it all, embarrassing the poor thing, not to mention her. Eventually worked her up to a restrained smile. The day she can laugh on her own over something like that is the day I weep tears of joy for her. Will she understand why she's laughing by then?

Tried to find out more about the naked man. Tom said he'd talk to the reporter he had cover it. Got an assignment out of the call, too. Beauty Pageants shouldn't be expended on somebody getting his, they've got enough horny photogs on the staff. Could have used it last month when atrophy was threatening. Then again, the libido has been down since that morning last week and I'll be out soon unless I replenish. Man, didn't know anything could affect me like that—like having a 500 hp. high-performance engine eager for opening out and not being able to gear it up to top speed. Passenger's been understanding and all, but you know you've given her better rides. He also wants to see my beach transparencies for a Sunday cover. The cash would arrive conveniently, I'm sure, just as Mr. Econopolous is dragging me down the stairs with the typewriter still clattering in my lap. Bump, bump, bump. Frock-coat Milne to read at mother's shriveled breasts. Good market among ghetto readers? Karl, with your score and a quarter behind you what would you give to be able again to read Winnie-the-Pooh with Carol's wide-eyed, though myopic, enchantment, without blending the fantasy with the more murky colors of reality? Lewis Carroll's cynical eyes saw his fantasies not only on his angry level but also as Alice was to see them, so maybe the thing is to deal in complements. Yes, bittersweet chocolate has always been your favorite.

Second rejection slip this week. Spent the afternoon at an office window with a camera, waiting for a girl to jump. Enough of that. The Beauty Pageant this morning: two dozen nubile late-teeny boppers sticking out their chests in vying for the definition "Miss Pointy-Boob 1968." Ten pork-jowled Chamber of Commerce phlegmers playing 3-D skin flicks on their retinas and nudging one another as the firm flesh titters by. And criterion? Why they actually took points off if a girl had space between her thighs when her knees were together. Buy Easter Seals! Man, what the hell are a woman's knees doing together anyway? So between their Greek predilection for symmetry and their American fetish for motherly mammeries they picked the kid with the most even teeth, most retroussé nose and most conical ice cream cones under her bathing suit, who unwired into a hand-at-mouth round-shouldered slouch when she was announced and fell into bouncing squeals. They passed up the Puerto Rican chick with the haughty, hungry eyes and hair to her waist and the pepper-headed black girl with the panther-sleek body that made the others look like eight-year-olds. They defined Beauty as bubblegum-snapping vapid frippery. Would like to see a beauty contest judged and composed of paraplegics and lepers so the definition would have to work around the obvious for once. Just how lucky am I that Carol has such a soft, delicate beauty? Aren't I bound to over-appreciate the soul when it's in such a lovely body? Come now, Karl. Come off it. That girl so lovely up there in her fluttering yellow summer dress, still "beautiful" by pedestrian standards an instant before impact, after which it was impossible to tell what color the dress was: how strongly would it have affected you if she had been an obese—possibly soulful—hairy-eared grandmother? Go ahead, convince yourself you wouldn't be revulsed if Carol were to unbandage in your bed after a deforming accident—go ahead. Your kind of liar is the worst, you fool. He always ends up self-righteous as well as self-deceiving.

Carol's work is getting to her again. Picked her up at the office and drove her downtown for a bite, thinking of an unhassled evening. Short-lived hope. Couldn't see working it up to another well-why-the-hell-don't-you-become-a-librarian-or-something-if-you-can't-take-it? scene, so I just let her blot her eyes and kept on eating. "Oh (which always comes out southern-fried and served in two syllables), Mr. Morrison sent around another memo today. This time it's a list of the clever ways we're supposed to determine if the husband is still living with the recipient: checking the closets for men's clothes, the bathroom for whisker residue in the sink, even asking the children out of Mama's hearing. Karl, I can't do that. The department lets them keep little enough dignity as it is. I explained to Mrs. Clay why I had to snoop around but she didn't seem to understand, just kept following me saying 'Yes Ma'm,' like she always does. And then that new case, Mrs. Atkins: she and all seven of the little ones are pitifully anemic—been feeding them starch again. And Mr. Torres missed his clinic appointment again for his teeth. There's no depending on some of them. I'm so frustrated every turn of my head because I can't do all that has to be done and seeing so little progress, and so exhausted over doing all I can. Sometimes I feel nothing I do is worth anything," as she peeled off her twenty-dollar kid gloves. If I were a humanist I'd probably garrote her for the Greater Good. Ah, my lovely simp, basting yourself in over-concern so you won't dry out of sympathy. The only non-glandular difference between us is that I recognize my profoundly self-centered indifference for what it is and willingly wear its apathy, while you ignore the honest impulses of your own indulgences and wind your morbid over-compensations around you like a shroud. You think of compassion as a responsibility rather than as a choice. Some day when you're not pulling in seven-thou-plus per annum for meting out society's legislated measure of caring to its sub-stratum, some day when you're free-lancing compassion on your own behalf, instead of acting as an agent for the rest of us, and are willing to examine your darker feelings and look more closely behind your responses, *then* tell me of your concern for your fellow man. I'm tired of arguing with you, Carol, tired of defending my "inhuman indifference to the suffering around us," tired of trying to pry your eyes open and struggling to rub your nose in reality. And when I'm tired I sleep.

Drove to the paper to pick up my check this morning. Tom fired me for not getting shots of the girl who jumped. No more assignments. The bastard. Didn't bother asking him about the other thing. Have the other two papers to occasionally sell to, anyway. Shitty time for it to happen.

If that fucking fag down the hall doesn't stop measuring my ass every time I go to the john, I'm going to punch his face in.

Cloistered myself for thirteen solid hours yesterday, intravenous coffee and all, to finish that strategic chapter. Dropped idea of using the naked man scene for dominant image. Can't write that yet because I don't understand that yet, and don't understand, fully, my reactions to it. Did good job. Buoyed me up all day. Well, hardly whole day. Carol came over to cook supper and I was reading her *New York Times* while she hummed over the hot plates. Read this one story buried inside, broke out laughing, read it again, were tears in my eyes as I doubled over there on the floor. Carol came over drying her hands, already laughing in sympathetic vibration, drawling "Whatevuh cayan be so amusing?" as she picked it up and read about the fellow who wanted to kill himself but was worried his mother would not be able to live down what the neighbors would think about having a suicide son, so he jumped from their tenement window with her in his arms, leaving her dead and him only injured. She dropped the paper as though she were holding something obscene, then looked into my eyes as though it had crawled over and changed into me. "How could you—how could you ever laugh about something like this? Karl, how sick are you?" Maybe I laugh because it's not me, maybe I laugh because it could be me, at any rate I laugh because I am slapped into responding strongly and better to laugh than to cry. "I suddenly see something evil about you. It frightens me." Carol, Carol, that's not you responding, that's who you feel *should* be responding. "I don't really know you." The world's sorrows today, sack cloth and stigmata tomorrow. "There's really such a cruel person underneath that mask you wear." Ah, one short month and you sound to the depths of my soul. She grabbed her sweater, purse, and left saying nothing more. I returned a while later to find two blackened, smoking pots and a new crack in the ceiling plaster above my bed. She hung up on me when I phoned at her office this afternoon. I assume it's over.

Someone complained to Mr. Econopolous about typing and loud music late at night. Would love to sneak a public address speaker under that queen's bed and feed in 120 decibels of Sousa marches some 3:00 a.m. Haven't been in a mood lately to fantasize other tortures for him, like nailing a Sophia Loren poster to his door or nightly slipping beneath his door the *Kama Sutra,* page by page (like religious tracts to convert his visitors). Depression in me breeds the humanitarian harmlessness of torpor.

Did some writing in the park yesterday. And the day before. And the day before that. Today is raining. Greying, oozing rain, squeezing dust to salivatic paste. Writing on paper dappled by leaf shadows, did I get off the breakdown scene less stark than if I had been staring at a cockroach crawling up a rusting radiator? Don't think so. There is usually enough Yin and enough Yang in both scenes to abstract an abundance of either. And while there was a little boy flying a kite in front of me and the laughed-out syllables of the frisbee players to enter my head, it was the diarrhetic poodle I choose to focus on, that thin-thighed mini-skirted girl's white poodle—no, not the poodle: the wide tan stain under its tail.

Got a surprise check today from *Leer & Lech* for some smut they kept around for close to a year. Had forgotten about that one. Twenty bucks will get the week's rent paid and some gas in the car so I can cruise tomorrow night and maybe sell something. I recall how Carol glanced down at a page of this scrawled diary last week and asked why there were no dates. I told her to drive through Idaho some summer keeping her eyes on clocks, to see just how arbitrary time was. She didn't understand. No reason why she should know something so specific, but I waved off explaining. Next I would have been affronted at her not thinking thoughts simultaneous with mine. My interpersonal demands cannot be granted outside the grave. However do I delude myself that I'm actually trying to reach people? She asked me what I wrote in it. I told her I wrote about things that happened during the day and sometimes things that might have. "Why don't you save the things you only imagine for your fiction?" she asked. I said look at your life and your actions closely enough, darling, and you'll see they are fictions once your understanding gets through with them. She didn't understand that: maybe her puzzlement is truth?

Talbot Street, a half-dozen blocks from here, exploded into shards of glass and frenzied people and flying stones and some gunfire and not a little bit of blood only eighteen hours ago. One angry fellow was shot to death in his car while trying to run down a policeman, and five looters and one policeman have been injured so far. Was grabbing cameras and stuffing film into my pockets before the radio report had it all out. Joined the trotting ranks of other professionals converging on the street to record the sounds of hurrying feet and cursing voices and the images of frightened eyes and twisted mouths. The reserves are pouring into the Armory, strumming their cold rifle barrels, waiting. It's only just begun. Four hours sleep. Going into it again soon as I finish this coffee.

Scribbling this in my car over a quick sandwich tonight. Scatterings of police cars flashing and dozens of helmeted cops before me here on Talbot Street. Just advised by one outside the car sipping from my offered thermos to remove the press card from my visor if I'm going to leave the car here and don't want to come back to it burned out. Do I quote that friendly kid here, the apprentice cop, leaning on my door saying how he's "itching to crack open a few more spade skulls," or do I pay more attention to the fuming guy this afternoon clenching his riot gun, saying "Christ, I hope no idiot makes me kill him. Got my fill of that shit in Vietnam." What if I had heard just one of them? Always thought of the rioters as jeering, taunting mobs confronting a tight string of hose-wielding, club-swinging brutes. But there's been little of that. The small groups that do form are quickly broken up by the mere arrival of the police. There's been no surging, hysterical mob welling up streets to take over City Hall. Just isolated outbreaks of store burnings, window-smashing and quick looting with occasional reports of rooftop bombardments or sniper fire when police and fire apparatus arrive. This sporadic violence takes a smoldering homogeneous anger, not the abrupt brush-fire mass-hysteria sort. So the cops have been camped here up and down Talbot Street, the main shopping district, while fires blaze all around it on side streets. Every few minutes a cruiser will tear off for some other part of the ghetto where trouble is reported. I've accompanied one of the police cars a few times but there's nothing more each time than perhaps a dozen running people, men, women, kids, black, white, carrying armloads of sport coats, portable TVs, lingerie, jewelry, drugs, trampling glass to powder and tripping over dropped clothing still on hangers. Two cops were posted at every sporting goods shop we passed, and not, I assume, to protect the golf clubs. I feel a stranger among all this kinetic and potential violence, and as though my limbs are not my own when I rush somewhere and lift my camera to my face. I have this constant uneasiness whenever there is a loud noise or a yell, or whenever we pass a burning storefront or angry faces: a feeling as though I am about to be blamed for these happenings. But no blame ever comes. The police shout and fire their guns in other directions, and the furious black faces shout and curse beyond me. I sense myself there only by function: a slate, a recorder. I stare through my lens as through a window. I am not really there. On both sides of me are people involved with one another through their hatreds, their sputtering frustrations. My only emotional involvement is occasional fear. I freeze into celluloid an instant of panic or of fury, yet I feel none of either myself. I tell myself I must stick my lens into the pain-distorted face of a boy bleeding to death in a gutter so that people may learn from this and perhaps prevent it from happening another time, yet I learn nothing myself in or from that action. I see people running on a flame-lit night street and I see hundreds of naked men running toward me screaming for help, and I do nothing.

Five days since my last entry. Too much has happened since. I lie here in a hospital bed only now able to keep a pen in my hand and tack down thoughts that have been wandering in and out of my head. Minutes after writing the last page I chased after a hook-and-ladder heading to a fire on Eliot Street and jumped on when it slowed for a tight corner. The supermarket was blazing out of control when we arrived. Clusters of people, children to old folk, stood around, jeering at the firemen as they scurried to a hydrant. The police hadn't arrived yet. I took pictures rapidly. A young man helped a woman lift a shopping cart heavy with canned goods over the fattened hose. One fireman shouting orders cupped his hands around his mouth to be heard over the noise of the crowd. I kept shooting. People were running on all sides of me. Then the first brick was thrown. It crashed through the windshield of the fire truck. Then more came, rocks and debris from the crowd, bricks from rooftops. Then I heard gunfire and one fireman near me clutched his leg. Everyone was yelling and hurrying for cover. I was standing near the truck and turned to dive under it when I fell over something and felt myself dissolve into a white flash of pain. I came out of the coma only yesterday, surrounded by flowers from strangers, by patronizing doctors and fawning nurses. It was hours before anyone would tell me what happened. Then one of the nurses brought me the copy of *Life:* full page, color, a fireman bent over my bloodied form which had its arm around a small unconscious boy I was lying atop. It appeared I was protecting him with my body. Touching. A photographer had arrived with the police minutes after it happened. They must have identified me from the old press card in my wallet, because I was captioned as being on the *Journal.* Tom had evidently gotten hold of my film the day the magazine came out because they double-trucked some of my pictures in that evening's edition, and with my things there was a generous check, weak explanatory note and an offer of a staff position. Carol came that evening. It took several repetitions to get through to her that I was a hero only by virtue of stark panic and clumsiness. But she still insisted I would have protected the kid if I had seen him. For over an hour she refused to accept my real reactions, so I had to tell her about the naked man. I explained in what a rush I was to get back to the city with the film that night, engraving deadline and all, when I was speeding down that stretch of country road. I told her how peaceful, how quiet the tree-lined roadside was with the unobscured stars above, and how jarring so much as a building would have seemed then: when ahead in my lights appeared this naked man, waving his arms desperately above him, this paunchy, hairless, moonlit-livid carcass sucked into my headlights, then disappearing. I said how I could see nothing in my rear-view mirror and for a sleepy moment thought it might have just been inside my head—I had seen it for only two or three seconds—then that it had to have been some shrieking maniac, and how by that time I was so far past him I figured if he was in trouble someone else was sure to stop. Then how the next morning I read about a man bathing while his house caught fire, who had to leave by a window and couldn't get back inside because of the smoke, who ran way out to the roadside for help because there were no other homes close by and who lost count of the cars that passed him without stopping while his wife and three children burned to death behind those glowing trees. I told an impassive Carol how for days I could not keep my mind from going through what he must have gone through then, seeing himself a surreal frame in a surreal film, unbelieving, a banking executive dancing naked on a roadside while his world crackled behind him. Finally I was through, sweating, weak, and there was silence from both of us. Then Carol, sweet Carol, caring Carol, empathizer with Mankind, softly hosannahed my concern as heralding entry into the ranks of the compassionate, and proclaimed my act was, after all, not as heinous as it might have been, since I was not the only person who had passed him that night.

Docs say no long-range damage—bullet only creased head and lodged in shoulder. I'm glad Tom came, hat on head and unabashed smiles, this morning, because if it were tomorrow I might not have cursed and thrown the bed pan after him. The nurse says Carol can't understand why I won't see her. No, she can never. The boy came with his mother again this morning. I still couldn't tell them. He sincerely seems to like me, apart from thankful appreciation, so I guess it doesn't matter. A lot of things we suppose do, really don't matter. Glanced back and was reminded by something I mentioned having said to Carol, about how some of the things I jot down here haven't actually happened. Looked over some of the things in here through the eyes of some reader who didn't know which have and which haven't. Does it really matter if I threw a bed pan at Tom? Does it really matter whether there is a flaming fagot living down the hall? On another level, does it really matter if Carol exists (or existed)? Would it really have mattered if I had photographed

233

the girl jumping (if, in fact, there was such a girl)? For that matter (think hard and long, now) does it really matter whether the naked man existed, or actually confronted me, or whether he simply represented a potential confrontation. Really? Some of them? Hmmm. My fingers are sore, my eyelids are drooping, I am very tired. So I shall sleep.

From Image to Expression

in partial fulfillment
of the requirements
for the degree
of

MASTER OF FINE ARTS

by
Kenjiro Sashi
translated and edited
by

Henry H. Roth

from *Minnesota Review*

1

My study my work my life has been the past eight years. To be sure an artist is more than someone who works in a studio is more than one who lives in himself—to talk drink and eat with companions is good and necessary even to do this paper is like cautious conversation with a stranger but a stranger who can become interested and whom you can desire to interest. To stay alone too long takes away creativity makes the soul hollow the heart petty even the gift of talent will turn coarse and thick. So here oversimplified is what began in the summer of my seventeenth year—soon I am twenty five and my life in art just beginning; after four years in Mexico and this my first year in New York City. Attached to this paper is portfolio of work revealing what I have seen and what I begin to learn and use.

dear Torio

How little we knew as children yet the days were so happy and carefree. We were the best in our class destined for great roles in society. You will be a judge at thirty, I know. As for me happily I have taken the first step in my life, the first pitiful step to ordered power and realization of beauty and truth. Even partial control is in the distant future. I can not hurry the process, could not even if I wished. In America everything operates high pitched, but working in this country without real hope of reward is especially difficult. Everything ugly buoys up to the surface quickly exposed. Temperature is close to zero but not the cold weather we knew scaling the mountains or even the sudden winds that swept down the coast; here the cold is a dirt ice hard steel jabbing into my gut flinging itself against my heart and ribs again and again. Some times I think I would do anything to be warm a full day and night. The best I can manage is a bottle of cheap wine on the most brutal nights. The loft I share is without proper insulation, the radiator only futile stage prop; the canvas along the walls shakes as if I were out sailing; in rereading the letter this seems a joke but I fear sometimes I may not survive my first american winter. His woman mocks, tells me I am a child, constantly she challenges my indifference and questions my manhood. She never pulls the screen down when she bathes; in front of him she torments and asks me to bring in the bath towel. Akhi is a fool, she lives to wound him. He should kick her out someone will take her away from him shortly for she is promiscuous and very beautiful . . .

Thank you for the letter and the money but you must promise no more checks unless I specifically request. I only recount adventures and doubts to lighten the burden for a moment. But I don't need money as much as a new loft an easier job and a choice gallery to hang my work. I have cashed your check and again thank you but really simply share my tales old friend. I brought warm gloves and a fine meal today. Please continue to write. What news of my family.

2

For many years I do not really think in terms of reality and non reality. Family is so important in Japan, I am to go to school then one I shall stand with my father and when he retires I shall assume the responsibility of a large corporation. In that environment all style is limited and you can be happy and tranquil but impossible to think or do anything different. So I cut away from family and responsibility the moment this decision was reached my life and mind lightened as if opened by an invisible key. See first sketches in portfolio. Nothing was impossible. I know then that environmental situation is very influential on one's work; new experiences must alter the pattern of anyone but an artist must respect change and greet it enthusiastically. Traveling and living in many places these past eight years are exquisite experiences, and I am most fortunate. It is so difficult, even rude to discuss one's own work but I dare discuss here. For a young man who grew up in Japan to live in Mexico so different in language and customs and scene is a radical change physically and mentally. And here in America all that happened before is again erased and something new, beautiful and violent is occupying these moments.

My friend

Yes you were correct to write the truth about them for mother wrote me only yesterday. The business has gone to relatives not even close ones; my mother weeps but I do not mourn deeply the passing of such a cruel, savage man; he is a true symbol of our cold business institution, never did he have time for moments of kindness or play with me. My father would be at peace in this City that seems about to collapse under the weight of filth and strikes. Aside from a few people this savage city and its mob search out to destroy and kill; it is survival of the fittest. Very different from Mexico which accepts you as and says here I am, sleep with our women, take from our tradition what you will, look up at our sun and be forever changed and mad, take as much or as little, go or stay in peace. While New York City delivers formal card—you will die shortly, it promises, and no one will care and no one will bury you. You will rot until the next garbage strike is done and workers will then cart you away. Yet I am more excited but more frenzied than in Mexico and you will remember my letters from there I will use what strength cunning and skill I have to stay even. That is my definition of survival. Tell me of your life. And your women, surely there are women.

She wanted me to kill Akhi and live on his insurance and bank funds, I left in the middle of the night, melodramatically in the middle of the worst snow storm in ten years. In fury she spilled out most of my inks and ruined my best paper and two plates. But no matter I am fortunate to be rid of the mad couple. Akhi fought with me to stay! He sees I will not hurt him or sleep with his woman, but he is old and senile but also a gifted sculptor and his lifes work and age deserve honor so I said nothing but ran from them. Of course in retrospect the loft was warmer than the one room I have now and I do grieve for the ink and paper and plates she destroyed. The bitch and the sad old man; when completely drunk I feel sorry for them and wonder if she had killed him yet.

3

Image is a mysterious thing and the most important element in work of art and creation. In gladness of creation and anguish of creation our ways of handling such an intangible presence, for it is like inner reserve of body flooding out; yet is fleeting. How to react, how to catch it, how to retain the image; I seize upon a never ending single line, I hold on to this line and when I see it move in a sure theme, this is my style. In the end it is only quality and content not how you see or explain the image —but for me when I feel the line move I ride it and am about to burst. The image is clear and true for me and each time the rhythm is the same.

Dear Torio

you are better than brother for you see and understand so well and care what happens better than family that might be in competition with me. Fevers of Mexico have followed and a new plague from the city sent me to a clinic; the doctor told me I am underweight, anemic and have pleurisy. But not TB, he marveled and so did I, since the pain, coughing and blood seemed a definite crippling illness. Bad enough but not the end. I still must work packing and lugging cartons for SONY (the irony of my lowly position is never lost on me though you are too polite to comment). I am with a gallery, three of my etchings have been sold, I do not yet draw a monthly wage from the gallery but when it comes I shall flee the SONY warehouse. Tell me more about your young lady and name her my cautious attorney, I have met Maude and she wears those huge mod glasses, not a beauty but funny and sweet and young, I am not her first but surely no more than twentieth . . . . write soon.

4

The symbol I search for must contain the eternal and the infinite; those things that lived and died and do not live again. Once having given up life they can never lose it again; shells and skeletons. Their change is into permanent and lasting existence. My work seen by the portfolio has been concerned with this symbol. One day as a child of sixteen I went to my coast, the coast I had played and swam in many times, thousand of times however this time I came only to sketch. I saw waves as continuous never ending variation; rolling in and out again drift wood shells bodies of birds and other animals were scattered on the beach. It was not an unusual scene. However, this time I comprehended the marvelous contrast, here were static objects opposing dynamic waves. I saw the incredible beauty of natural formation created by erosion and other land marks of nature. I took the skeleton of an animal in my hand and looked through an empty eye socket. I saw the beach the dunes the sky and sea extending without limit. Since I discovered those skeletons that day almost ten years ago I have been fascinated by the empty world of bones and shells.

Dear friend:

At last a decent loft, very close to Wall street the heart of America, it is amusing to see the faces of those vested men I meet when strolling about. Wonderful narrow streets and sudden intersections; seems different in its formation than other sections of New York. The doctor in the clinic said I am free of any disease tho I feel quite weak and have difficulty breathing and sleeping. Have won an international prize and museums now wish to see and possibly purchase. I quit SONY without notice, and receive a modest monthly stipend from the gallery. The girl lives with me, I cannot call her woman though she is competent in housework, imaginative in cooking and original in love making. She still attends college fulltime; twice her parents have come here made scenes threatened cajoled. The last time the father was more calm he has seen my name in the NY Times and wanted to know what my work sold for. Every American I have met wishes to make a deal. I do not love Maude, but she is a delight and no trouble and so eager to please. Her language shocks me so I am sure she would bowl you over with her words. Though of the upper class her vocabulary rivals a seamans and I must laugh at how shocked I become. Things go well, tell me about your woman not the same details I do but some gossip. Will you marry, will you not marry?

5

Dear Dear friend:

Remember how much we loved the cinema not only those of our own people but the foreigner. Have you seen the kubrick film Dr. Strangelove? imagine me, straddling not the H bomb but a steady resolute line toward the eternal the infinite the finite the vague, the clear or the weightless the leaden. We leave for Mexico within the week. New York has won, but in winning gave up many token victories my career much enhanced some fame and money, and a pregnant mistress coed soon to be my wife. During our relationship these months there have been others for each of us; believe the child is mine the odds would seem to indicate my fatherhood. Trust you are not shocked by my comments, I have not changed so much but time is for the grabbing and women stand by also waiting. The parents are relieved to have her married and both of us out of the country.

That sun is better than any drug, any woman or orgasm of the two; surely my work will be even better. Maude says I will be a legend, I hope it will all be as living legend.

Have listed our P.O. number—please write often, you are my only contact, the only one I can talk to, I fear I am becoming addicted to woman impregnated daily, the line I ride is shaky, my image and expression of it never even partially fulfilled. I stand on coast of my childhood and looking through the eye of the skeleton is a caravan of people and leavings and still the view is exhilarating and original.

Of course my best to your bride.

My portfolio contains a series of skeletal remains done in Japan, a series marking the comprehension of the magnificent sun in Mexico.

And finally my most recent work the earth and cosmos series. . . .

The existence of the sun makes life possible for human and all living things. The ancients thought the sun as God and worshipped it. The fact that impressed me most deeply in Mexico was not the land the trees the people the desert but simply the existence of such a glorious sun. The sun rays seemed so terribly close, each moment of daylight a previous intimate experience. I felt the sun, before I only sense it for it was distant element. Now it was everything and all that was needed. I felt a power inside me to grasp first the sun then not only the sun but moon and stars. The entire cosmos was very near to me. The sun and cosmos, the mystery of their presence is what I ask of myself through symbols. Now my chief interest is with the earth the stars and the planets floating in infinite space. Such an eternal infinite existence is what I have tried to express. This, the core of my approach to art. But for the future I cannot say how best to improve the expression of it.

The Rhyme of Lancelot

Peter L. Sandberg

from *South Dakota Review*

He was sixty. She was fifty-five. Four years ago she had come into the bank to make a will, and he had helped her with it and during the course of things in a most natural way he had asked her to have tea with him at Mother Creighton's shop across from the bank, and she had accepted. They understood each other at once for they were both unhappy, and gradually they grew affectionate, and finally they grew intimate. The affair began in the fourth year of their friendship, and they carried it on through the three months of autumn. Like the season, it was getting old.

"What are you doing, Jame?" he asked. He sat in his shorts and sleeveless undershirt, and looked through the clean squares of the motel window to the place where the mountain began.

"Setting my hair," she said from the bath. "You're a caveman you know; it's a mess."

"We should go on our walk," he said. "Before we leave, I mean."

She came into the room where he sat, opening a bobby pin with her teeth. Her hair was soft gray. She wore a half slip and stockings, but her wrinkled breasts were bare and he looked at them thoughtfully.

"We don't have to walk," she said. "I always liked it though. It was part of us."

"Well of course we'll walk." He was agitated at her use of past tense so he fiddled with a Gideon Bible that lay on the writing desk. "Jame," he said.

"Yes."

"It's not like it was at first. I mean it's not as good as when we began."

She sat down at the edge of the bed, covering herself with her arms.

"I guess it isn't, Michael. But I thought it was still fun."

He opened and closed the Gideon Bible and he said, "Fun. You know, I think that's exactly the right word. Three months ago it was exciting for an old couple, and in so short a time it's gone to fun." He shook his head. "A few more months and it could be indifference. It could be our marriages all over again."

She had taken her lip in her teeth and he saw that she was upset. "It's not your fault, Jame," he said. He got up and put his arm around her. "It's not our fault; it's just the way things are, I guess."

"We've always understood each other," she said. "Perhaps we're just having a bad day."

He nodded. At times like this, she seemed like a stranger. Something was wrong. Either they had lost something, or they hadn't progressed. At the end of his life he was sensitive to the failures in a relationship.

"There's nothing at home for either of us," he said almost to himself. "The very best, the nicest we have is what we have here."

"I know it is."

"Jame," he said eagerly, turning to look at her again. "Do you know what it was like the first time between us? I felt like a god!"

She laughed and her eyes sparkled at him. "You're always dramatic," she said.

"I don't care, damn it, I mean it." He went to the window

and looked out again at the high slopes. "And now; well it's like getting to the top of something and having to come down. Let's fight it, Jame." He went back to her. "Let's not have a bad thing happen again."

"What will we do?"

"All right. Instead of taking our usual walk, which we've taken eighteen times, by the way, we'll do something different. Let's climb the mountain." He was pleased with himself; it was like throwing down the glove.

"Why we can't do that," she said. "There isn't time. It will be dark soon."

"We'll go tomorrow, first thing."

She laughed. "Michael, you crazy man. You know I have to be back tonight."

"Call. Make an excuse."

"I can't," she said. "Really."

He took her shoulders in his hands and stared at her.

"But Jame, what did you do the first time when we decided to come here?"

"I made an excuse," she said. "I guess I could make another."

That afternoon, for the nineteenth time, they took their walk arm in arm through the village; but now there were differences. Instead of looking in at the shoe shop and commenting on prices and styles, they went in and rented two pairs of boots and wool socks. At the market, where they usually stopped to sniff the fresh vegetable smells, they went in and spent almost an hour picking fruits and cheeses for an alpine lunch. They bought a pint bottle of claret and a small box of cashews. On the way back to the room, they made a brief stop at the pay telephone, and in the motel office arrangements were made to spend an extra night. For supper, instead of going to the usual restaurant, they drove into the next town and found a German beer cellar that served knockwurst and dark beer. Their time together in the room that night did not regain its lost dimensions, but it showed promise, and he fell asleep in the early hours satisfied that the direction of the affair had changed.

They awoke early, pleased to get up and be doing something.

He tucked his trousers into the wool socks so they looked like climbing knickers, and he wore a green flannel shirt and his reindeer sweater. She put on a blue wool skirt and blouse, and drew her socks up to her knees.

"Jame," he said. "You can't climb a mountain in your skirt."

"Well why not?"

"It just isn't done. We should have bought you a pair of slacks."

She laughed. "Well it's not a very big mountain is it? They say there's a trail to the top. Besides, it will be something new."

"That's right," he said. "And if things get rough I can give you mine, and go on in my shorts." He put his arms around her and held her close. "Things could have been different; if only we had met with our lives in front of us."

She put her hand over his mouth. "We promised not to go on about things that aren't possible."

"I know, damn it. There's no point."

They put on their coats and tramped through the village to have breakfast at the all night diner. She ordered a poached egg on toast, and he had a stack of pancakes, which he always considered a man's breakfast although they did not agree with him.

"We've put new life into us, Jame," he whispered to her over their empty plates. "It's good again."

"It's not like pumping up a tire," she said, but he saw that she was happy.

From the diner, they went across town to the city park where the trail to the mountain began. The sky was bright and western with a fine sun beginning to rise. He wiggled his fingers in his driving gloves and his toes in the good-fitting boots.

"Not cold?" he asked.

"No, I feel wonderful. It was a good idea of yours, Michael."

"Have you ever climbed a mountain before?" he asked.

She thought for a moment. "Never one this big," she said.

He smiled. "Neither have I. I'm glad it's you and me."

She touched his arm.

The trail was easy to follow, a slender line of dirt twisting upwards through the heavy forest of pines that covered the

lower slopes. At first they walked briskly, but soon they slowed
their pace and he reminded her that they were not young. She
walked along in front of him, her hands in her coat pockets.
He followed, watching the trees and stones for a while, but
soon losing himself in his thoughts. He thought about many
things, and when he thought about something particularly vital,
he gestured with his hands as though his mind were an or-
chestra and he were conducting. He loved Jame. It was a simple
orderly fact, the kind he liked, uncluttered and clean. He
wanted to know what Jame thought about him. He knew she
liked him very well, but he wanted to know exactly.

"Michael," she said. "Have you noticed the jays?"

"Yes, they're lovely," he said. "Proud looking devils."

"I saw a cardinal a while back, but you were woolgathering."

"Damn it," he said. "I've always liked cardinals. Be sure I'm
in on the next one."

They climbed on in silence. On the steep sections the trail
switchbacked, making it easier to gain elevation. The trees began to thin and the ground was strewn with rocks and boulders.
He thought they were going very slowly, but soon they began
to see patches of snow, and at one rest stop they had a view of
the summit, white against a dark blue sky.

Michael walked and waved his hands. It was hard for Jame.
She had not been raised to carry on with a man, and he thought
the lines in her face had grown deeper and longer in the last
three months. But it had been Jame who suggested the first
weekend, and he had been shocked and delighted for he never
thought they could be more than friends. And they were still
just friends. She always reminded him of that. Love was elusive
and full of sadness. He remembered the story of Paolo and
Francesca when Dante asked them why they were in hell and
Francesca said they had read the rhyme of Lancelot and sinned.
And Paolo had wept.

"Jame," Michael said, puffing badly. The last stretch had
winded him and he guessed the air was getting thin. "Let's
have lunch." They had been climbing three hours.

"Should I pick a spot?" she asked.

"Why don't you," he said.

They went a little way off the trail to a clearing where the sun beamed brightly on a carpet of pine needles and cones. She took a kerchief from the pocket of her coat and spread it on the ground. He brought out the fruits and cheeses and pared equal servings with a one-bladed silver pocket knife that the bank had given him in memory of something he had done; he could not remember what. Two chipmunks gathered to chitter for scraps while they ate their snack in the rich odors of pine sap and earth.

Sitting in the sun warmed Michael, and he was able to take off his driving gloves; and then all at once, as he began to peel an orange, it occurred to him that he and Jamie seldom talked to each other. They took their pleasures in mere presence, and he supposed that was the finest thing two people could do who had reached the eventide of disappointed lives.

He breathed in deeply the resin smell of outdoors and took a tangy wedge of cheese between his teeth. It was a damn nice picnic they were having. A very pleasant, happy time.

He had been born on the eastern coast, not far from Plymouth Rock. He had been raised in the New England traditions; he had married, and sired a son. He had spent thirty years working in a bank. He had been to the funerals of four generations of his family, and during his lifetime he had read of two wars and a police action. For sixty years he had known consciousness; he could measure the time easily, seven hundred and twenty months, three thousand one hundred and twenty weeks, twenty-one thousand nine hundred days. A long time. Yet, when he ranged the still clear beam of his memory through the long wilderness of lost years, he could say quite truthfully that eating a wedge of cheese on the slope of a mountain with his lady friend in the twilight of his time was one of a small total of moments that he could say had been happy.

"You know, Jame," he said. "I think a god watches over you and me."

"We're just old sinners," she said. "We'll be roasted on a spit one day." She looked very peaceful, he thought; the sun had brought an attractive flush to her cheeks.

"Why damn it," he said. "The old man, if he is up there, what could he find wrong with a picnic."

"The picnic's all right," she said. She looked momentarily worried, and he knew what she was thinking.

"You don't suppose the old peep can see through the motel roof, do you?" He grinned at her.

"Michael," she said quite sternly. "Don't court trouble with the Lord."

When they passed timberline, they could look down to the valley and see the buildings of the village nestled there, a few columns of smoke hazing up from chimneys. They walked very slowly now because the air was thin, and they were tired. Once, he saw a gum wrapper on the side of the trail and when he stooped to pick it up he felt a pain in his back and hoped that his disc wouldn't go out. They saw black ravens spiraling on air cushions up into the sheer sky, and horny lizards go tense on lichen-covered rocks as they passed. Then all at once and not knowing it would happen, they saw the arc of the summit ridge spread out before them like a scimitar moon.

"Michael," she said. "Isn't that the top? Over there I mean."

"Yes. We're almost there."

The ridge was covered with snow, and he led the way, letting his feet make their marks in the clean white powder. She followed in his train. In half an hour they had reached the top and could look back along the long path they had made in the snow that arced away from them.

She looked at it a moment, and then she said, "I think it's the most beautiful thing I have seen."

He had wanted to make love to her right there on the summit, but he knew it was too cold and they were too tired so he got out the claret and cashews and they had a snack.

Then he took her in his arms and kissed her a long kiss until his heart beat fiercely in the thin summit air, and when their lips came apart in a cloud of frosty breath she said, "I love you, Michael."

She had never said this to him before, and when he heard the words he knew how much he had needed and wanted to hear them. And it was right between them again. Whatever it was they had begun to lose yesterday in the valley, they had regained today on the mountain top.

For a long while he held her in his arms and gazed through the blowing strands of her hair to a world of mountains that ranged the corridors of his vision. Then, because there was nothing else to do, and because it was getting late, he took her by the hand and led her down familiar tracks.

Down in the Eighth

David Steingass

from Colorado State Review

Sunday morning stepping off the New Haven Rail and Road in Putnam: I know I'll never smoke again. I make medieval vows of abstinence. The girl in the drug store has no Coke-Cola, and she hasn't started coffee although it's almost nine. Fresh out of Alka Seltzer. No Sunday papers.

"Can't help it you're going to visit him," she says when I ask. "I never heard of Norman Smith, though I should of, I guess. I'm Phyllis Smith." And she shrugs at me.

I slide the same dime three times through the telephone coin chute before Phyllis Smith walks down along the counter and leans across to me.

"Hey. The operator's still in church. Until ten-thirty, today."

So I buy cigarettes, and light up beside the mail deposit box outside. The late August sun makes my skin crawl, and I wait on the brink of something. The world is turning all the time and the next time around I'm on for sure, at the depot. Dryrot dust comes from the planking of the building, grass grows between the track ties, and sunlight stabs into a small, central spot far away in my skull. The world is spinning, the world, and I am just a little ahead of it this morning. Spin on, great ball, spin. Just now it is a broadside curve dropping inside and low: hard enough to get a clear swing at on a good day.

And the man across the street is blind, deaf, and dumb, but I do not realize it immediately. "Best way to Woodbridge?" I ask him, but he is staring at my kneecaps. He sits crosslegged before an appliance store display window full of knobby white surfaces and smooth contours. Suddenly he stabs his hand at me. An Oracle. He spreads out a patched, braille street map of Putnam and fingers me to a bar, a church, a shoe repair shop, the drugstore, moaning after each one and swinging his head back and forth. Then he starts shaking a tin cup and squeezing Salvation Army slowly from his concertina, while I back off quickly as I can, feeling the whole town peep through frontroom curtains over coffee.

Coffee, steeped and drained to save mankind. But all I can think of doing is squooshing the depot as if it were a puffball. It looks full of dust. Quick estimates: each foot this morning is a rod long. Three good crunches should do it. But how to get them there? Each toe catches when I step, and I totter, hanging in air a second, my head an electric arc machine.

I go instead into the shoe repair shop, hoping to smell stain and leather, but as soon as I open the door there is a tiny bell jingling over my head. I stumble and spill my suitcase over the floor. It's all right though, for I have almost everything replaced when the shoeman comes in from the back door. I hope he talks like a cobbler. I notice he has a coffee mug in hand.

"I'm sorry," I blurt as the huge leather apron limps wildly into the room, and he snaps a quick hard-eyed glance. The left ear and most of his hair is gone, and his head is red as a steamed lobster. Along the wall are WWI photos under glass: all kilts and trucks and trenches.

"And how might you be this fine morning, young fellow?"

"I'm sorry I have no shoes."

"There's the shoes all over your feet for a start."

"Yes, but they're new. I've only worn them for movies, you know. Things like that."

"It's always the way of it. Nicest things we have, and we hide our shoes for the dark."

"Would it be possible for you to believe," I begin to realize words coming hard, "that I haven't had a coffee this morning?"

"Sure, lad? This's my first, come to think. You'd better hurry. Phyllis closes the drugstore at nine-thirty Sundays, and she's got a nice pot there."

I am a medical doctor, quite formal and studied, trying to diagnose difficult symptoms. The case is puzzling, the terms from a field I am in total ignorance of. I blame deadhead instructors.

"The fact is I've been there, and there's no coffee, I'm afraid."

"Is that it, lad? I was sure Phyllis made coffee Sundays."

"What I really want to know is how to get to Woodbridge. I've got a friend there."

"Well, Woodbridge." He turns away to files hunched along the wall, full of geologic survey maps, opens one and studies a green sheet. He lurches back suddenly.

"No good lad. I just can't remember, but then I've been here but ten, fifteen years."

"Yes. Well, I thought as much. If you could just hold the bell on my way out."

Then I am raising my foot for the third stomp. Dryrot slouches through the air, and his tinkling bell announces that the Oracle is prepared to grant my interview. When I arrive on the scene, however, he has flown with tin cup, concertina, and blindness.

Full of summer pay in a bar off Grand Central, I had a night to kill before visiting Norman Smith in Connecticut. Slapping a ten on the bar (onyx), I was out-of-town money. Summer money following the season: Miami, Maine coast, Atlanta, back again.

"Martinis. Dry. Tell me when this goes."

Ready for anything, I was. Then I took two two-dollars-ten-cents in dimes (twenty-one) for the people I knew in the big city, and prowled to the phone booth. Nothing. Not a soul at home all down the list.

"Ten's gone, Mac." I hadn't had a martini since June.

"Plenty money. Don't stop." Second time around a guy answered who got me sick on cherry stone clams on their half-shells the year before. Suggested we meet at "Pappa's." I held out for my bar, best damn one in town, where just now two Mayflower men were trying to booth a summer camp counselor. Ruddy, bleached hair, a lanyard around her neck with a big green plastic whistle. Cherrystone gave me his address.

"Keep your voice down up the goddam stairs though, will you?"

I stalked the subway late at night alive for life, dead to signs and stops. The hours roared away. I doodled my instruction sheet, constantly aware of the nuances the world was making. Toward morning a rodent got on, making two of us in the car. He was maybe five feet, heavy beard I noted, for my PhD thesis. I grabbed wallet and keys close, and shouted to him. He shouted back, then pulled out a gas credit card slip and made writing motions. Maybe he's a cop was all I could think, ready to cover tracks. "I'm lost," I wrote, signing my name carefully.

He backed off like a cornered animal as the train slowed, and leaped off. "Scheister!" screamed the flying rodent. I noted the remark with a asterisk.

The New Haven clanked out of Grand Central at six. I smouldered gin and picked olive fragments from my teeth with a match book cover, and every inch of the ride was the Grand Canyon Quartet of my skull. Command performance. The Connecticut hills darted before the rising sun faster than the eye dared follow, so I watched thirty-four empty seatbacks sway. Above Stamford, a kid about fourteen got on carrying a football and a blue Air France bag. His hair flamed out and his face was bas-relief in dark freckles and steely little blue eyes. I concentrated on the bag and thought of a boy in New York the day before, before the martinis. Right on the street he tugged my arm. I thought he was epileptic. Or lost. Or worse. I perched him on my suitcase, eagle scout that I am, and prepared to earn another merit badge.

"Don't be upset now, little fella. We'll find somewhere in this great big town." He shoved an envelope at me.

"Sign it, will you mister?"

It took a moment to register. Ballplayer, of course. I instantly touseled his hair good-naturedly. "Sly devil," I said, having to admit that he was pretty sharp to see through my disguise. "You've got to tell me who I am first."

"M-e-l-r-o-s-e," he spelled as I wrote. "Jackie Melrose," and I saw tears film his eyes when he sprinted away.

"Hang in there, champ," I said. "Keep up the old workouts."

This kid was prep school: banlon crew shirt, saddle pumps, a certain slant of nose. And he jumped so suddenly that the bubble gum almost popped from his mouth.

"Well, goddam it anyway! Here you are!" He charged to the seat beside mine and I raised a hand to my ear. "It's really you, isn't it?"

"It really is."

"I mean, what the hell you doing here with a big game in Philly this afternoon? Get canned?"

"No, not at all." I could see he suspected something. I had to pull an excuse to save the team's honor. Anything not to lose a fan. "I'm going to see my grandmother, who is very sick."

"Not what the paper says," he pointed to the Sunday sports' page headlines and picture. "Hey, what's the matter. You hung-over or something? Clean that gunk out of your eye. Shape up! now."

"Putnam next," the conductor shouted.

It was the voice more than anything, finally. Like steel, portable table legs sliding over concrete. He didn't deserve the team's favors. I asked out. "Want an autograph before I go?"

"What the hell?" But he hurried a piece of paper from the back of his pants.

"Thomas C. Scott," I wrote, and watched him double-take me through the window, open-mouthed, as the train bounced away.

Down in the Eighth

Frustrated by the Oracle, I wind down the street past the post office in a hollow under a few elms, all of it fenced in granite blocks. Beyond, the street switches back so sharply it seems to end in junkyard. Truck skeletons, building partitions: the end of the world. Destruction and desolation.

Without a moment's hesitation, I drop the fallout shelter door behind me and strike out. It is all we have left, I resonate in pioneer determination, expecting to turn up a girl survivor any partition now. We must retain faith in ourselves, no matter how our bodies ache.

"You can't go in there, buddy," the cop car says, sidling up beside me.

For a second, I consider the possible results of using my leg irons to smash through to him.

"Get out of there!"
"Sorry. Just trying to find a friend."
"Well, he ain't in there. This's town property," he points to a sign. "You can't read, I see."

My lawyer stands before the cop and calls him an illogical and slanderous idiot.

"Sorry," I say again, just for the record.
"Where's he at? Your friend."
"Woodbridge."
"Little off base, ain't you?"
"The train doesn't go to Woodbridge."
"Train can go to hell for all of me! Out of town, huh?"
"Yes. Now, his name is Norman Smith. You might know him as Lonestar, his nickname."
"I don't know nobody by Lonestar. Look, fella, Woodbridge's out along the switchback. I cruise here every twenty minutes,

256

and I don't wanna see you here the next time around. We don't like hitchhikers much, either."

Friend of my heart, I moan out along the switchback, burping gin. Friend and comrade, show me a sign if you are indeed not pulling my well-worn leg.

Memories of the 1853 rendezvous outside Jackson's Hole: buffalo robes and agency rotgut. Beaver plews. Bronzed Ute women. The Lonestar with his new Kentucky breechloader, and me parting on a swirling ridge of fog at daybreak. "Next year," he says, "beat it up to my country. God, it's sweet land, though. Up above the Tetons where the Rosebud curves into the Little Bighorn, and to hell with these agency traders. Soon's the ice blows out, I'll look for you, hoss."

I think of course he said Woodbridge, but I am actually too tired to put down the bag and check my wallet.

"Woodbridge where you're going?"

I look into the open passenger door of a roadster, about '27, spit-shine front to rear, with white walls. Visions of Capone appear, but I have heard the magic Woodbridge words. "Yes," I say, and look to the driver, dressed in black, with a red beard. I want to run.

"Climb up then. Bag in back, I guess. I'm Alan Hartwell, Lutheran minister in Putnam. Come to think of it, I didn't see you in services this morning, did I?" All Sunday jokes. We shake hands.

He knows Woodbridge. He knows Norman Smith. He knows that nobody in the family goes to church. More, he doesn't seem to care, but I become Martin Luther groveling in the meadow, having just received the heavenly bolt. Lonestar, I will say. Friend, you must see the right and true way before it is too late. Come with me to the peace that surpasses all things.

"Well, friend Tom, this is my turnoff. Your Smith is just up the long hill. Around the bend you'll see the house."

I call out walking up the driveway and drop my bag. Lonestar walks out on the lawn, smiling. "Why didn't you call from Putnam?"

Down in the Eighth

He has stacked up points on me every round, and is starting to take flashy chances for the judges. Just as he twitches into range, I bury a quick left on his belly button. The right crosses over his heart and he drops. The fans are suddenly wild with my recovery on a very slow start. The blood is all with me. I am fast and loose as ever, and just before the end of the eighth, I work him to a neutral corner, catch him a jab, and put him down for good.

Smitty's Haven

Joanne Zimmerman

from *Western Humanities Review*

It came to Smitty's attention that a tenant was finally moving into the vacant room in Mrs. Hadley's boarding house. Old Mr. Newman had dwindled and died in that room, and it had taken Mrs. Hadley months to get rid of the heavy smell of medication and death, although she had used pine scent, magnolia spray, incense and deodorizers.

Old Mr. Newman had been carried out stiffly horizontal. Now someone else's mortal trappings were being carried in—a woman, Smitty could see by the clothes in a plastic bag lying across two cartons in the front hall. He had no particular sentiment about this, being a man who easily accommodated himself to change.

It had barely made a ripple in his routine when his wife had packed a suitcase and left him four years earlier on a quiet evening while he watched television. He hadn't even noticed until he went to bed and realized that no one shared it with him. Lacking a housekeeper then, he selected a few things that had contributed most faithfully to his comfort, and moved with them five blocks away to Mrs. Hadley's boarding house. He gave his employers the change of address, and continued going to the same tavern after dinner to drink a couple of beers and watch television, and kid around with the waitress, Sylvia, and the bar tender. Occasionally when he left there to go home to bed, he turned right, in the direction of his former apartment—not for more than a step or two—before he turned about in wonder, and headed for bed at Mrs. Hadley's.

Smitty lingered in the front hall, a short stocky man in brown slacks and a stiff grey wool jacket which he zipped as though preparing to go out, then un-zipped. He had already glanced through the letters on the oak table near the door, but he scrutinized them again, one by one, though he did not often receive mail, and was not expecting a letter. He stared intently at the umbrella and one red glove that had lain side by side on the table since midsummer. He was waiting for, ready for, news—the kind of news that just might come in a letter, or with the arrival of a stranger.

The new boarder came down the stairs for her belongings. He had not speculated beforehand on her appearance; he had no preconceived notion of her, therefore he was only slightly surprised that she was dark-skinned; dark-skinned, dark-eyed, a small nose with a widely flaring nostrils, a bitter-sweet expression around her full mouth. There were no other Negroes at Mrs. Hadley's, or in the immediate neighborhood, now that he thought about it, but he did not see why there should not be.

She had put the clothes bag over her arm without looking at Smitty, and was bent over to pick up one of the boxes by the cord that tied it.

"Can I give you a hand?" he asked.

"I'd appreciate it if you could take one of these—that is, if you're going upstairs anyhow," she said crisply.

"Take 'em both," Smitty said, reaching for the cartons. He expected to pick them up with no effort, and was surprised when they were heavy. "Wow! What is it, money?"

She laughed. "No, books."

"Certainly must read a lot."

"I'm a school teacher," and looked at him cautiously.

He followed her up the stairs, and could not help noticing

that her brown calves were well shaped, but that as for the rest, there was barely enough to hang her clothes on. He set the boxes down in the center of her room and glanced around. Fresh paint, a new rug, clean curtains—Mrs. Hadley had finally exorcised old Mr. Newman, and now the room had the temporary strangeness, the emptiness of transition—no longer Mr. Newman's, but not yet hers either, keeping to itself for a little while. Through the smell of fresh paint, the invigorating cold air from the open window, Smitty detected an elusive light perfume that emanated from Miss . . . Miss. . . . He looked squarely at her, noticed that her hair was slightly grey, that her eye lids were tired, lines around her eyes and mouth.

"My name is Smith," he offered seriously.

The lines around her mouth accentuated her swift smile. "A good name, but not unusual. Happens to be my name, too."

Smitty laughed. "Miss? Mrs.?"

She shook her head. "Miss."

"Welcome to Hadley's, Miss Smith." He extended a strong hand. "Anything I can do for you, let me know." There didn't seem to be anything further to say.

Smitty trotted down the stairs again, on his way to the tavern. A bitter wind stirred whorls of old papers, dry leaves and grit around his ankles. He was glad to be in the warm beery dark room. He took his habitual seat, facing the television but not so close that he had to strain his neck looking up at the set mounted high over the bar. Sylvia, the waitress, brought him a beer.

"Greetings, little man."

"How goes it," he asked, without taking his eyes off the screen where shadowy figures struggled.

"Not bad. Not bad." Her mouth that was slit too wide in her plump face barely opened when she spoke. "Could be worse. I thought you weren't coming when I saw 'Gunsmoke' had started without your permission."

"Yeah. That wasn't nice of them."

"I thought maybe they finally installed television in that moth-eaten mansion where you live."

"Not a chance. And if they did, you know I'd come back here anyhow."

"Yeah? For what?"

"You got a bigger screen."

She snorted. "You're not just kidding I got a bigger screen. I got the biggest screen you ever saw. I'm going to show it to you sometime, too. You just be a patient boy."

"I'm trying."

"You just keep trying. You'll make it, too. I kid you not." Her speech leaped from high to low pitch, regardless of meaning, but the mask of her face remained unchanged. Sylvia had a reputation for her dead-pan humor. Smitty laughed immoderately at everything she said, feeling lucky to be one of the ones she bantered with, searching out and finding innuendo in her least phrase.

She wore a white nylon uniform, nearly transparent except for the collar and pockets, worn over a white nylon slip, which was clearly over white nylon brassiere and pants. The icy fabric strained at the buttons which held it together down the front, bosom and belly pushing for nudity. She leaned all this against the table briefly. "When you can take your eyes off the silver screen I got a good joke for you, Smith." She moved on, having established Smitty in the ranks of her followers.

The light reflected from the screen flickered across Smitty's square-lined face, his stubborn cropped hair. Behind his eyes, a small original light, not a reflection, sparked to life. "A good name, although not unusual." He smiled.

An hour later, at the closing commercial, he realized he was not aware that the story had been brought to a satisfactory conclusion, and he knew he had been dozing. He got stiffly to his feet, stretched, picked up the change on the table, leaving a quarter for Sylvia. As he left she emerged to scoop up the tip and call to him, "Bye, now! Don't do anything I wouldn't do."

"That's giving me a lot of lee-way," he returned snappily, turned up his collar, and went home.

The next evening the faint elusive perfume in the hall led

Smitty right to Miss Smith's door. He tapped lightly before he had a chance to consider. The door opened immediately.

"Hi. How are you?"

"Fine. How are you?" She stood aside so that he could enter the room, leaving the door ostentatiously wide. The boxes of books remained where Smitty had put them. The clothes bag and a small suit case on the bed. Only the desk looked as though she had made use of it and meant to stay—two neat stacks of papers and an old water glass with sharpened pencils in it.

"I just thought I'd see if there was anything I could do for you? Anything you need? I mean, I'm going out, and I could pick up something."

"You're very kind," she said seriously. "I don't believe there is anything, however."

"You new in this neighborhood?"

She stiffened, clasped her hands, turned her face slightly, and looked warily, side-long at him. "Yes. Why?" The two words were widely spaced.

"Just want to get you acquainted if you're new," Smitty said simply. "There's a good drug store two blocks that way," he pointed. "Got everything. Even books. Open all night, too, if you ever want a sandwich or a cup of coffee. If you want a beer, there's a tavern this way," he gestured with the other hand. "A couple of them."

Her smile was immediate and brilliant, showing her white teeth. "Well, thank you. There is nothing I need now, but I will certainly remember all you say. I'll never forget it, in fact."

"You can always ask me." He turned toward the door. "That's my room right there. Good night."

"Good night, Mr. Smith."

He zipped the grey jacket and went outdoors. He knew he was still smiling, not that anything was so funny, not like Sylvia's jokes, but that he felt fine, he just felt like smiling. He used the same smile to greet Sylvia.

The following evening he washed up, but did not go out. He looked around for some pretext for being in his room when it was not yet time for sleep. There was nothing to look at, nothing to do. He stretched across the bed, folded his hands under his head and stared at the ceiling. He heard the latch of a door click, leaped to his feet, and opened his own door, but hers was closed. The bulb had burned out and the hall was very dark. He picked up his grey jacket, put it on as he went slowly down the stairs. It was a shivering cold night, a few shreds of clouds blowing between the elusive stars. It occurred to him that it would be pleasant to have someone walking with him. To keep himself from holding out his arm to her, he jammed his hands deep in his pockets.

Sylvia said, "Honey, you don't have to keep your hands in your pockets. If you want to hold your pipe, put it on the table."

"Christ, you got a dirty mind."

"I notice I don't have to explain things to you. Anyhow, what did I say? It's you taking it dirty." She brought his beer.

He had better luck the next evening—happened to meet Miss Smith in the hall, and they went upstairs together, and continued to her room. Smitty sat on one of the cartons while she hung up her hat and coat.

"What do you do for a living, Mr. Smith?"

"Call me Smitty. Everybody does. Why, I'm a carpenter."

"A carpenter! How fine!" She smiled her teacher's smile at him, as though he had just received 100 and a gold star for effort.

"Fine? Yes, I suppose so. It's fairly steady. I like it all right. I never had much education. I mean, like you, to go to college to be a teacher. Now, that's my idea of fine."

"The world needs carpenters as well as teachers. Jesus himself was a carpenter."

"Lots of times I wish I'd had more education. To satisfy myself, and to help other people. I never realized until now how much I live for myself. I mean, there's nobody in my life I do anything for."

"On the contrary, a carpenter always builds for other people. Gives them shelter, satisfies a very basic need, a real craving we all have for a home."

264

"Do you think of it that way?"

"Absolutely. And I think if you weren't meant to be a carpenter, you wouldn't be one. If you were meant to be a teacher, that's what you would be. A teacher deals in the abstract, in intangibles, things you can't see or feel, like the future. A carpenter is a man who pounds a nail and makes a house grow. When it is done he can touch it. He can walk into it and say 'There it is. I built it.' "

Smitty rose to his feet, swollen with pride. "That's it! That's exactly it! I've always felt that way, but I never really knew how to say it. I have the hands, Miss Smith, and you have the words." He sped out the door.

"Good night," she said softly. "My name, incidentally, is Lorene."

Smitty stood in the center of his room, smiling, feeling wonderful, approving himself, approving all Smiths, and all the rest of the world. He wanted to go right back and get some more of that build-up. He wanted, in exchange, to give her approval and gratitude for making him feel so good, for being so fine herself. He wanted to do something grand for her, build a house for her, board by board, nail by nail. He wanted her to move into that house, and he wanted to move into it with her.

He did not really want to be put to sleep by beer and television, but he could not stay in the confines of his small room so close to hers. As he went down the street to the tavern it occurred to him that he had never built anything for himself.

"Greetings, little man." The room stank of stale beer. It was dark enough to hide filth. Faint lights around the bar made a jagged glitter of bottles mirrored.

"Cut this 'little man' crap, Sylvia, will you?"

"Why, you should be pleased." She feigned injured feelings. "You know what they say—a little man is like a sturdy bush—all root."

"All right. Cut it out," he said gruffly.

"What, the root?"

"No. All the crap. Give me a beer."

"Always building for other people, and never anything for myself," Smitty thought, as he sipped the beer, kept his eyes on the screen without seeing it, so as to exclude Sylvia. "How many years I been a carpenter? Twelve? Thirteen? And nothing to show for it. No house, no money in the bank, no friends, no family. So I built a lot of things. I got not a one to show. Just a lot, a lot of evenings drinking beer with a lot of different people. (I got a beer-belly to show for that, at least.) A lot of television shows. A lot of nothing. What is it?"

"You want another beer?" She gave the table top a swipe with a rag and set down a wet bottle. "I got a good joke for you, Smitty."

"Tell me a good joke, Sylvia. I need it. I'm in a terrible mood."

"There's this colored fellow and his girl in bed, see."

"Colored girl?"

"Sure. And he's humping her and humping her, all night long. About every twenty minutes. You know, like you dream of."

"Yeah."

"So finally, about two in the morning, he pats her, and she don't even budge. She's all in. So he gets up, puts on his clothes. 'So long, cold ass' he says, and leaves."

Smitty waited. When he realized he had heard it all, he said, "Christ, Sylvia. What kind of a joke is that? That's a helluva dumb story."

"You think so?" she shrilled. "Shows how much you know. What's the matter with you anyhow?"

"I just think that's a helluva dumb joke, that's all," he said glumly.

"I'm gonna show you you're wrong, Smith. I'm going to tell it to Dan over there, and everybody else who comes in here tonight, and you listen to them laugh."

Smitty tried to concentrate on the television program, but he could not block out Sylvia's greeting to her customers, the ensuing silent attention to her story, the explosions of laughter; more and more morose as laughter puffed and eddied around

266

him, excluding him from the companionship of his fellow-drinkers. When he felt the cold air across his shoulders that meant another customer, another audience, had pushed the door open, he got up abruptly and left, not quite fast enough to avoid hearing one further guffaw that sped after him down the street, sharpened and aimed at him.

The next evening, in the stack of mail, there was a letter to Smith. Smitty took it in amazement—Miss Lorene Smith—and carried it up the stairs. He reasoned that she must not be home yet, if the letter remained in the day's mail. He decided to keep it until she came in and then deliver it to her personally, but he felt there was no real justification for doing that. He tapped the letter against the fingers of his left hand, decided to slip it under the door, and as he did so, the door opened.

He straightened up and held out the letter. "I brought you your mail. Happened to see it because it said Smith. Caught my eye, don't you know. I nearly opened it." He stood in the doorway.

After a long interval Lorene said, "Won't you come in?" Smitty entered, closed the door, then opened it and left it wide open. The only chair was at the desk. He would not sit on the bed. He sat on the carton.

"You're busy. I can see you have lots of papers to mark."

"It's my own fault." She laughed. "I gave them all tests today."

"How are all the children doing?" he asked seriously.

"Oh, some better, some worse." They sat in silence. Smitty watched her like a good television play, with pleasure and interest, observing, not especially needing to relate to her in other ways. But a woman is not like television. "What do you do with yourself in the evening, Smitty?" she asked.

"Nothing much. Watch a little teevee, drink a couple of beers, chew the fat a little. You know what I mean? Doesn't seem to be much else to do. Just pass the time until it's time to hit the sack. Got to get up pretty early, you know."

"Yes. I hear you leave when I'm just getting up."

"That right?" He was charmed that she was aware of his presence. "I hope I don't disturb you."

"Not at all."

Then silence, restraint, returned. This time Smitty said, "Well, I'll get going. I know you got a lot of work to do." At the door he turned half-way around. "Some time, when you're not so busy, I'd like you to come out with me for a beer, or coffee. Think you could?" he said over his shoulder.

"Do you really mean it?" she said softly, swiftly.

"Why, sure. I'll remind you. Some other evening. I go to this same tavern all the time. Swell bunch there. Good night."

It came about on many evenings that Smitty had something to say to Lorene, something to ask her about in the hall if they met by chance, some reason to tap on her door and talk to her for a few minutes. He found that as the afternoon at work wore on, he was looking forward to that moment. He could visualize her swift smile, hear her soft voice reply, as five o'clock crawled closer.

But there were also evenings when he belabored his brain, and could not hit on a pretext for knocking at her door. Then he would lie across his bed, staring at the ceiling, finding fantastic pictures in the water-stained old paper—flowers, cats, lovers coupling, aerial views of mountain ranges on the moon. Finally he would give up hope for that evening, and fill the time before sleep at the tavern. Once he fell asleep, woke angrily in the middle of the night, cheated, close to tears. At the sound of a latch he would leap to his door to confront her.

"Ah, Smitty. Are you going out?"

"No. Well, that is, yes. Really I was looking for you. I hoped you'd go out with me for a beer or a cup of coffee."

"Thank you. But I'm afraid not. I have so much work to do. Papers to grade, and all."

"They really work you teachers, don't they?"

"Yes. It's really not so bad. It's good to be busy." Her door closed, leaving the hall dark.

Smitty sighed deeply, storing his lungs with the delicate scent of her. He went downstairs, sliding his hand along the bannister she had just touched.

He had no urgent messages for Sylvia. For something to say, he asked, "What'd the Bears do today?"

"I don't know. I don't know if they played. Hey, Al, what'd the Bears do?" she called to the bar tender, then interpreted his mumbled reply for Smitty. "He says they didn't play either." She leaned against the table. "All you fellows think about is football and broads, broads and football. Don't you ever think about nothing else?"

"What else is there?"

"I dunno, but there ought to be something."

Smitty laughed, wanting to feel like laughing, wanting to feel the good feeling of being included in her circle of men-of-the-world. Sylvia wandered off and he riveted his eyes on the television screen, seeking distraction and tranquility. But wherever he looked, and whatever he tried to think about, he was back at the boarding house in the room at the end of the hall, sitting on one of the cartons of books, talking to Lorene. Not this kind of fencing he did with Sylvia, but really talking, exploring his mind and hers with words. "I might just as well not come down here," Smitty thought, disconsolately finishing his beer.

After the next beer, in his mental televised interview, he had substituted his own brown chair for the book carton he usually sat on, and was at his ease. "Why do you suppose she don't unpack those boxes?" Smitty thought. If she should be planning to move again soon! He got to his feet—he wanted to rush right home to make sure she was there. On the way he stopped. "Sure she's there. What a fool you are, Smith. Some carpenter. She doesn't unpack those books because she has no book shelves. Mrs. Hadley never had a smart woman with books before."

He whistled during the time he worked on the shelf—sawing, hammering, painting it apple green—his magic that would keep Miss Smith contentedly at Hadley's. He refused to think that she might move and take the shelf with her, or leave it and him. She could not. He carried it to her carefully, holding the underside of the shelf since the paint was still tacky, but he could wait no longer for it to dry. His anticipation of her pleasure could not be sustained further.

A gift was certainly a valid reason for knocking confidently at her door. He spoke as soon as the door began to swing. "I made something for you," he grinned.

She did not answer with a smile. "For me? You made a present for me?" She stared at Smitty.

He had to draw her attention to the shelf. "Yes. Look. A book shelf. For your books. Now you can unpack them, and get the boxes out of the way."

"Why, Smitty! How wonderful! You made it for me." She was radiant, just as he had in advance visualized the look in her eye, but it almost was the sparkle of a tear.

"Ah, ah. Don't touch." He held out a warning hand, spotted with apple green. "The paint isn't quite dry. I just couldn't wait any more to give it to you."

"It's perfect." Then she was suddenly soberly quiet. The bitter-sweet expression of her mouth returned. "Still I wish you hadn't."

"Why not?"

"I don't want you to do anything for me," she answered violently.

"Don't you like it?" incredulously.

"Oh, Smitty." She held out her hand, and her smile returned. "I love it. It's perfect. It's just that I don't think you should spend your time and effort on me," she glowed at him.

"Why not?" He held her hand for the first time. The skin was supple. "I *want* to spend it on you. I have no one to spend it on *but* you."

"I'm not worth it," she whispered.

"I think you are. I sure think you are." He plunged down the stairs and outdoors.

A fine icy mist drizzled from the sky. As Smitty approached the tavern the neon announcement skittered nervously: "The . . . The . . . Haven . . . Haven . . . The Haven . . ." He held his hand to his face, still inhaling the delicate perfume imparted to his own by Lorene's hand. Without slowing down he passed the tavern. He could not hold a beer in his hand that night; he could not sit still and watch television, no matter what

270

was playing. He could not kid around with Sylvia. He didn't even want to think about her, but he couldn't help thinking that she would have plenty to say about his absence the next day. He stood still. "What the hell, Smith. Who are you kidding? She won't give a damn if you're there or not. If it isn't you wearing out their chairs, it's somebody else, and that's the truth." He strode on at top speed, passed a tavern half a block further. "Now what I mean is, I could go in to this one, and it would all be the same—a warm room, smell of beer, a television going full blast, and a sporty waitress with a lot of crummy jokes. Or not. But it don't make any difference. That's the point. You see what I mean (he nearly said, Lorene)? It don't make any difference—no one cares. No one cares if I turn in to this tavern, or that one, or none. Makes no difference to anybody where I turn, if I stay or go. Christ, that's awful!"

He put his head down, but did not slow his pace through the glistening dirty streets, until he found himself on the block where he had lived with his wife. "And how about that?" his thoughts continued, furious in retrospect. "She could be married for seven years, and leave just like that! I bet she never even thought about me after that." He had not felt anger at her until now. He lifted his face to bellow in rage, felt the shock of icy rain, and only sobbed. "What did I do for her? We lived together; we lived side by side; we shared an apartment—and I think we never really looked at each other." Not, that is, in the way he had looked at Lorene, into Lorene, into something radiant, tragic, and maddening. "We never made it for each other, my old lady and me. We were a couple of hot kids, and when that was gone, we were like strangers. Like not even the same family. The only person I ever met who makes me feel like she's my own family is soft and brown and smells like a God-damned bunch of flowers."

He was standing in front of a red brick apartment building, possibly talking aloud. He ducked into the entrance. His name was not on one of the cards next to a row of black buttons. None of these people could even know that he had once belonged here, had a key, went up the dark stairs every night to an apartment, and came down every morning for years. Someone was coming down now. Smitty wanted to shout to this unseen person "Stop! Where are you going? Why? Time is passing!" But he knew he would sound like a crack-pot. He knew he didn't even have any business there, and pretended to be studying the names on the bells—even discovered one that was vaguely familiar (he could not recall what the people were like, but he remembered they had a nice little dog), did not look up as someone passed in back of him quickly. If the stranger had clapped him on the shoulder in recognition he would have wept.

After a safe interval Smitty left, too. He could not determine what his feelings were—exalted, wild, depressed—he felt them dully through a spongy thickness in his brain. All he wanted was to get back to Mrs. Hadley's and go to bed with a shot of whiskey so he could stop shivering.

He slept fitfully. When his alarm clock rang in the morning he sat up on the side of the bed to turn it off, but lay down again, unable to hold up his ringing head. "Just till this dizziness passes," he thought, and dozed. He thought he heard a light tap at the door, but perhaps he had dreamed it. To be safe he croaked hoarsely, "Come in."

Lorene opened the door, smiling. "I knew I hadn't heard you go out this morning. I always listen for you. Are you all right?" She entered the room.

To Smitty it was as if she swooped in on wings. "I felt kind of dizzy this morning. I guess I caught cold or something."

She put her hand on his forehead. "You're feverish, Smitty. Let me get you something." She returned with aspirin. "I have to go now, but I'll tell Mrs. Hadley to bring up some tea. Stay in bed today. I'll look in on you this evening." Smitty submitted blissfully to her commands.

He slept on and off during the day—waking or dreaming, his thoughts were the same. Toward evening the old frame house creaked alive, doors slammed, footsteps resounded on the stairs. Smitty roused, switched on the light, and she entered, carrying a tray of soup, toast, custard, tea and crackers. She brought her own pillow to put under his so he could sit up in bed to eat. His head throbbed, but he could answer truthfully that he felt fine. He reached for her hand, held it to his warm cheek. "Gee," he said, "thanks. This is wonderful. You're wonderful. You're a wonderful woman."

"I am not at all," she answered sadly. "I have been dreadful . . . the very worst imaginable."

"Aw, you're kidding. I can't believe that." He felt stupidly like laughing, and was fearful.

"I know you can't. I cherish you for that reason, but now I want to tell you. I must tell you." She pulled the straight chair next to the bed and sat down.

Smitty waited, horrified, afraid to hear, wanting to hear, a confession he could not imagine; admission of sin, vice, depravity, was inconceivable.

"I have been so bad. I fell so low. I came to despise myself," she chanted. "My sin was in my heart, and there was no visible sign. I looked unchanged, the world did not change around me. I wanted it to. Can you understand? I despised myself, and I wanted other people to despise me, too. I did not want love and respect from those around me when I did not deserve it. I wanted to be punished. I longed for punishment in order to be humble, to learn humility, but the world did not punish me. So I arranged my own punishment. I wanted to burn in hell until I was humbled, so I tried to arrange my own hell."

Smitty struggled up to lean on one elbow. The muscles of his neck stood out with the effort and tension. "What did you do?"

"I moved here," she said calmly.

He fell back to the pillow gasping with laughter. "It's not *that* bad!"

She continued gravely, "You don't know. You're not a Negro. I am. I am the first Negro in this boarding house, in this neighborhood. Strangers look at me with loathing, and I say 'Good— for I am loathsome to myself.' People go out of their way to be insulting, mean, spiteful, and I say 'Fine, I deserve it.'" She folded her hands calmly.

Smitty looked at her incredulously, "But all you're learning is that those people are a bunch of bastards. They are the ones that should be punished, not you. I don't believe you could ever do anything bad. I know you couldn't. You're too hard on yourself. I've met a lot of people in my time, and you're the kindest, most wonderful person I've ever known." He pressed his head against the pillow, turned his sweating face away from her, but continued to speak. "You're the first human being who has ever meant anything to me."

"I came here to punish myself, to erase my arrogance, and find humility. And the first encounter I had was with you— your good, friendly, helpful gesture the moment I moved in. Your consideration for me. Your regard for me as an individual. You have ruined my hell, Smitty, made it evaporate, because for you it does not exist, and when I am with you it does not exist for me, either. You have made it bearable—even pleasant. When others are cruel, I think about your kindness. I have tried not to avail myself of it, but I don't want to hurt you. I had to explain because this hell is becoming too—not even earthly— but heavenly." Tears streamed down her cheeks and she made no effort to wipe them.

Smitty could see now that the lines around her mouth that were so ready to outline a smile had been etched by weeping also. He tried to concentrate on what she had said, on the con- fession of guilt and sin, but he could not—he was fearfully happy with the intimations of her feeling for him. "Lorene. Why shouldn't you be happy? Why should we make it hell for each other? There is enough of that. If we can help each other, if we can mean something to each other, why shouldn't we?"

"Oh, Smitty, I don't deserve it," she wailed, knelt beside his bed, held his hand between hers. "I was so wrong. You have taught me how wrong I was. When I thought I was looking for punishment and rejection, I was hardening my heart, I was only keeping arrogance alive. I'm humbly grateful to you for helping me learn how wrong I was. I was truly lost, but now I will be a whole person again, thanks to you." She put her head down, letting her tears dry on his pillow. He stroked her thin neck, felt the live texture of her fragrant hair.

"I don't know about all that," he whispered. "I just want to be something to you. I love you. You are everything to me."

She only shook her head. "No, you don't know," she whispered. "You don't understand."

As soon as he was well, Smitty knocked on Lorene's door in the evening, without needing an excuse. "I thought maybe you'd like to. . . ."

"Yes, I would. Very much. I can see that the children will be neglected." She gestured toward her desk. "My good fortune is their bad luck." She laughed.

"They have you to themselves all day. Now it's my turn. They won't mind a little neglect." He beamed at her.

In the street he took her hand, pulled it through the crook of his arm. Smitty was defiantly on guard at the approach of the first pedestrian, but this man hurried by without a glance. A woman passed them, then another man. Smitty nudged Lorene, chuckled in sheer delight.

"I want you to meet my friends—there's this girl Sylvia at the Haven. She's a swell gal, great sense of humor, million laughs, all the time." He stopped and faced Lorene. "You understand, she never was anything to me. No one ever has been until now." She seemed hardly to hear him. He continued, "In a way, I don't have any friends. I don't have any family either. You have to be my friends and my family." He laughed. In his huge happiness he did not sense her misgivings, her apprehension.

In the tavern he sat at his usual table, but with his back to the television. Sylvia sauntered over. "Hi ya, little man. Long time no see."

"Yeah. I been sick. I had the flu or something. But it's all over. And I'm better than ever." He grinned at Lorene. "This is Miss Smith," he said proudly.

"How do you do. What'll it be?" She leaned on the table, one hand on her hip.

"Want a beer? Two beers."

Sylvia ambled to the bar. Smitty took Lorene's hand. He wriggled with uncontainable joy. He could not smile broadly enough. Sylvia returned, gave the table a swipe with her cloth, precisely, carefully set down one bottle and one glass in front of Smitty.

"Yeah. Where's the other one?"

"I'm sorry, Smith," she said in her dead-pan sing-song, "We can't serve beer to minors." She turned away.

Smitty hooted. "What did I tell you? Didn't I tell you she had some sense of humor?" delighted that she had at once included Lorene in her circle of gulls.

When she did not return with the second beer, Smitty called to her, "All right. A joke's a joke. You win. A fellow could die of thirst."

"So die." She ambled toward them, her expression mask-like, steely. "I kid you not. No beer to minors."

"Oh, come on, Sylvia. A joke's a joke. Lorene is no jail bait. She's a school teacher." He felt a hideous premonition; trapped in the situation, he tried desperately to kid his way out. "And old enough to know better. Like you. Same as you."

"Not the same as me, bucko." Sylvia faced Lorene, put a hand under her chin, tilted her face upward and scrutinized it closely for a few seconds. Lorene submitted quietly, eyes downcast, hands folded in her lap, a light smile in the corners of her mouth. "Not even old enough to know better," Sylvia said finally. "Can't be served in *this* place."

Biographical Notes

CYNTHIA BUCHANAN was raised on a ranch in Arizona. She has an M.A. in creative writing from the University of the Americas in Mexico City, and spent last year in Spain on a Fulbright Fellowship in creative writing. She is presently working on a novel, *Fortune Dundy,* and shorter pieces.

JERRY BUMPUS is married and lives with his wife and two young daughters in Spokane, Washington. He was born in Illinois, educated in the Midwest, and has taught all over the West, as well as a year in Kobe, Japan. He has published about 30 short stories and a novel, *Anaconda.*

RAYMOND CARVER was born in Clatskanie, Oregon, and educated at Humboldt State College and the University of Iowa. He is married, has two children. His poetry publications include *Near Klamath* and *Winter Insomnia,* and he has had stories in many of the literary magazines. This year he received a Discovery Grant from the National Endowment for the Arts.

RICK DE MARINIS was born in New York, raised in California, and got a B.A. and an M.A. from the University of Montana, where he taught composition and creative writing for two years. He is now teaching at San Diego State. More usually a poet, he has published in a number of little magazines. His story reprinted in this volume is his first work of fiction.

J. M. FERGUSON, JR., lives in Columbus, Ohio. A college English teacher for six years, he is now a Field Editor for Odyssey Press. His work has appeared in *New Mexico Quarterly, Transatlantic Review, Arizona Quarterly, South Dakota Review, Cimarron Review,* and elsewhere.

FRED GARDNER grew up in Bedford-Stuyvesant, Brooklyn, and attended Harvard, where he was an editor of the *Crimson* and graduated in 1963. He worked as an editor for *Scientific American* for three years, then began setting up anti-war coffeehouses for GI's near Army training bases. He has written a book about the Presidio Mutiny case, and writes regularly for *Hard Times,* a political newsweekly. He also writes songs.

GARY GILDNER was born in West Branch, Michigan, won All-Parochial basketball honors in high school, got a B.A. and an M.A. from Michigan State, and teaches in Des Moines, Iowa. His first book of poems, *First Practice,* was published last year.

JAMES B. HALL is Provost of College V at the University of California, Santa Cruz. His stories have appeared in a wide variety of publications, and a great many of them have been anthologized.

CURTIS HARNACK was born in LeMars, Iowa in 1927, and attended Grinnell College and Columbia. He served in the Navy late in World War II (out of Port Chicago) and has worked a year for the U.N. Secretariat. He has taught at Grinnell, the University of Iowa, and Sarah Lawrence. He lives in New York City, is presently working on a novel, and has published *The Work of an Ancient Hand* (1960), *Love and Be Silent* (1962), and *Persian Lions, Persian Lambs* (1965).

ROBERT HENSON teaches at Upsala College in East Orange, New Jersey. His work has appeared in many little magazines, including *Shenandoah* and the *Michigan Quarterly Review*.

JOHN HERRMANN, a native San Franciscan, has taught fiction writing at the University of Montana and the State University of New York, and is now visiting professor in English in Iran at Pahlevi University, Shiraz. He has received summer fellowships to Yaddo and the McDowell Colony and hopes to finish his first novel this year in Switzerland.

GERALD LOCKLIN teaches at California State College at Long Beach. He has published widely—poems and stories—in the little magazines, plus two collections of poems, and has just completed a novel.

PETER LORD is twenty-three years old and lives in Montreal, home of the Habs. He is at work on a book of poetry entitled *joyce*.

WILLIAM MINOR was born in Pontiac, Michigan, in 1936. He has M.A.'s in drawing and painting and in English, is currently teaching English at Wisconsin State University-Whitewater, and is working on a novel, *The Chuckleheads*. His woodcut prints have been exhibited nationally, and his poems and stories have appeared in many little magazines.

THOMAS W. MOLYNEUX teaches at the University of Delaware. His stories have appeared in several of the littles. He has had a Rockefeller Grant and has completed a novel.

WILLIAM MOORE is married, lives in New York City, and has a teen-age son. His story reprinted in this volume was his first published piece.

JOYCE CAROL OATES won the National Book Award for Fiction in 1970. She has a new book of short stories, *Love Stories,* just published, and a new book of poems, *Love and Its Derangements.*

BILL RODRIGUEZ is a former cabbie, newspaper editor, busboy, and radio producer. He is married, writing, and teaching English. His work has appeared in *Four Quarters, New England Review,* and the *Congressional Record* (8/9/65, p. A4391).

HENRY H. ROTH is married and has twin girls and a son. He has published more than 50 stories, continues to write them, and has finished two novels.

PETER L. SANDBERG lives with his wife in a small cabin on the shore of a New Hampshire lake. He is a lecturer in English at Northeastern University in Boston, teaching the fiction-writing seminar. His work has appeared in *Short Story International, Literary Review, Literary Cavalcade,* and *Saturday Review.*

DAVID STEINGASS had a first book of poems, *Body Compass,* published last year and is working on a second poetry ms., a book of short stories, and a novel about South California. He is presently reading, writing and traveling across the country.

JOANNE ZIMMERMAN is married and has three children. A substitute teacher in the Chicago area, she writes on days she doesn't teach. Her stories have appeared in a dozen littles, and a novel, *Lily! Lily!,* will be published in the near future.

Distinguished Stories 1964–69

1964

Raymond Carver	The Student's Wife	*Carolina Quarterly*
Daniel Curly	Love in the Winter	*Colorado Quarterly*
Crispin Cusack	The Runner	*Virginia Quarterly Review*
Stanley Elkin	The Guest	*Paris Review*
Irvin Faust	Googs in Lambarene	*Carleton Miscellany*
Len Fulton	The Line	*Dust*
James W. Groshong	The Gesture	*Antioch Review*
Mike Grumley	Mirror Negative	*Cheshire*
Maureen Howard	Sherry	*Hudson Review*
Dennis Lynds	A Blue Blonde in the Sky over Pennsylvania	*Hudson Review*
James McConkey	The Crossroads near Frenchburg	*Sewanee Review*
Georgia McKinley	The Mighty Distance	*Kenyon Review*
Larry McMurtry	There Will Be Peace in Korea	*Texas Quarterly*
John Metcalf	Consequences	*Prism International*
Leonard Michaels	Sticks and Stones	*Massachusetts Review*
Jay Neugeboren	The Application	*Transatlantic Review*
Flannery O'Connor	Revelation	*Sewanee Review*
David Ray	Esse	*MSS*
Henry H. Roth	The Fat Guy	*December*
Laurel E. Speer	Routine Operation	*Minnesota Review*
Peter Taylor	The Throughway	*Sewanee Review*
Lee Wallek	A Grain of Sand	*Flagrante Delicto*
Robert Wilson	While We're Young	*December*
William Wiser	Gambler's Chances	*Antioch Review*

Distinguished Stories 1964–69

1965

James Conaway	The Abcedarian	*Texas Quarterly*
R. C. Day	No Hard Feelings	*Kenyon Review*
William Fifield	Second Fiddle	*Texas Quarterly*
Philip L. Greene	One of You Must Be Wendell Corey	*Partisan Review*
Hugh Hood	A Solitary Ewe	*Literary Review*
Josephine Jacobsen	On the Island	*Kenyon Review*
M. M. Liberman	Letter from the Thirties	*December*
Helen Luz	"I've got to find one . . ."	*Grande Ronde Review*
Dennis Lynds	Why Girls Ride Side-saddle	*Minnesota Review*
Amado Muro	More Hobo Sketches	*Arizona Quarterly*
Grace Paley	Living	*Genesis West*
George Petrides	Pax Africana	*Red Cedar Review*
Abraham Rothberg	Pluto Is the Furthest Planet	*Yale Review*
Ronald S. Rubin	The Banks of Mississippi	*Transatlantic Review*
Daniel John Schneider	A Very Nice Young Man	*Minnesota Review*
Andrew Simmons	Sorrow in the Morning	*University Review*
V. Stack	The Day She Saw Things as They Are	*Panache*
Susan Taubes	The Sharks	*Virginia Quarterly Review*
Walter S. Terry	The Bottomless Well	*Georgia Review*
Victor White	The Hotel	*Southwest Review*
Joseph Whitehill	One Night for Several Samurai	*Hudson Review*
Joy Williams	The Roomer	*Carolina Quarterly*
George A. Zorn	Mr. and Mrs. McGill	*Perspective*

1966

Gaston Bart-Williams	My Friend	*West Coast Review*
George Blake	A Place Not on the Map	*Literary Review*
Raymond Carver	Will You Please Be Quiet, Please?	*December*
Albert Drake	In the Time of Surveys	*Northwest Review*
Ernest J. Finney	The Investigator	*Epoch*
Robert Fox	A Fable	*Midwestern University Quarterly*
H. E. Francis	One of the Boys	*Southwest Review*

Ernest J. Gaines	My Grandpa and the Haint	*New Mexico Quarterly*
Jan Garden	Ride into Dark	*Quixote*
Keith Gunderson	Two Prose Poems	*Epoch*
Norma Klein	Side Effects	*Quartet*
Conrad Knicker-bocker	Diseases of the Heart	*Kenyon Review*
Thomas McAfee	This Is His Living Room	*Midwestern University Quarterly*
Leonard Michaels	City Boy	*Paris Review*
Marvin Mudrick	Cleopatra	*Hudson Review*
Howard Nemerov	The Nature of the Task	*Virginia Quarterly Review*
Joyce Carol Oates	Where Are You Going, Where Have You Been?	*Epoch*
J. D. O'Hara	Once More into the Breach, Dear	*Western Humanities Review*
Robert Ramsey	In the Corncrib	*Red Clay Reader*
Kent E. Thompson	The Man Who Cried Faith	*New Campus Review*
I. G. Thorsteinsson	The Bronze Maidens from Bellevue	*Vagabond*
Joseph Whitehill	The Round Brass Elevator	*Hudson Review*

1967

Norbert Blei	The White Balloon	*Midwestern University Quarterly*
Theodore Bloom	A Four-day Wait	*Quarterly Review of Literature*
Brock Brower	Storm Still	*TriQuarterly*
Jerry Bumpus	A World of Beautiful Children	*Colorado State Review*
Mark Costello	Murphy's Xmas	*Transatlantic Review*
Olivia Davis	Loss and Chaos	*Kenyon Review*
Ralph Davis	The Son of the Sad Fat Wordman Goes North	*Lillabulero*
Joan Didion	When Did Music Come this Way? Children Dear, Was It Yesterday?	*Denver Quarterly*
Andrew Fetler	In Line for Lemonade	*Malahat Review*

Carolyn Gaiser	Differences	*Paris Review*
John Bart Gerald	Alabama Jacks	*Ararat*
James B. Hall	Getting Married	*Virginia Quarterly Review*
Robert Hazel	White Anglo-Saxon Protestant	*Hudson Review*
Arlene Heyman	Something that Would Grow	*Epoch*
Helen Hudson	The Listener	*Antioch Review*
Glenn F. Jackson	How Much Do You Love Me?	*Quartet*
Marion McCreedy Leaman	Perverse Echo	*California Review*
Nancy C. Mackenzie	The Wrong Silence	*Prairie Schooner*
Ben Maddow	You, Johann Sebastian Bach	*Hudson Review*
Hilary Masters	The Game in Season	*Quarterly Review of Literature*
Jack Matthews	A Story Not about Richardson	*Ante*
Alden Nowlan	Humbly, for Fyodor	*Prism International*
Nancy Huddleston Packer	Early Morning, Lonely Ride	*Southwest Review*
Henry H. Roth	Of Frail Pigeons and Red Roses	*Quest*
Evelyn Shefner	The Invitations	*Colorado Quarterly*
Robert Joe Stout	Christmas at Aunt Sarah's	*Quest*
Joy Williams	Baby, Tonight I Rolled Pinto Lee	*Colorado Quarterly*
Margery Wood	The Bride	*Epoch*

1968

John Bennett, Jr.	Of Banjos and Flowers	*Transatlantic Review*
Jerry A. Bitts	The Teachers' Party	*Trace*
George Blake	A Modern Development	*Kansas Magazine*
Norbert Blei	The Hour of the Sunshine Now	*Minnesota Review*
Robert Bonazzi	Light Casualties	*Transatlantic Review*
John Chambers	The Morning Mr. Spelina's Great-Great-Grandfather Danced All Night at the Ball	*This Magazine is about Schools*

J. M. Ferguson, Jr.	Summerfield	*Descant*
Franklin Fisher	Normal	*Western Humanities Review*
K. C. Frederick	"Whose Country Have I Come to Now?"	*Epoch*
Kurt Higgins	The Coward	*Jeopardy*
Matthew Hochberg	Throne	*December*
Madison Jones	Home Is Where the Heart Is	*Arlington Quarterly*
Barbara Jump	The Fool Discovered	*Malahat Review*
Matthew W. McGregor	Porkchops with Whiskey and Ice Cream	*Virginia Quarterly Review*
Ian T. MacMillan	Light and Power	*Georgia Review*
David Madden	Traven	*Southern Review*
Jack Matthews	Love Song for Doris Ballinger	*Carleton Miscellany*
Leonard Michaels	Manikin	*Massachusetts Review*
John R. Milton	A Small Betrayal	*Western Review*
Joyce Carol Oates	By the River	*December*
Andrew James Purdy	Master of the Courts	*The Smith*
Henry H. Roth	Dance!	*Prism International*
Miriam Rugel	Paper Poppy	*Kenyon Review*
Robert W. Schultheis	The Fall	*South Dakota Review*
David Spriggs	The Autopsy	*Duel*
Peter Taylor	First Heat	*Shenandoah*
Steven Turner	A Nail in the Heel	*Arlington Quarterly*
John Vachon	You Can Make a Million	*Panache*
Gordon Weaver	Reasons I Insist You Call Me by My Right Name	*Latitudes*
John F. Zeugner	The Tennis Player	*Perspective*

1969

Daniel Eigerman	The Girl and the Island	*Quartet*
William Knight	Richard P. Watson	*Literary Review*
Walt McDonald	Three Sisters	*New Campus Review*
Botticello Marbo	The Sea Farm	*Mt. Adams Review*
James Mechem	A Strange Lassitude	*Zeitgeist*
Gerald Mulligan	Busrides	*Epoch*
Philip F. O'Connor	Gerald's Song	*Western Humanities Review*
Henry H. Roth	Ryan	*Jeopardy*

Distinguished Stories 1964–69

E. J. Scannell	Brown	*Arlington Quarterly*
Doug Spettigue	Edge of Christmas	*Fiddlehead*
Lowell Uda	When My Father Nags, Chee!	*Colorado State Review*
Krishna Baldev Vaid	We Indians	*Western Humanities Review*
Sol Yurick	Do They Talk about Genet in Larchmont?	*Confrontation*

Magazines Consulted

The following magazines were read in selecting stories for this anthology. Some of the magazines are no longer active, some may have changed addresses. For an up-to-date listing of addresses, consult the *Directory of Little Magazines* (DUSTbooks, 5218 Scottwood Rd., Paradise, Ca. 95969—$2.50). Editors of little magazines are asked to send their publications to Box 274, Western Springs, Ill. 60558, for reading for next year's collection.

Abyss, Box C, Somerville, Mass. 02143
Aesop's Feast, 207 W. Fowler Ave., West Lafayette, Ind. 47906
Ann Arbor Review, 2118 Arlene St., Ann Arbor, Mich. 48103
Ante, Box 29915, Los Angeles, Ca. 90029
Antioch Review, 136 Dayton St., Yellow Springs, Ohio 45387
Approach, 114 Petrie Ave., Rosemont, Pa., 19010
Arizona Quarterly, Univ. of Arizona, Tucson, Ariz. 85721
Arlington Quarterly, Box 366, Univ. Sta., Arlington, Tex. 76010
ARX, 12109 Bell Ave., Austin, Tex. 78759
Aspects, Box 3125, Eugene, Ore. 97403

Bennington Review, Box N., Bennington College, Bennington, Vt. 05201
Beyond Baroque, Box 675, Venice, Ca. 90291

California Review, 280 E. Mountain Dr., Santa Barbara, Ca. 93103
Carleton Miscellany, Carleton College, Northfield, Minn. 55057
Carolina Quarterly, Box 1117, Chapel Hill, N.C. 27514
Chicago Review, Univ. of Chicago, Chicago, Ill. 60637
Cimarron Review, 203B Morrill Hall, Oklahoma State Univ., Stillwater, Okla. 74074

Magazines Consulted

Colorado Quarterly, Hellems 124, Univ. of Colorado, Boulder, Colo. 80521

Colorado State Review, 360 Liberal Arts, Colorado State Univ., Ft. Collins, Colo. 80521

Confrontation, Long Island Univ., Greenvale, N.Y. 11548

Consumption, 4208 8th N.E., Seattle, Wash. 98105

Corduroy, 406 Highland Ave., Newark, N.J. 07104

Cottonwood Review, 118 Kansas Union, Univ. of Kansas, Lawrence, Kan. 66044

December, Box 274, Western Springs, Ill. 60558

DeKalb Journal, DeKalb College, 555 Indian Creek Dr., Clarkston, Ga. 30021

Denver Quarterly, Univ. of Denver, Denver, Colo. 80210

Descant, TCU Station, Fort Worth, Tex. 76129

Desperado, 60 Bessie St., San Francisco, Ca. 94110

Discourse, Concordia College, Moorhead, Minn. 56560

Duel, Sir George Williams Univ., 1455 Maisonneuve Blvd., Montreal 25, Quebec, Canada

Edge, Box 4067, Edmonton, Alberta, Canada

Epoch, 251 Goldwin Smith Hall, Cornell Univ., Ithaca, N.Y. 14850

Evidence, Box 245, Station F, Toronto, Canada

Fair, 1642 N. 8th St., Terre Haute, Ind. 47804

Fiddlehead, Univ. of New Brunswick, Fredericton, N.B., Canada

Freelance, Box 1128, Washington Univ., St. Louis, Mo. 63130

Georgia Review, Univ. of Georgia, Athens, Ga. 30601

Goodly Co., 724 Minor Ave., Kalamazoo, Mich. 49001

Greensboro Review, Univ. of North Carolina, Greensboro, N.C. 27412

Hudson Review, 65 E. 55th St., New York, N.Y. 10022

Husk, Cornell College, Mount Vernon, Iowa 52314

Illuminations, El Rito, N.M. 87530

Impulse, Rockland Community College, 145 College Rd., Suffern, N.Y. 10901

Jeopardy, Western Washington State College, Bellingham, Wash. 98225

Kansas Quarterly, Rm. 358 Watson Library, Lawrence, Kan. 66044
Kenyatta, 1442 N. Sedgwick St., Chicago, Ill. 60610
Kenyon Review, Kenyon College, Gambier, Ohio 43022

Latitudes, 1760 Queen St., North Bellmore, L.I., N.Y. 11710
Laurel Review, College Box 47, Buckhannon, W. Va. 26201
Leprechaun Review, Box 2324, French Quarter, New Orleans, La. 70116
Lillabulero, Krums Corners Rd., R.D. #3, Ithaca, N.Y. 14850
Literary Review, Fairleigh Dickinson Univ., Rutherford, N.J. 07070
Little Review, Box 2321, Huntington, W. Va. 25724

Malahat Review, Univ. of Victoria, Victoria, B.C., Canada
Mandala, 818 Terry Place, Madison, Wis. 53711
Massachusetts Review, Memorial Hall, Univ. of Massachusetts, Amherst, Mass. 01002
Mikrokosmos, English Dept., Wichita State Univ., Wichita, Kan. 67208
Minnesota Review, Box 4066, Highland Sta., St. Paul, Minn. 55116
Modine Gunch, 506 Memorial Union, Madison, Wis. 53706
Moonlight Review, Box 1686, Brooklyn, N.Y. 11202
Mt. Adams Review, Box 6054, Cincinnati, Ohio 45206

New Campus Review, Metropolitan State College, Denver, Colo. 80204
New Renaissance, 9 Heath Rd., Arlington, Mass. 02174
North American Review, Univ. of Northern Iowa, Cedar Falls, Iowa 50613
Northwest Review, 129 French Hall, Univ. of Oregon, Eugene, Ore. 97403

Panache, 153 E. 84th St., New York, N.Y. 10028
Paris Review, 45–39 171 Place, Flushing, N.Y. 11358
Partisan Review, Rutgers Univ., New Brunswick, N.J. 08903
Perspective, Washington Univ. P.O., St. Louis, Mo. 63130
Prairie Schooner, 219 Andrews Hall, Univ. of Nebraska, Lincoln, Neb. 68508
Presence, c/o English Dept., SUNYAB, Buffalo, N.Y. 14214
Prism International, Univ. of British Columbia, Vancouver 8, B.C., Canada
Pyramid, 32 Waverley St., Belmont, Mass. 02178

Quarterly, Montclair State College, Upper Montclair, N.J. 07043
Quarterly Review of Literature, 26 Haslet Ave., Princeton, N.J. 08540
Quartet, 186 Ridge Rd., Utica, N.Y. 13501
Quest, Box 207, Cathedral Sta., New York, N.Y. 10025
Quixote, 315 N. Brooks St., Madison, Wis. 53715

Red Cedar Review, 325 Morrill Hall, Michigan State Univ., East Lansing, Mich. 48823
Red Clay Reader, 6366 Sharon Hills Rd., Charlotte, N.C. 28210
Riverside Quarterly, Box 40, Univ. Sta., Regina, Canada

Sewanee Review, Sewanee, Tenn. 37375
Shenandoah, Box 722, Lexington, Va. 24450
Sketch, Rm. 210, Pearson Hall, Iowa State Univ., Ames, Iowa 50010
Smith, 15 Park Row, New York, N.Y. 10038
South Dakota Review, Box 111, Univ. Exchange, Vermillion, S.D. 57069
Southern Humanities Review, 210 Samford Hall, Auburn Univ., Auburn, Ala. 36830
Southern Review, Drawer D, Univ. Sta., Baton Rouge, La. 70803
Southwest Review, Southern Methodist Univ., Dallas, Tex. 75222
Sou'wester, Humanities Div., Southern Illinois Univ., Edwardsville, Ill. 62025
Spectrum, 916 W. Franklin St., Richmond, Va. 23220

Tamarack Review, Box 159, St. K, Toronto 12, Canada
Tangents, 3473½ Cahuenga Blvd., Hollywood, Ca. 90028
Tempest, Univ. of Wisconsin, Milwaukee, Wis. 53201
Texas Quarterly, Box 7517, Univ. Sta., Austin, Tex. 78712
Toucan, 1520 South Blvd., Kent, Ohio 44240
Trace, Box 1068, Hollywood, Ca. 90028
Transatlantic Review, Box 3348, Grand Central Sta., New York, N.Y. 10017
TransPacific, Antioch College, Yellow Springs, Ohio 45387
TriQuarterly, Univ. Hall 101, Northwestern Univ., Evanston, Ill. 62201

University of Windsor Review, Univ. of Windsor, Windsor, Ontario, Canada
University Review, 5100 Rockhill Rd., Kansas City, Mo. 64110

Vagabond, Box 2362, New Orleans, La. 70116
Virginia Quarterly Review, 1 W. Range, Charlottesville, Va. 22903
Voyages, 2034 Allen Pl., N.W., Washington, D.C. 20008

Wascana Review, Wascana Pkwy., Regina, Saskatchewan, Canada
West Coast Review, Simon Fraser Univ., Burnaby 2, B.C., Canada
Western Review, Western New Mexico Univ., Silver City, N.M. 88061
Western Humanities Review, Univ. of Utah, Salt Lake City, Utah 84112

Yale Review, 28 Hillhouse Ave., New Haven, Conn. 06520

Zeitgeist, c/o General Delivery, Saugatuck, Mich. 49453